THE MEMPHIS MURDERS

THE
MEMPHIS
MURDERS

by Gerald Meyer

A CONTINUUM BOOK

The Seabury Press | *New York*

The Seabury Press
815 Second Avenue
New York, N.Y. 10017

Library of Congress Cataloging in Publication Data

Meyer, Gerald, 1940–
    The Memphis murders.

    (A Continuum book)
    1. Murder—Memphis—Case studies. I. Title.
HV6534.M4M45   364.1'523'0976819   73–17880
ISBN 0–8164–9202–6

For Pam,
    wife and friend,
        with love and gratefulness

Contents

1

The Dumas Case

AUGUST 14, 1969. A hot and brilliantly sunny Thursday in Memphis, Tennessee; a quiet day in the middle of a quiet week. The front page of the morning *Commercial Appeal* carries no local news. President Nixon has given a dinner in Los Angeles to honor the Apollo 11 astronauts, recently back from the moon. American Special Forces personnel have been accused of murder in Vietnam, Washington is speculating about possible candidates for a vacancy on the Supreme Court, and in Northern Ireland Catholics and Protestants are fighting in the streets. Dull news from the faraway world on a steamily tranquil day. Nothing seems to be happening anywhere. Memphis dozes.

At the Hermitage Apartments on South Cooper Street, everything is normal. People come and go slowly in the heat, departing for work and returning home, delivering things, visiting friends, running errands. The Hermitage is a new development on the borderline between an affluent neighborhood of large homes and a decaying area of small bungalows; its builders, hoping to set it apart from the poverty directly to the north, have taken pains to make it as attractive as possible. A dozen brick buildings in mock colonial style form a large grassy courtyard shaded by tall trees, and in the center of the courtyard is a swimming pool. In the afternoon several young women come out of their apartments to swim. Later some of them leave to prepare supper. They are replaced by young men home from work and eager to cool themselves in the water. The shadows grow longer and finally merge into dusk. After dark the last swimmers go indoors. Another day seems to have ended routinely.

In Apartment One at 1133 South Cooper, a first floor apartment whose bedroom windows are visible from the swimming pool, an apartment past which people have been walking at intervals all day, a man and a woman lie dead. They have been murdered. Roy Dumas's body, hands and feet strapped together, is on a twin bed under a window at the corner of the building. The body of his wife Bernalyn is tied to a bed in another corner room. On this quiet day, in the midst of all the tranquil activity around them, the Dumases have been strangled. They lie in their silent rooms for hours, in the late afternoon and the evening and finally in the dark, and their bodies stiffen and grow cold.

These are not "ordinary" murders, murders of the kind that policemen handle almost every day, murders with clues and motives and rationally answerable questions. Nor are they isolated murders, tragic but limited in their implications; they will be followed by other murders leading one by one to a savage, bloody climax. The discovery of the bodies of Roy and Bernalyn Dumas will mark the beginning of the most terrifying period in the history of Memphis, a bizarre period of twenty-nine days in which some lives will be destroyed, others will be forever changed, and an entire city will be brought to the edge of madness.

Bernalyn Kelly Dumas had awakened early as usual on the last day of her life. She ate a quick breakfast, bathed and carefully arranged her hair, and selected a freshly pressed white twill uniform from among several in her closet. She left the apartment shortly after six o'clock, walked four blocks north to Young Street, and caught the Number Two Fairgrounds bus to Baptist Memorial Hospital, where she was at her desk on the eleventh floor in time for the 6:45 duty call. Mrs. Dumas was nursing supervisor for a surgical ward of fifty-one beds, and she had a well-earned reputation for crisp efficiency. It was important to her that she always be at work on time: her promptness, she knew, guaranteed that her subordinates would be equally prompt. She was as precise and meticulous in her work as in her personal habits, though she was not a martinet. Tall and dark-haired and still trimly built in her forty-sixth year, she was well liked by the people who worked for her, a good supervisor and pleasant company so long as everything was done correctly.

Thursday was as uneventful on the eleventh floor of Baptist Hospital as in the rest of Memphis, and Mrs. Dumas did not often have to leave her desk. At eleven o'clock in the morning, she received a telephone call from Mrs. Bill Miner. Two months before, the Dumases' son Mike had married Mrs. Miner's daughter Tanya. Today was Tanya's birthday.

"We're having a little dinner party to celebrate," Mrs. Miner said. "It's nothing fancy, really, but we'd love to have you and Roy join us." Bernalyn Dumas was delighted, and she quickly accepted the invitation. She was eager for an opportunity to get to know her son's new in-laws, who lived in the fashionable Germantown district on the edge of Memphis. She liked the Miners but had not seen much of them since the wedding.

Later, in noticeably high spirits, Mrs. Dumas had lunch in a room near her duty station with a friend named Joanne Hill, also a nurse. She talked happily about the birthday party, and about how much she liked Tanya. "I've already bought her a present, thank goodness," she said. "It's dress material. I'll take it with me tonight." Lunch was interrupted by another personal call. Mrs. Dumas took it, then sat down again with Mrs. Hill.

"That was Roy," she said. "He's upset because the car isn't ready yet, and he doesn't want to go to the party. That's probably just as well. Sometimes he has trouble talking clearly, and Bill Miner is a little hard of hearing. They're not always the best company for each other." She laughed, seemingly not annoyed by her husband's unwillingness to join the celebration. She was never easily annoyed.

At 2:45 P.M. Mrs. Dumas was relieved by the evening supervisor, but she remained at her desk for another half-hour to clear away some paperwork. At 3:15, while preparing to start for home, she received her third personal call of the day. She talked quietly for perhaps a minute, then hung up the phone and turned to Joanne Hill.

"I already have one present for Tanya," she said. "I don't see any need to get another one, do you?" This time, for some reason, she did seem irritated. Mrs. Hill got the impression that the call had been from Mike Dumas, though later he would deny having talked with his mother at any time on Thursday. The call would remain one of the day's many mysterious events.

At 3:20 Mrs. Dumas stepped onto the elevator and waved goodbye to Mrs. Hill. "I'd better hurry," she called as the doors began to close, "if I'm going to fix my hair before the party." She rode down to the lobby, walked quickly to Madison and Dudley Streets, and got on an outbound bus at 3:26 P.M. Fifteen minutes later she got off at Cooper and Young and walked south toward home past ponderous church buildings and a dismal series of ramshackle little homes. The brick walls of the Hermitage, impressively and reassuringly middle-class, were visible at a great distance as she approached. She increased her pace to make the green light at Southern Avenue, slowed a bit to step carefully across two sets of railroad tracks, then began hurrying again. She was almost home.

Olga Mae Lindenmayer, a seventy-six-year-old nurse who had worked at Baptist Hospital, was riding eastbound on Southern Avenue with her son when she noticed a woman in white dress and stockings crossing the street ahead. "Why, that's Bernalyn Dumas!" she exclaimed. "I wonder what she's doing here. She lives way over on LaBelle—let's see if she needs a ride." Mrs. Lindenmayer's son Bill turned left onto Cooper and stopped his car at the edge of the Hermitage. Bernalyn Dumas saw them and stopped walking.

"Hi!" said Mrs. Lindenmayer. "Can we give you a lift? Looks like you're a long way from home."

"Well, hi there," Mrs. Dumas answered, her thin face smiling. "Thanks so much, but I'm already home." She pointed at one of the apartment buildings, half a block away and up on a high green lawn. "We live there now," she said with a hint of pride.

The two women chatted briefly, but Bernalyn Dumas seemed nervous and eager to go. "I've really got to run," she said. "Thanks for stopping, though. It's nice to see you looking so well." She waved and started walking again, clutching her large leather purse under her left arm. As Bill Lindenmayer pulled away, his mother turned in her seat and waved goodbye. She had been the last person to talk with Mrs. Dumas.

Dr. Patsy Erwin, who lived across the hall from the Dumases, was sunning herself at the pool as Mrs. Dumas came briskly up the concrete steps at the front of the Hermitage. She watched Mrs. Dumas turn left onto the walk leading to her front door and disappear around the corner of the building. The fact that Bernalyn Dumas was hurrying did not seem odd to Patsy Erwin. She did not know Mrs. Dumas well but knew that she led a busy life, that she had a family and a demanding job and was going to school at night. Dr. Erwin stayed at the pool a while longer and then returned to her apartment. Instead of walking around to the front door that Bernalyn Dumas had used, she crossed the lawn to her back door. It was next to the Dumases' back door, but as she went inside she did not hear anything unusual. She had been the last person to see Bernalyn Dumas alive.

Roy Dumas had not left home on Thursday. He sometimes did not leave home for days at a time. A tiny, fleshless man weighing less than a hundred pounds, he was unsteady on his feet and did not have the stamina for ordinary work. His arms and legs were as thin as a child's, his face was as nervous and sinewy as a very old man's, and no stranger would have guessed that he had once been a combat hero. But he had, in the Second World War. He had won the Bronze Star, the Purple Heart and a Presidential Citation, had lost part of his stomach as a result of wounds, and had never fully recovered. In the summer of 1969 he was fifty-eight years old and had not held a regular job in more than fifteen years, but he was receiving one hundred percent disability compensation from the Veterans Administration and worked at home as a tax accountant and notary public. Those two sources of income, combined with his wife's salary, provided a comfortable life for the Dumases. They had been able to send their only child away to good schools, and now that he was grown and married money was available for other luxuries. Their three-bedroom apartment at the Hermitage was the most stylish home they'd ever had, and it was nicely furnished. One of the bedrooms, the middle one, was Roy's office.

Some time after his wife left for work, Dumas got out of bed and took off his green pajamas. He dressed in a pair of blue-gray slacks, a light blue pullover shirt, a pair of brown shoes and a sporty three-colored belt. He took his morning medicine, had a light but leisurely breakfast, then turned on the big color television in the living room and went into the front hallway to get the morning paper, leaving the door ajar behind him when he returned. A card on the door bore his name and advertised his business services. It was a sore point with Roy Dumas, that card. At his previous homes he had put a sign on the front lawn, and it had sometimes attracted new clients. But when the Dumases moved to the Hermitage in August, 1968, he learned that outdoor signs were not permitted there. A small card on an inside door was not very helpful.

The living room draperies were pulled shut, but instead of

opening them Dumas turned on a lamp. He sat down on the sofa and looked through the paper. SPARKLING HEROES' FEAST CROWNS DAY OF TRIBUTE FOR NATION'S MOONMEN, said the big headline at the top of page one. On an inside page was the latest story about the murder of actress Sharon Tate and four other persons at a mansion in California. That had happened just five days ago, on Saturday, and it had been sensational news over the weekend. Now, still unsolved, it was becoming a little tedious. Thursday's story said the killings had been "ritualistic."

Dumas folded the paper and put it on the coffee table, already cluttered with stacks of magazines. He and Bernalyn had been looking at home movies the night before, and the projector was still out. Rolls of film were scattered on the floor near the end of the sofa. The room needed tidying up, but Dumas was in no hurry to begin such chores. First he wanted to check about his car.

The car, a one-year-old Dodge, was being repaired. Dumas had banged it against a parked car on August 6, and since then it had been at the Economy Body Shop. It was supposed to be ready on Thursday, however, so at 10:30 he telephoned to see if he could pick it up.

"We're just putting the finishing touches on it," said Hiawatha Swift, an employee at the shop. "It ain't ready now, but we can have it ready for you by five if you want."

Disappointed, Dumas asked to talk with the manager, and Swift told him the manager was not in. "All right then," Dumas replied impatiently, "I'll be there at five." He hung up sharply to express his disgust.

Shortly after 10:30 that morning, mailman Marion Harris entered the hallway at 1133 South Cooper and put the morning's assortment of letters and circulars into the building's four boxes. He noticed that the door to the Dumas apartment was open slightly and that the television inside was turned on at a high volume. He returned minutes later with some Sears catalogues, dropping them on the floor with a loud bang. Roy Dumas's door was still open and the television was still on.

The apartment directly above the Dumases' was occupied by four girls, all twenty years old. One of them, Sue Caldwell, came home for lunch at noon. She parked in the courtyard at the back of the building and entered her apartment through the back door, but at twenty minutes after twelve she came down the front stairs to get the mail. She too noticed that the door to Apartment One was open a few inches and that the television was playing noisily. She saw nothing to indicate that anything unusual might be happening inside. Almost certainly nothing was, because forty minutes later Dumas telephoned his wife to tell her about the car and learned about the birthday party for Tanya.

When Sue Caldwell returned to her job at Memphis State University, her roommates Wanda Turnbo and Jean Hardesty were still at home. From one o'clock until one-thirty the two girls remained together in their living room, watching the day's installment of "Love Is A Many-Splendored Thing." Then Jean Hardesty, who worked nights, went to bed. Wanda lay on the floor in front of the television watching another show, and before it ended at two o'clock she heard someone knock on the door downstairs. It was a hard, loud knock, but that seemed natural because the television in the Dumas apartment was still disturbingly audible. Wanda had her own set turned to an unusually high volume to keep the downstairs noise from interfering with her soap opera.

Sometime within an hour after Wanda heard the knock, Jean Hardesty came sleepily into the living room. "Did you hear that?" she asked. "I thought I heard a man yelling downstairs. It woke me up."

Wanda hadn't heard anything. She turned off the television and the two girls listened intently. The television in the Dumas apartment was still on, and that was all they heard. After a moment Jean shrugged and went back to bed. At

2:45 Wanda went swimming. While she was gone Roy Dumas's television was turned off and the building became totally silent.

Mrs. Betty Rogers, night switchboard operator at police headquarters, was on duty when the Dumas call came in.

"Memphis police," she said slowly. It had been a dull shift up to now, and Mrs. Rogers was a little bored.

"Send the police," a young man's voice cried. "Send me the police. My mother has been raped and murdered."

Mrs. Rogers transferred the call to station 524, the dispatcher's office. Lieutenant Frank Kallaher picked up his phone as soon as it began to ring. "Dispatcher," he drawled. He was not expecting anything important.

"Send me the police. My mother has been raped and murdered."

"You're reporting a killing?" Kallaher reached for a pencil and noted the time. It was 9:55 P.M.

"A murder, yes. My mother. Send me the police."

The voice was hysterical now, repeating the same words over and over again. Kallaher had trouble getting the address.

"Hold it a second," he commanded. "Where are you?"

"My mother's apartment. 1133 South Cooper. Apartment One. Send me the police."

"Stay right where you are and keep calm," the lieutenant said. "I'm sending cars right now. They'll be there in a minute, so don't touch anything. I'll send an ambulance for your mother."

"Send *me* an ambulance, too," cried the voice on the other end of the line. "I'm in a state of shock."

Patrolmen Dick Reed and Bob Furr were at South Cooper and Central Avenue when they heard Kallaher's order for cars 19, 20 and 159 to proceed immediately to 1133 South Cooper. Reed picked up his transmitter and pressed the talk switch.

"This is car 23," he said. "We're in the neighborhood of that call on Cooper. We can get there right away if you want us to."

"Affirmative, car 23. Go ahead."

Seconds later Reed and Furr stopped in front of the Hermitage, found the building at 1133, and went in the front door. When Furr knocked on the door of Apartment One it swung open, and he stepped inside just as officers from another car entered through the kitchen door at the back. A terrified teenage girl was at the back door. "Mike's mother," she screamed, pointing at a doorway. "In the bedroom!" Reed and Furr went the way the girl had pointed and found the body of Bernalyn Dumas. Patrolman Larry Shipman followed, then went down the hall looking into other rooms. "We've got another one," he said when he returned.

A young man in a suit and tie had come in through the kitchen door and was in the living room when Shipman spoke. "Oh, no!" the young man cried. "Is my daddy dead too?"

Captain Robert Cochran, commander of the police department's homicide bureau, had returned from a trip to Florida Thursday afternoon. He was at home, relaxing and looking forward to three more days of vacation, when his telephone rang at 10:10 P.M. He picked up the receiver and hoped for the best. Not many people had his number, and his calls often involved bad news.

"This is Sam McCachran," a familiar voice said. Lieutenant McCachran was acting night commander in the homicide bureau. "Sorry to bother you at home, Captain, but we've got trouble down here. We've got a mess on our hands."

"What have you got?"

"Two people killed in an apartment. A man and wife named Dumas, I think. The guys at the scene say it looks like ligature strangulation. It's a real goddamn mess."

Cochran wrote down the address. He knew his vacation had just ended.

"I'm going there now," he told McCachran. "You better call Dr. Jerry, if you haven't already. And make sure that apartment gets sealed off. Oh, call John Carlisle, too, and ask him to meet me there. I'm on my way."

When Cochran arrived at the Hermitage, a crowd of almost a hundred persons was gathered outside the Dumas apartment. Inside, too many policemen were standing around waiting for the investigation to begin. Some of them were smoking, which angered Cochran, and he ordered everyone except two homicide detectives to leave. As he feared, however, the murder scene had already been compromised in at least a small way. There were cigarette butts in ashtrays in several places around the apartment, and later it would be impossible to determine which had been there when the bodies were first discovered and which had belonged to policemen.

Cochran was a tall man with the physique of a professional wrestler, a former Marine with a craggily rough face under thick black hair. The bridge of his nose, bent inward as a result of an old football injury, completed the picture of a heavy-handed Southern lawman. But the appearance was deceptive. Cochran had a quiet manner and was a perfectionist in his work. Sloppy investigation always made him angry, though he tried not to show it. To him, smoking by a policeman at a freshly-found murder scene was inexcusable.

Cigarette butts were small problems, however. The big ones were in the bedrooms. Cochran took a quick look, stepping gingerly so as not to disturb anything, and realized immediately why Sam McCachran had called him. He left the apartment and went back out into the front hallway, where things were almost out of control. The crowd outside was becoming noisy, and reporters from newspapers and television stations were trying insistently to get inside. Cochran

knocked on the door of Apartment Two, and when Patsy
Erwin answered he explained the situation and said his men
needed a command post. She put her apartment at his dis-
posal. A few minutes later Dr. Jerry Francisco, the Shelby
County Medical Examiner, arrived at the building followed
by John Carlisle, chief investigator in the Shelby County
office of the state attorney general. Cochran took both men
with him into the Dumas apartment to begin a thorough exploration. They started with Mrs. Dumas's bedroom.

It was horrifying, even to veterans like Cochran, Francisco
and Carlisle. They had been through many investigations together but never had seen anything quite like this. The bedroom seemed arranged for dramatic effect, as if the killer had
intended the greatest possible shock for whoever discovered
the murders. The body of Bernalyn Dumas, the most conspicuous object in the room, lay nude and spread-eagled on
its back on a double bed pulled slightly away from the wall.
Three nylon stockings—one brown, one tan, and the third
gray—had been used to tie her right wrist to the bedpost.
Her left wrist was tied to the other bedpost with a red scarf
and a fourth stocking darker than the other three. A pair of
white panty hose had been wrapped around her mouth to
form a gag and knotted tightly at the throat. These panty
hose, and the whole lower half of Mrs. Dumas's face, were
covered by a white wool dickey pulled up almost as far as her
nose.

Mrs. Dumas's white dress had been unsnapped in front
and folded to both sides. Her slip and bra and garter belt
had been cut open in a vertical line from neck to hem, her
panties had been cut along the same line and then horizon-
tally across the crotch, and everything had been pulled aside
so that the entire torso was exposed. The feet were not tied,
and the knees were spread apart and raised slightly. Mrs.
Dumas's white stockings had not been removed. The bedspread under the body and some of the clothing were stained

with what appeared to be two different dark substances, but the stains were small and the body did not appear to have been mutilated. A purse lay open beside the bed, its contents strewn about on the floor. Near the purse was a large and fancily patterned rayon handkerchief folded into a triangle; its ends were tied together.

"This looks like a mask," said Cochran. Dr. Francisco did not reply. He was bent over the lower part of the body, examining it closely. Carlisle stooped to look at the handkerchief, stood up, and nodded without expression.

Two jewelry boxes were open on a dresser. Like the drawers in the room, they had been ransacked. Near them lay a big butcher knife with a curved heavy blade eight and a quarter inches long. The blade was tarnished but not bloody. A few inches away was a pair of surgical scissors covered from the tips of the blades to the finger holes with a dark gummy-looking substance. When Cochran called Francisco's attention to the scissors, the doctor bent over them, sniffed, and wrinkled his nose.

"That's what I was afraid of," he said. "This is a bad one."

There were twin beds covered with matching spreads in Roy Dumas's room. One was cluttered with clothes, coat hangers and magazines. The body, so small and pitifully frail that the massive Cochran could have lifted it with one hand, lay twisted face down on the other. Dumas was fully dressed except for his shoes, his feet were bound just above the ankles with a pair of maroon suspenders, and his hands were tied behind his back with brown suspenders. His mouth was gagged with a red wool scarf and a gray nylon stocking, one end of which was knotted with ferocious tightness around his throat. The left side of the face was bloody, and spots of blood were visible on Dumas's shirt and trousers, on the bedroom rug, and on a wall. A pair of white panty hose, knotted and stained with blood, lay at the foot of the bed. On the floor Cochran noticed a large blue and gold handkerchief folded and tied like the one in Mrs. Dumas's bedroom. This one had a price tag attached to it; it had been purchased at Goldsmith's Department Store for three dollars.

"Another mask," Cochran mused. "Two masks."

Carlisle exhaled noisily and shook his head. "Looks worse every minute," he said.

The three men went to the living room. Atop the television they found a pair of brown gloves stained with a dark substance. Francisco sniffed and frowned disgustedly. A black dickey like the white one covering Mrs. Dumas's mouth was on the sofa, and a billfold was on the floor under a chair. The billfold had been emptied, but a thick stack of credit and identification cards was on the floor beside it. Carlisle lowered himself to his hands and knees to look at the cards. "Dumas's," he said when he stood up.

Fire and Police Director Frank Holloman and Police Chief Henry Lux, when they arrived and saw the bodies, asked Cochran if he wanted them to assign more men to his bureau. The captain said no, he'd rather stay with his own team of specialists and put them all on twelve-hour-a-day shifts. That meant a lot of overtime, but Holloman and Lux immediately consented. They asked Cochran what else he wanted.

"Nothing right now," he said, "except if you could talk to the press. I haven't got time for that." Bob Cochran resented having to talk with reporters when he was busy on a major case.

It was almost midnight when Holloman and Lux went outside for a press conference. Squinting into a flood of television lights and talking through an incoherent barrage of questions, they confirmed some of the basic elements of the story. Mr. and Mrs. Dumas had been found dead in separate bedrooms; they had been found by their son Michael, who had notified police; both victims had been bound, but the cause and time of death were not known. The crowd pressed in closer, trying to hear, fathers in sport shirts raising small children to their shoulders for a better view. They might not have been so eager if they had known that detectives had asked news photographers to take pictures of the crowd on the chance that the murderer had stayed to watch the excitement.

The reporters continued their questions but got few answers. Holloman, a long-faced man with a bushy crop of graying hair, described the killings as "atrocious and revolting," but he didn't explain what he meant. Instead he turned and went back into the building, and when Lux followed the press conference was over. In the Dumas apartment investigators were taking pictures, listing the victims' belongings, and beginning to dust for fingerprints. Dr. Francisco was freeing Bernalyn Dumas's hands from the bedposts and preparing to send the bodies to the morgue. In the command post across the hall, detectives were being assigned to canvass the Hermitage and the surrounding neighborhood. Mike Dumas was in the command post, being questioned.

An hour after midnight the *Commercial Appeal*'s presses began cranking out a Friday morning edition emblazoned with a huge headline: SON FINDS BODIES OF PARENTS SLAIN IN SAVAGE CRIME. The accompanying story was a crazy quilt of the things said by Holloman and Lux, unconfirmed rumors, and imaginative expansions upon hints dropped by some of the officers who had reached the scene first and later had been sent outside by Cochran. The lead paragraph flatly stated, without qualification or attribution, that the bodies of the Dumases were "so bloodied that police were not sure immediately how they were killed." Unidentified policemen were quoted as saying that Mrs. Dumas had been raped and that recent murders in Los Angeles—the Sharon Tate killings—had been committed in "similar gory fashion." One paragraph, noting that Holloman had not stated the cause of death, went on to assert that this was because "the scene was so gory." An unnamed detective was quoted as saying, in a way that echoed the latest news from California, that the Dumas murders were "ritualistic."

The story was a botch, the kind of mistake that most newspapers can make when time is short, information is scarce, the event is a big one and reporters on the scene are not extremely careful. Spread across the front page of the metropolitan area's only morning paper, it jolted Memphis. Reinforced by similar television accounts, it helped to send rumors sweeping across the city. Roy Dumas had been castrated and his wife cut to shreds, according to one grapevine account of the killings. Other versions included gruesome descriptions of how the killer had used table legs, baseball bats and broken bottles to disfigure his victims. There was much talk about the Tate case and much fear that the same killer was now in Memphis.

The whole city was frightened. Some residents of the Hermitage moved out before sunrise Friday. They backed trucks up to the doors of their apartments, loaded them with furniture, and sped away.

The homicide bureau included a total of thirty-one men at the time of the Dumas murders, but four were on vacation. At 8:15 A.M. Friday the twenty-seven available men were assembled in the bureau's day room on the second floor of the headquarters building and told that until further notice they would be working twelve hours a day with no days off. Further vacations were cancelled. Then Cochran briefed the men going on duty about what had happened during the night. The apartment had been searched, photographed and dusted. A minute description of the apartment and everything in it had been tape recorded by Lieutenant Glynn King, and when typed the description would fill almost a hundred single-spaced pages. Every item that might provide a clue or prove useful as evidence had been seized; this included two cans of the Dumases' garbage and the contents of the trap under their bathroom sink. Autopsies and other tests were in process. The walls of the apartment had been sprayed with ninhydrin, a chemical capable of raising fingerprints on rough surfaces. Detectives would be assigned to remain in the apartment day and night until all possibilities there had been exhausted; the ninhydrin might take two weeks to produce results.

Seven detectives were sent back to the Hermitage at the end of the meeting, two to get a list of all cars parked there and five to begin a door-to-door search of every building within two blocks. They were instructed to learn who lived in each building, where each resident worked, whether anyone had seen anything suspicious on Thursday. Railroad tracks, parking lots, garbage cans, alleys and yards all were to be explored. Anything unusual was to be brought to headquarters and checked out.

The list of things to be done was enormous, and all of them had to be done as quickly as possible. A "Dumas workroom" was set up in the homicide bureau, and a detailed map showing every structure within a five-mile radius of the Hermitage was mounted on the wall. Color-coded markers were used to indicate houses where burglaries had occurred, houses where suspicious characters lived, houses that had been visited and checked out by investigators. The goal, which would require many weeks, was to check every house on the map. On other walls detectives hung a map of the Hermitage and a floor plan marked to indicate the location of every potentially significant item found in the Dumas apartment.

In any city, only "big" murders receive this kind of attention. The Dumas case was a big one from the start because it was so mysterious, because it frightened so many people, because the publicity put the police department under sharp public scrutiny.

Roy Dumas's files contained the names of his clients, and every one of them had to be found, questioned and checked. A list of everyone who lived or worked at the Hermitage or was there for any reason on Thursday had to be compiled, and everyone on it had to be investigated. There were other lists, too: known burglars and sex offenders, Bernalyn Dumas's acquaintances at the hospital, all of the victims' friends and relatives. Authorities in Tennessee, Mississippi and Arkansas were asked for the names of any criminals or mental patients recently released or escaped who might be capable of a double murder.

Mike Dumas, twenty-one years old and a senior at Memphis State, was questioned all night and all morning and part of Friday afternoon. Detectives asked him everything imaginable—questions about his own background, what he knew about his parents, what he and they had been doing Thursday. When the detectives ran out of questions they asked the old ones over again, each time probing for more and more detail, and Dumas remained cooperative. He was a graduate of Kemper Military School in Missouri, he worked in the data processing department of a downtown bank and was studying computer technology in college, and overall he was no stranger to precision. He seemed unoffended by the detectives' most exact questions.

He had gone to school Thursday morning, Dumas said. His wife Tanya picked him up at noon and they drove to her parents' home in Germantown. At three o'clock he left there and went to his own apartment on Steve Road, intending to study, but at 3:30 a friend named Bill Dismukes stopped by. Dismukes, trying to sell Mike Dumas an insurance policy, didn't leave until 5:15. Mike returned to his in-laws' home at 5:30 for dinner, and at six o'clock he tried to telephone his parents but got no answer. That was annoying but not frightening, because Roy Dumas was far from being a prompt man. Mike left after dinner to go to a seven o'clock class, and when he returned at nine his parents still had not arrived. Worried now, he called his mother's duty station at Baptist Hospital to ask if anyone knew where she might be. No one did. He called his grandfather Kelly in

Toone, Tennessee, to see if Bernalyn and Roy might have gone there. They hadn't. Finally he called the emergency room at Baptist Hospital and police headquarters to ask if his parents had been involved in an accident. So far as anyone knew, they hadn't. When Mike announced that he was going to drive to his parents' apartment to see if anything was wrong, Tanya's sixteen-year-old sister Angelique and her brother Bill Jr., fourteen, volunteered to ride along.

Mike Dumas had lived with his parents until his marriage early that summer, and he still had a key to their kitchen door. He parked his car at the rear of the building, unlocked the door, and went through the kitchen into the living room. When he called out, no one answered. He went into his mother's room and saw her on the bed. "Mom!" he shouted, but she did not respond. Her face was completely covered by the white dickey, and when he pulled it down and touched her forehead he realized that she was dead. He ran screaming to the living room, fell down, then got up and ran through the front door to the hallway. Still screaming, he pounded on Dr. Patsy Erwin's door; she opened it a crack, but when she saw Dumas's distorted face and heard his unintelligible cries she became afraid and refused to release the chain. "Bitch!" Dumas yelled. He ran back into his parents' living room and telephoned the police. After talking with Lieutenant Kallaher he dropped the phone, ran out the back door, and fell down again. Angelique Miner started into the apartment to see what had happened, but Dumas told her to stop. He was still on the ground when the first officers arrived, and Angelique was the girl who screamed when Patrolman Furr came in through the front door.

Every part of Dumas's story was comfirmed, and at three o'clock Friday afternoon he was permitted to go home. Exhausted and relieved, he put on his jacket and left the downtown headquarters building. As soon as he was on the stone steps outside, photographers and reporters began taking his picture and shouting questions. Frustrated by police officials' refusal to discuss the case, embarrassed by Director Hollo-man's insistence Friday morning that the murder scene had in fact not been bloody, they had been waiting impatiently for some new development.

The questions asked by the reporters were simple enough, compared with what Dumas had been asked by police, but he had been advised not to give any information to the press. So he tried to push his way down the steps to where a patrolman was waiting to drive him home. He was still dressed in the brown suit and blue shirt he had put on for his wife's birthday party Thursday afternoon, but he looked surprisingly fresh. He was a handsome youth, tidy and crisp like his mother. His necktie was still drawn up tight, and his straight dark hair was neatly combed. His eyes, however, betrayed his exhaustion. They were drawn back into his skull, and dark circles were visible behind the frames of his glasses. When the reporters did not move aside for him, he seemed momentarily confused.

"I'll tell you a statement," he said suddenly, his voice trembling slightly. "I'll tell you one. It's a shame that those two people can't live on this earth." Then he broke free and got into a police car. It was a brief quote but a good one, and soon it was in the news. The papers and television stations did not report, however, that Mike Dumas was being handled as a highly possible suspect. He was the Dumases' only child, and he had found their bodies in an apartment to which he had a key and which appeared not to have been forcibly entered. Relatives are always suspect under such circumstances—especially when no one else is.

In fact, the police had no solid suspects. The investigation was unwieldy from the beginning because it had no focus, and it could not be focused until a firm motive or suspect or clue had been found. Having none of these, the homicide bureau had to continue to look everywhere. Detectives checked the history of the Dumas family as thoroughly as possible, thinking that a reason for the murder might lie somewhere in the past.

Bernalyn Dumas, the investigation showed, was Roy Dumas's third wife. He had been born in Bald Knob, Arkansas, in 1911, married for the first time in Louisiana in 1938, and was divorced in 1941. He married again in Arizona in 1943, and that marriage ended in divorce in April, 1947. He served in the Army during the war and was badly wounded by exploding shrapnel. Bernalyn Kelly was born in Athens, Tennessee, in 1923 and graduated twenty years later from the Deaconess Erlanger School of Nursing in Chattanooga. She served during the last months of the war as a nursing lieutenant in the Women's Army Corps and met Roy Dumas in 1945 at the Kennedy Veterans Hospital in Memphis, where she was stationed and he was a patient. They were married in Hernando, Mississippi, on May 5, 1947, and later they moved to St. Louis where Bernalyn took a training course in psychiatric nursing at Barnes Hospital. Their son was born in St. Louis in 1948.

The family returned to Memphis after Michael's birth, and in 1951 Mrs. Dumas began a successful career at Baptist Hospital. She became assistant head nurse in 1952, head nurse in 1957, and ward supervisor in 1959. Since 1967 she had been taking night courses toward a master's degree at the University of Tennessee.

From the early fifties until 1966, the Dumases had lived in a small frame house at 2092 LaBelle Street. It was not an attractive house, and the neighborhood was even worse: railroad tracks and factories were visible from the front door. They sent their son away for high school, and when he graduated and began college in Mississippi the Dumases moved into an apartment. In 1968 they moved again, to the Hermitage. They were active members of the Lindenwood Christian Church and leaders of the Shelby County chapter of the Disabled American Veterans; Roy served as the chapter's chaplain, and Bernalyn was vice commander of the women's auxiliary. They seemed to have had few friends outside the DAV and their church, and they were among the oldest residents at the Hermitage, where most of the apartments were rented by single people and newly married couples. They were regarded, one of their young neighbors told reporters, as "a quiet, respectable, elderly couple."

Not everything about the Dumases was quite so routine. Since 1960, detectives discovered, Roy had been involved in eighteen reported automobile accidents, and it appeared likely that still others had not been reported to authorities. Too weak to drive competently, and candid in admitting as much, he nevertheless had persisted in driving. A Sears Roebuck salesman informed police that two days before his death Roy Dumas had attempted to purchase a .38-caliber Smith & Wesson revolver and had become indignant when told that Tennessee law required a waiting period between purchase of firearms and delivery. No one knew why he had suddenly wanted a pistol, though detectives spent many hours searching for an explanation.

On December 23, 1967, Michael Dumas had been involved in a collision that caused the death of a one-month-old child. Detectives were intrigued to learn of that incident, and they explored the possibility that someone in the baby's family had decided to kill Dumas's parents in revenge. But they found an earlier case involving Bernalyn Dumas even more interesting. In August 1953, almost exactly sixteen years before her death, Mrs. Dumas had awakened in her bedroom one night to find a burglar searching for money. When she shouted at the intruder, an old report on the incident indicated, the man ran to a kitchen window and tried to climb out. Bernalyn Dumas pursued him, shouting for him to stop, and he turned back and struck her in the head with a frying pan. The blow severed the optic nerve in one of Mrs. Dumas's eyes and she underwent two serious operations as a result, and thereafter she was able to see only with the help of thick glasses—glasses which police found on the floor of the bedroom where she was murdered. The burglar had been caught, and in 1954 he was sentenced to fifty-four years in prison on one hundred and seven counts of burglary, ninety counts of larceny and one count of assault with intent to murder. The last charge stemmed from the striking of Mrs. Dumas. The burglar served thirteen years in the state penitentiary at Nashville and was paroled in 1967.

There were things worth exploring in all this, suggestions that someone might have decided to take revenge on one or another of the Dumases. All the possibilities were explored, and all of them proved fruitless. Even the burglar was found and cleared. Later the *Memphis Press-Scimitar*, the *Commercial Appeal*'s sister publication, ran a front page story naming the burglar and saying that he was being hunted. The "suspect" heard about the story and, frightened by it, telephoned police headquarters long distance to ask what was going on. He was told not to worry; a detective had been too talkative and a reporter had misrepresented his words.

Every morning Cochran met with Holloman, Chief Lux and Chief of Detectives Joe Gagliano for at least an hour to review the Dumas case. At least once a day he held a meeting of detectives in the homicide bureau to discuss what they had done and what remained to be done. Almost without exception, progress could be measured only in negative terms. Officers were turning up and quickly exhausting an abundance of possible leads. Many came from persons living at the Hermitage.

Despite its name and apparent tranquility, despite the handsome quiet of its antique brick walls and oak-shaded lawns, the Hermitage had a long and varied record of crime complaints. Perhaps it was a convenient, too tempting target for residents of the poor neighborhood to the north. Over the past two years there had been frequent reports of burglaries, peace disturbance incidents, even muggings. In the summer of 1968, when the killing of Martin Luther King put white Memphis in fear of a general conflagration, a security guard had been hired at the Hermitage. Later, when calm returned, the guard was dismissed. Early in 1969, in response to demand from tenants, the management had put new and more secure locks on the doors. Incidents and complaints had continued, however, and as a result some residents had moved out even before the Dumas murders.

About 3 P.M. Thursday, shortly before Bernalyn Dumas left work and started home, police had received an anonymous report of a prowler on the Hermitage grounds. Officers had been sent to investigate but had found nothing. Late Thursday night, in interviewing persons living near the Dumas apartment, detectives were given more than fifteen different accounts of suspicious persons seen in the area that day. This was a predictable result of imagination mixed with sudden fear, and most of the stories were hopelessly vague. The most specific was about a Negro woman who had often been seen parked for long periods of time in a Thunderbird sedan at the Hermitage. Detectives managed to find the woman. She worked for a detective agency owned by a retired Memphis policeman and had been gathering information to be used in a divorce case.

Cochran's men continued to throw out their nets, but when pulled in every net was empty. One by one the names of possible suspects came up, and one by one they were cleared.

Nothing could be found to indicate that the apartment had been forcibly entered. The metal frame of a screen on one window was bent but shrouded in cobwebs. Nothing could be found to indicate that Bernalyn Dumas had been followed home by the killer, or to prove that the killer was already in the apartment when she arrived. Only one unidentifiable fingerprint was found. It was on a knife under a cake dish in the Dumases' kitchen, and it was insufficient for a check against FBI files. Memphis police checked it against the fingerprints of local burglars and thieves and sexual deviates, and against prints found at all other crime scenes in the city, but it was never matched.

Many surfaces that should have borne at least the Dumases' fingerprints turned out to be utterly clean, and the ninhydrin on the walls turned up nothing useful. Nothing pointing to the identity of the killer, not even a single strand of hair or one smudged footprint, was discovered. Everything found in the apartment was identified as having belonged to the Dumases. So far as their son could determine, none of their belongings had been stolen.

Three dollars were found in a side pocket of Bernalyn Dumas's purse. Aside from that, police found almost no money in the apartment, but the Dumases had never kept much money at home. Robbery did not seem an altogether satisfactory motive.

The autopsy results, as they became available, proved gruesome but not remarkably helpful. The cause of death was indeed strangulation, and the injuries to the left side of Roy Dumas's head indicated that he had probably been struck before his death by a right-handed person. A far more alarming fact was that Bernalyn Dumas's vagina and rectum both had been penetrated and cut internally with a sharp instrument, almost certainly the pair of surgical scissors found on her bedroom dresser. The gummy-looking substance on the scissors proved to be fecal matter. The stains on Mrs. Dumas's clothes and bedspread were blood and fecal matter. Test results failed to prove that she had been raped.

The gloves found on the television set in the living room had belonged to Roy Dumas. The stains on them were blood and fecal matter.

According to Dr. Francisco, broken blood vessels on Mrs. Dumas's wrists indicated that she had been alive when tied to the bed. But she was probably dead when mutilated with the scissors, Francisco added. He had taken fluid from the eyes of both victims in an effort to determine the time of death, but the test results indicated that they had died

Thursday morning. This was dismissed as an obvious mistake, and on the basis of other evidence the time of death was set at anywhere between 1:30 P.M. and 7:00 P.M.

Francisco, a compactly built man with short hair and eyeglasses, was accustomed to difficult cases. In 1968 he had performed the autopsy on the body of Martin Luther King, and his intelligence and care in that case had been admired and praised. Memphis policemen liked working with him, and his stature in their eyes rose still higher when he achieved a new triumph in the Dumas investigation. He took one of the mask-shaped handkerchiefs, analyzed traces of saliva on it, and was able to determine that the mask had been worn by someone with type A blood. Roy and Bernalyn Dumas both had type O blood. Francisco's announcement seemed to provide the first solid fragment of information about the killer. The doctor was not able to determine, however, whether the other handkerchief mask had been worn by a second person.

None of this information was given to the press. Joe Gagliano, chief of detectives and more accessible than Cochran, was questioned persistently by reporters wanting to know more about the case. They were particularly curious about the rumors concerning what had been done to Mrs. Dumas. "We'll say she was sexually molested," Gagliano said. "Period." In answer to most questions, he simply said "No comment." Frank Holloman did the same thing, as did Chief Lux, and the rumors spread and became more colorful.

Pet stores and animal shelters in and around Memphis experienced a sudden jump in the demand for dogs, especially large dogs. The Doktor Pet Center on Plaza Street was sold out within forty-eight hours after the bodies were discovered.

In his office at the homicide bureau, Bob Cochran continued to put his information together in new combinations to see what had been learned. Very little, actually. Practically nothing could be ruled out except suicide. The killer could be black or white, young or old, male or female. Possibly there were several killers.

Every piece of physical evidence except the bodies was bundled up for shipment to the Federal Bureau of Investigation laboratories in Washington. The homicide staff, still working seven days a week, broadened the range of its inquiries and reached deeper into its files of robbers, burglars, rapists and sexual irregulars. Gradually the number of possible suspects and clues grew smaller. The scissors used to mutilate Mrs. Dumas were proved to have been hers. Detective Jimmy Dugan, a young and aggressive newcomer to the homicide bureau, surprised his superiors by tracing the butcher knife found in Bernalyn Dumas's bedroom and establishing that Roy Dumas had purchased it. Then Dugan began tracing the big handkerchief mask bearing the Goldsmith's price tag, and by going through thousands of the store's sales slips he determined that Dumas, not the killer, had bought it. The suspenders, the stockings, everything used in the killings had belonged to the Dumases. Dr. Francisco had examined the knots used to bind the victims and told Cochran that they were not unusual in any way.

Over the weekend, relatives began to arrive in town for the funeral. The services were to be held Tuesday morning at Memphis Funeral Home, and afterwards there would be a formal military burial at National Cemetery nearby. Roy Dumas's medals would be displayed beside his casket. Lieutenants Barry Linville and Tommy Smith were told to attend the funeral and watch for suspicious persons; perhaps the killer would attend too.

Roy Dumas's brother Eugene arrived from Springfield, Missouri. His sister, Mrs. Llewellyn Lee, came from Bellflower, Missouri. The day before the funeral they and Michael Dumas issued a public statement urging the killer or killers to surrender to police and seek psychiatric treatment.

"Whoever brought this terrible tragedy to Memphis and to our beloved needs help," the family said. "It was a terrible thing and a sick act and we have trained people who can help them. We harbor no hatred, but we don't want such a thing to happen again, so we ask the guilty parties to come forward and seek help." The statement was printed in the afternoon's edition of the *Press-Scimitar* and Michael Dumas was shown reading it on the evening news. It was a touching appeal, and almost everyone in the city saw it or read it or heard about it.

It touched Mrs. Leila Jackson, an eighty-year-old widow.

It touched Glenda Sue Harden, twenty-one years old and recently engaged to be married.

It touched Mary Christine Pickens, fifty-nine years old and alone.

And it touched Mary Putt, though she had troubles enough of her own. She was watching television when Michael Dumas was shown reading his family's appeal. She was moved by what she saw and annoyed by her husband's cynically male response.

"That's just a come-on," Mary's husband said. "There probably is something wrong with a person who would kill two people like that, but if he turned himself in they wouldn't do anything for him. They'd just lock him up and throw the key away. They don't really help people like that."

Mary shrugged. She didn't know anything about such matters, and her husband didn't either.

2

A Delta Girl

MARY PUTT'S presence in Memphis during the summer of 1969 was the result of a long series of accidents and mistakes. Almost all of Mary's life, in fact, had been shaped by accidents and mistakes, by unexpected events and by things that on the conscious level at least were totally unwanted. It was a life out of control, a confusing and disappointing and frightening life following a random course at high speed to certain catastrophe. It had been that way long before her own acts and the acts of others brought Mary to Memphis in 1969; the pathetic, disgusting and tragic things in which she became involved that summer were simply an inevitable collision with her own foredoomed reality. If they had not happened in Memphis they would almost certainly have happened somewhere else, probably at about the same time. Accidents and mistakes had produced a momentum that virtually nothing could check.

Accidents affect every life importantly, and mistakes alter most lives to some extent, but in Mary's case both were so decisive that choice and independent action were overwhelmed. There is actually no point at which it can be said without qualification that Mary had freely chosen to be living as a wife and mother in Memphis at the time of the

Dumas murders. She was a headstrong girl who prized independence to an extraordinary degree, but she had lost it quickly and entirely before she was even old enough to vote. Because this happened in part as a result of her own actions, she was not an altogether innocent victim. Because in several ways she victimized herself, her life is complicated and puzzling.

Mary wanted freedom and adventure and a colorful life. But she was female, and she grew up in the South, and the double standard for young men and young women has been more durable there than in any other region; when she was growing up, it was still possible for a girl who did the things that boys were expected to do to be ruined as irredeemably as any Victorian maiden. Outside the South, Mary's story probably would have developed quite differently. Even in the South it might not have been so dismal if she had been born just a few years later. But Mary was a girl who learned to think and behave like a boy in a world that expected the sexes to follow distinctly different paths. That is why, despite her own hopes and efforts, she lost control of her life and really was ruined. She defied the laws of her culture and paid with her future for doing so.

She was born in 1949 in Sledge, Mississippi, a tiny and decrepit village in a kind of timeless zone south of Tennessee and east of Arkansas, a region of old and isolated and shrinking towns scattered over a flat delta landscape. It is cotton and soybean country, a place where wild kudzu vines cover the low hills and form strips of jungle along roads and highways and have to be burned off the fields, where the soil is dark and fertile but only those families who own the land benefit from its bounty. In the late nineteen-forties, for all but a tiny minority of aristocrats, it was still pure Yoknapatawpha County, still almost completely untouched by postwar change or the economic shifts that elsewhere were creating a New South. If anything, the delta was for many of its people an even harsher place to live after the war than it had

been before technology began to make human labor superfluous. For poor white families like the one into which Mary
was born, it was a place where a life of comfort and prosper-
ity was almost unimaginable and nothing more tangible than
custom preserved a sense of superiority over the vassal blacks
who had not yet been driven or lured away.

Mary's birth, because it added to the burdens of a family
already struggling to survive in the archaic feudal world of
northeastern Mississippi, was not an unmixedly joyous event.
Her parents were living on a farm in Tunica County at
the time, scratching a livelihood out of sharecropped land,
but Mary was born in Sledge because her mother, Annie Lee
Matthews Bulimore, had gone there near the end of her
pregnancy to have the help of relatives when the baby arrived. Annie was forty-one years old then, a tough and proud
woman with freckled fair skin and high cheekbones under
graying red hair, and her life had been hard even by delta
standards. She had two other living children, a son twelve
years old and a daughter seven, and a new and late edition to
the family was cause for worry. Sharecroppers depended entirely upon physical strength for what little they were able to
earn, and the Bulimores were no longer able to take continued good health for granted.

Mary's father, Richard Bulimore, had like his wife a sense
of personal dignity undamaged by the physical circumstances
of his life—an inner sense of balance that belied stereotypes
of the benighted savage redneck and won and held respect
even when he was penniless. The son of English immigrants,
he had owned farmland when he was young but had lost it
during the early years of the Depression. Almost fifty years
old in 1949, he was a big, handsome and imperturbably
good-natured man laboring without complaint to support his
family by raising cotton on land controlled by owners whose
agents came every year to claim a painfully high percentage
of his crop. The little house that came with his farm in Tunica County was hot in summer and cold in winter, and on

rainy days the Bulimores had to put buckets on the floor under the places where the roof leaked. The need for share-croppers was diminishing by the time Mary was born, and some delta families were already leaving for factory jobs in the North and in some of the South's larger communities. But Richard and Annie Bulimore were rooted in the cotton-lands. They preferred the life they knew, leaking roof and all, to strange work in strange places.

Before long, in any case, migration became impossible. Mary contracted spinal meningitis while still very small, and for a time it appeared likely that she would be permanently crippled. Her parents were able to find medical help for her, her brother was instructed to exercise her legs for long pe-riods every day, and gradually her condition improved. She learned to walk at an unusually late age, but the important thing for the family was that she walked at all. She was al-most fully recovered and was developing into a bright and robust child when her father suffered a physical collapse that would, with later complications, keep him an invalid for the rest of his life.

Mary loved her father more than anyone else she ever knew, and after she was grown she retained clear early memories of him as a figure of great physical strength. In fact, however, he must have always had a vulnerable consti-tution. A costly illness in his young manhood had been one reason for the loss of the share of his parents' land that he, one of several brothers, had inherited. In the early years of his marriage Bulimore had worked as a commercial fisherman, netting and selling the huge catfish of the lower Mississippi, but here again his health failed him and after re-current attacks of pneumonia he was forced to leave the river and turn to sharecropping. He was fifty-five years old, and Mary was just old enough to begin school, when he fell vic-tim to a lung disease that required two operations and left him too weak to farm or fish. His wife believed that this ill-ness had been caused by the fact that Bulimore, unable to afford to rent a tractor, had found it necessary to spray his land with boll weevil poison by hand, the hose around his neck and the nozzle near his face. Inhaling clouds of poison, Annie was sure, had wrecked her husband's lungs. Something, certainly, had destroyed his health permanently; in later years, as his condition slowly deteriorated, he lost a lung and part of his stomach and was at intervals dangerously close to death.

Cotton plantations have no place for sharecroppers who cannot work, and so after his collapse Bulimore was ordered out of his house. He took his family a few miles east to Sarah, a little town in Tate County, because Annie had brothers there and the area was so depressed that rents were almost negligible. They found an empty old church building at the edge of town, rented it for ten dollars a month, and settled in for a life even more constricted than the one they had known before. The church had five enormous high-ceilinged rooms, and even after the Bulimores moved in their few beds and chairs it still looked abandoned. It had electricity but no running water or central heating, so the Bulimores had to carry in wood by the armful and water by the bucket. Little Mary found it a lonesome, spooky place to live. During the day her father, usually too sick to get out of bed, was often her only company.

Throughout most of her childhood Mary had no awareness of being poor, because in Sarah there were no wealthy families to serve as points of comparison. The town had never been prosperous, and by the mid-fifties it was sinking deep into squalor, many of its houses left empty in the wake of accelerating emigration from the delta to the cities. Most of those who remained behind were, like Mr. and Mrs. Bulimor, piously fundamentalist Baptists and Methodists who never missed church on Sunday and regarded the drinking of beer as a high order of evil. For all of them, life was hard. After Mary's father was disabled the Bulimores began to receive twenty-five dollars a month from the state welfare department, but even in Sarah that was not nearly enough to support a family. Annie went to work at the only jobs she could get—picking and chopping cotton in season, commercial fishing at other times. It would have been hard work for a young man, and Annie was now in her late forties. But she kept at it season after season and then year after year, and once when a family friend asked if she was disappointed by the turns her life had taken she looked at him blankly as if she couldn't understand what he meant. She was doing the job that God had given her, supporting her husband and trying to get her children raised. The only thing worth regretting was that sometimes work and worry made her treat the children with a harshness she did not intend. She lacked the time to mother her children and to discipline them too, and so, because she wanted to give them what she thought they would need, she concentrated on discipline.

As she grew up, Mary developed very different perceptions of her parents. Her father, cheerful through all his ailments, continued to seem a kind and protective figure who never criticized her, often praised her, and was always quick to forgive her trespasses. Her mother, who went out every morning to do a man's work for low pay and came home each night to an oversized home in need of cleaning, became in Mary's eyes a kind of demon who seemed never pleased, never satisfied, never affectionate except when her youngest daughter became ill and needed nursing. At those times Annie became very loving, and she would apologize for her sternness. "I imagine I am hard on you, girl," she would say, "but sometimes I just get to the point where my nerves can't stand anything. I only want what's best for you." Mary, confused by these changes in her mother's moods, began to resent being cared for. She acquired an aversion to taking medicine, to admitting illness, to staying in bed when she was not feeling well.

She began to blame everything on her mother. When her

older brother quit school after the tenth grade and went
north to a factory job in "the city," Memphis, she thought it
was because he wanted to get away from Annie. When her
sister married at sixteen and moved to another delta town,
Mary thought she had done so to get away from Annie. Mary
envied her brother and sister because they had, she believed,
escaped to a better life. She too wanted to escape, and naturally the path that her sister had taken seemed at first far
more accessible than her brother's. Marriage was the easiest
way for a girl to get away.

Before she reached her teens, however, Mary became
aware of a fact that many girls do not learn until too late:
that marriage is at best a risky means of escape. Her mother's
grinding life was the first clue, of course, but it was not a
persuasive one because Mary could not identify with her
mother or consider her sympathetically. But she saw girls not
a great deal older than herself, girls in Sarah and on farms
nearby, who had left school in their mid-teens to get married
and found themselves trapped with children of their own
in homes as poor and dreary as the ones they had so eagerly fled.
Something in Mary was able to draw a lesson from what she
saw around her, and the lesson was confirmed when her own
sister's marriage ended in divorce after two years and one
child. Something in Mary was imaginative enough to decide
at an early age that her brother was the example to be followed. She made up her mind to do better than her brother,
to prepare herself to escape. She would finish high school before going.

High school opened Mary's horizons and presented her
with status problems that she had not previously experienced. She had gone to grade school in Strayhorn, a ten-mile
bus ride from home but otherwise no distance at all from the
world she had always known. Like Sarah, where the most
prosperous resident was the woman who ran the post office,
Strayhorn was a decaying hamlet dependent for survival
upon jobs in the few small factories being established in the

area by firms in search of cheap labor. Not many of the children had been much better off than Mary, and her homemade clothes had attracted no attention. But the high school at Coldwater, thirty miles from home, was different. It had a thousand students, some of whose parents had money, and at the beginning of her freshman year Mary became acutely aware that not everyone lived like the people in Sarah. Her clothes were not like those of her more affluent classmates.

Life was a bit less difficult for the Bulimores by this time. Mary's brother was becoming a success in Memphis and was sending money to his parents. Mary and her mother and father had moved out of the church building into a small, unpainted wooden house in a gully near the highway that ran through Sarah, and Annie had rented a shack behind the house to two roomers. The monthly checks from the welfare department had increased to fifty-five dollars, and so the family was not so hard-pressed as it had been a few years earlier. There was little money to spare for clothes, however, and Mary wanted new clothes badly. She was determined to have them, and so she found a part-time job at the Blue and White Restaurant in Tunica, sixteen miles from Sarah.

The Blue and White was one of the best restaurants in the northern delta, a gathering place for planters and brokers and other members of local society's thin upper crust. Mary was only fourteen years old when she was hired, but she was already a tall and shapely redhead and she looked at least sixteen. She enjoyed her job and worked hard, and the owners were so pleased with her that on nights when they needed an extra girl on short notice they would send a car all the way to Sarah to pick her up. On a good night—Christmas Eve was always best—Mary could make more than twenty dollars in tips, and it wasn't long before she was one of the best-dressed girls at school. The job cut into her study time, but she didn't care about that. She didn't really enjoy school, and she was clever enough to get solid passing grades with little effort. It cut into her social life, too, but she didn't care about that either. The sophisticated big spenders at the Blue and White were far more interesting than even the ruling elite at Coldwater High, and Mary was delighted to find herself moving up in the world so rapidly.

High school and the restaurant broadened Mary's world. California broadened it still more. She went to California at the end of her sophomore year for a long visit with her sister, who had remarried and was living in Modesto. That summer was the happiest time in all of Mary's life, and for more than two months, as she told friends later, she felt "like a butterfly set free." Her sister and brother-in-law gave her spending money, bought clothes for her, and demanded nothing. They gave her the opportunity to discover things whose existence she had never suspected.

She bought a bikini, the first she had owned, and wore it almost every day to the beach at the Modesto reservoir. At the beach, and at parks where teenagers gathered, she met boys unlike any she had known in Mississippi, and the more exotic they seemed the more they fascinated her. Her favorite was a quiet Mexican youth named Jose who spoke little English and was the son of migrant farm workers. He took Mary to his home, and his mother taught her to make tortillas. He took her to the fields to pick fruit, and when he laughed at the slow way in which she pulled apricots down from the trees Mary laughed too. At the beach she met a college student from Hawaii, a sky-diver who told her about the islands and about jumping out of airplanes, and Mary told him that someday she would see and do those things herself. At a teenage hangout in Modesto she met a Hell's Angel who called himself Little Jesus and wore a gold ring in his ear. He seemed dangerous and dirty at first, but after they became acquainted and he took her riding on his big motorcycle she decided that he really was a nice boy.

It was all exciting, and Mary felt that she was beginning to understand people and see how interesting the world could be. When the summer ended she refused to go home. Mississippi was backward and boring, and all the boys there were hicks with white socks and slicked-back hair and nothing to do. She wrote to her mother and announced that she was going to stay in California, finish high school, and then get a job or go to college. By return mail Annie Bulimore warned that she would go to California herself if necessary, hitchhiking if she couldn't raise the bus fare, to bring Mary home. So Mary got on the bus and went back to Mississippi, to Coldwater High School, and to the Blue and White Restaurant. She knew that after two more years she would be free.

By the beginning of her junior year, Mary was a fully formed and complex young woman whose personality was stretched in different directions by conflicting impulses. She hated life in Sarah and wanted to be out in the bigger world that she had briefly experienced, but she was grudgingly willing to remain in school because she knew that a diploma would be necessary for a full and final escape. She wanted to please her mother and be accepted by her, but she thought it was impossible to do either. Unlike any girl she had ever known, she had absolutely no expectations of love, marriage, and a happy family life. When she heard other girls talk about wanting to get married and have babies she thought they were fools. She knew something of sex by now, and she liked what she knew well enough. But she did not associate it with love. She did not associate anything with love. The idea of romantic love was as meaningless to her as quantum physics—and far more annoying, since the girls around her were not constantly talking about quantum physics. She wanted to graduate and travel and be totally free forever.

For the time being, stuck in Mississippi, she vented her frustration by rebelling. In her first two years at Coldwater High she had been a quiet, uninterested member of her class, neither receiving nor demanding much attention from anyone. Now, back from California and filled with scorn for her classmates and fear that maybe she was as big a hayseed as they, she became a troublemaker. She chose her friends from among the students who had reputations for wildness because at first they were the closest substitutes she could find for the teenagers in Modesto. Determined to do what she wanted to do when she wanted to do it, Mary broke all the minor rules at school. She smoked, she left the campus at lunchtime, she was insubordinate; as a result she was often in trouble, often on probation, and occasionally suspended. None of this worried her, and as she became known as a daring girl—that's how she hoped she was known, at any rate—she found that she enjoyed being a kind of celebrity. Even being on suspension, she discovered, was fun. She would get up in the morning as usual and catch the school bus, and in Coldwater she would catch another bus to Memphis and spend the day there before returning to Coldwater in time for the last bell and the ride home. Her mother, who saw Mary get on the school bus early in the morning and get off late in the afternoon and nothing more, never knew what was going on.

Usually Mary was careful not to do anything really bad at school, if only because her dislike for the place was exceeded by her desire for a diploma. But her determination to be independent, and her idea that an important part of independence was never permitting anyone to take advantage of her, sometimes had serious consequences. One day, when she was undressing in a locker room before gym class, another girl mischievously raised a shade so that several boys were able to see in. Enraged, Mary shoved the girl's head against the window and broke the glass, forced her backward across a table, and was beating her on the head when a teacher pulled her off. Luckily, the girl was not injured and Mary was merely suspended for three days which she spent happily in Memphis. When she returned to school she paid for the broken window by doing clerical chores in the principal's office. Mary liked the principal because he seemed to like her. She would smile at him and open wide her blue eyes, and he seemed to be charmed. Keeping him charmed was good insurance.

It was not so easy at home. Mary and her mother could not get along peacefully, and as Mary grew bolder the situation became rapidly more unpleasant. The first serious conflict erupted not long after she returned from Modesto, when she began to receive letters from her Mexican friend Jose. The letters were a garbled combination of Spanish and English, and Mary had to take them to the school library to translate the Spanish parts. She treasured them, however, and she was hurt and angry when Annie complained volubly, that she was neglecting her studies to correspond with "a greasy wetback Mexican." They fought, and soon Annie was tearing up Jose's letters as they arrived and any letters that she found Mary writing to him. "I'd rather you went out with a nigger than one of those crazy Mexicans," Annie would scream. They continued to battle over the letters until Jose stopped writing, and then that particular conflict between mother and daughter came to an end.

There were other conflicts, though. Annie Bulimore had vague but high aspirations for her youngest child, and she seemed to have something unpleasant, something critical to say about the boys who came to the house. No boy was good enough, it appeared, and eventually Mary tired of trying to find a boyfriend whom her mother would accept. She went in the other direction, accepting dates with young men who were so much older than she, so notorious and unmannerly, that they were certain to send Annie into a frenzy. Dates with such men were satisfying to Mary in more than one way. They expressed her contempt for the dull conventions of life in Sarah, and they were weapons in the continuing quarrel with her mother.

Her first new boyfriend was a twenty-four-year-old auto mechanic renowned for his drinking and wild behavior. A friend of Mary's had dated him and reported that his reputation was well deserved, and so when he asked Mary for a date she did not hesitate to accept. He wore white socks and combed his hair in the oily country style that she wanted to despise, but he took her dancing at the night clubs near Moon Lake. The Moon Lake district had a reputation for wildness, too, and that made Mary enjoy it all the more. She dated the mechanic until December and then started going out with his brother, a soldier on leave from the Army. The triangle created some confused feelings.

On Christmas Eve, Mary returned home from a date with the soldier and went to bed. About two o'clock Christmas morning the mechanic and another man drove down into the gully where the Bulimore house stood and threw lighted firecrackers under what they thought was Mary's bedroom window. Then they drove back up onto the highway and began driving back and forth, peeling rubber and trying to make as much commotion as possible.

They had been wrong about the window. The bedroom belonged to Mary's parents, and Richard Bulimore was awakened from a bad dream by the exploding firecrackers. He was in a period of relatively good health at the time, strong enough to get out of bed, load his shotgun with birdshot, and labor up the hill to the highway. When the car roared past again, Bulimore cut loose with both barrels. The mechanic screamed and raced out of town, and Mary never saw him or his brother again. She didn't miss them. She had cared no more for them than for any of the men she dated.

Her closest friend was Sandy Woodson,* a girl who had a speech impediment but somehow could sing like Brenda Lee. They went together to night clubs where Sandy would go to the bandstand and sing, they always had fun, and sometimes they fell into misadventures that appeared funny in retrospect. One night they double-dated with two boys who drove them out onto a country road, parked, and made some rather blunt demands. Mary and Sandy said no, and when the boys became more insistent they got out of the car. The boys drove away, leaving them to walk home in the dark, and Mary didn't reach Sarah until one o'clock in the morning.

* a pseudonym

Sandy, who lived in another town, went on alone and didn't get home until dawn. A few days later, however, she was laughing about the whole episode. To Mary, Sandy seemed the ideal carefree girl, exactly the kind of girl Mary was determined to be.

But not long afterwards Sandy quit school abruptly and went to Chicago. Later she wrote to say that she had married. Mary was despondent over both events; her best friend not only had gone away, she had ruined her life. If such things could happen to Sandy Woodson, Mary feared, they could happen to anyone.

Sometimes, sitting on the porch at her parents' house, Mary saw hoboes come out of the tall grass and jump onto the freight trains that slowed as they passed through Sarah. She always wanted to go with them.

The bus ride from Sarah to Memphis was short and inexpensive, and Mary went as often as possible. Memphis was the great metropolis at the northern edge of the delta, an awesome and worldly place, and she loved being part of it. She discovered Overton Park and learned that it was easy to meet boys with motorcycles there by asking them for rides. The Memphis boys had more money and were more sophisticated than the boys back home, and some were almost as interesting as her friends in California. The best of the lot was Tommy Peck,* who had the biggest kind of Honda made and took Mary for breakneck rides through town and out into the country. Sometimes, with Mary clinging to his waist, he sped eighty miles to a wide-open night club called the Casa Benita in Clarksdale, Mississippi.

The summer of 1966 was the most prosperous time in Mary's life and almost as much fun as her months in California. She found a job in the fountain room at Baptist Memorial Hospital in Memphis and was able to live rent-free at the home of her "Uncle" Edward Reed, who was not actually related to the Bulimores but had been raised by Mary's parents

* a pseudonym

and was regarded as a member of the family. Her salary at the hospital was $280 a month, and she made enough in tips to pay for her meals and other necessities. She tried to save part of each paycheck for her last year of high school, but most of her new money was quickly spent on clothes, visits to beauty parlors, and things that she didn't need but wanted. She bought a camera and a portable typewriter—the most expensive possessions she had ever had. Her social life, in the first weeks of the summer, was divided between dates with Tommy Peck on his Honda and flirtations with medical students at the University of Tennessee near the hospital. She liked the foreign students best, especially one dark-skinned young man with large liquid eyes who was, someone told her, a Persian. She spent many hours trying to arouse the Persian's interest but had little luck.

During the summer Mary's father became gravely ill and was brought from Sarah for treatment at Baptist Memorial. A frail man in his late sixties by then, he seemed to be in danger of dying, and Mary visited him every day before and after work. She and her mother, also up from Sarah, sat at his bedside by the hour. They talked to pass the time, and for the old man's sake they kept their talk as cheerful as possible. Gradually, by stages so imperceptible that Mary scarcely noticed, a young orderly who worked in the ward began to join the conversations. He said his name was Clifford Putt, and that he was from Virginia and had no family or friends in Memphis. He was twenty-one years old, trimly built and nice looking with neatly combed blond hair and a smooth boyish face, and he seemed lonely. Annie and her husband were both delighted by his earnest friendliness, and soon he was calling them Mom and Dad and coming to stay with them in the hospital room after work. He said he had nothing better to do, and that he was happy to have some company himself. After a while he began taking Mary out on dates.

Clifford's car was old and ugly and slow—"the rag," Mary dubbed it—and he was not nearly so adventurous as her favorite boyfriends. But he always spent his money freely and was willing to do anything Mary suggested. When Richard Bulimore was discharged from the hospital and Mary returned home to begin her senior year at Coldwater, Clifford started driving to Sarah regularly on visits. It was hard to know exactly why he came, because often he paid more attention to Mary's parents than to her. He brought them little gifts, asked about their health, and talked with them politely for as long as they wished. Mary liked him, but not in any special way, and when he began to drop hints about getting married she ignored them. When the hints developed into proposals, she managed to introduce Clifford to one of her friends from high school, hoping that he might become interested in her. The friend, Retha Redd, was a plain and quiet girl who lived in the nearby town of Blue Goose and didn't get out much because her parents were old and expected her to stay home and take care of their home. Mary thought that if she could get Clifford and Retha together she would be doing everyone, herself included, a favor. But Clifford was not interested.

Dating Clifford had one great advantage. It made things agreeable at home. Annie was enchanted by Clifford, and she seldom missed an opportunity to assure Mary that he was "just the nicest boy in the world." Annie treated Clifford like a favored son, and when he got into trouble she responded with a mother's loyalty.

One night Clifford telephoned the Bulimores from Memphis and said he had been arrested. He had been accused of stealing forty-eight dollars from the wallet of a patient at the hospital and needed twenty-six dollars in bail. Annie borrowed the money and got her brother to drive her into the city. When she returned home she said that Clifford was very repentant about what had happened and had promised to stay out of trouble. "Everybody deserves a second chance," said Annie. Clifford left the hospital but got another job, and early in the fall the police arrested him again and charged him with trying to break into the warehouse where he had been working. He was convicted of burglary and sent to the state prison at Nashville. Mary was sorry for him but felt no personal loss. Clifford was just another boy, and far from the most interesting one she knew.

Most of her senior year followed the pattern Mary had set for herself after returning from California. She worked at the restaurant, studied as little as possible, and maintained her pose of tough independence. Her boyfriend that winter was Hot Dog Walker* from Sledge. Hot Dog was big, surly and crude. He was almost twenty-five years old and had a reputation for wild behavior, and Mary liked him and liked being seen with him. One night the two of them rode Hot Dog's motorcycle into the Coldwater High gymnasium and disrupted a varsity basketball game; that assured Mary's fame. Another night, shortly after buying a new Mustang, Hot Dog took Mary for a fast ride on the highway and collided with a cow. When he got the car under control and brought it to a stop its front end was smashed, the windshield was shattered, and the cow lay dead on the hood.

"Well," Hot Dog drawled, his hands still on the steering wheel, "this Mustang sure tore that cow's ass." Mary laughed until the tears came. She was sure it was the funniest thing she had ever heard. When Hot Dog took off for Texas a few months later, she missed him. Clifford was writing to her and her parents from prison, but Mary didn't often write back. She didn't often think about Clifford. Annie, relieved by the disappearance of Hot Dog Walker, seemed to be talking about Clifford constantly.

In the spring of 1967, Annie Bulimore went on the bus to California. Her older daughter and son-in-law, who had decided to move back to Mississippi, had invited her to come to Modesto and ride home with them in their car. Mary stayed at home with her father and stopped looking for reckless, disreputable boyfriends. With her mother gone, she no longer

* a pseudonym

had anything to prove. She went out almost as often as before but no longer stayed out as long as possible. And when Annie returned, Mary was so close to graduation that she forgot about trying to make trouble.

Mary's mother had often told her that when she graduated from high school she could begin doing whatever she wished, and these promises had helped her to look forward to her diploma as a certificate of liberation. But when graduation day finally came and Mary's class organized an all-night bowling party, Annie said no. The party wasn't to start until one o'clock in the morning, and Annie said that was too late. In place of the party, Mary was taken to a night club by her sister and brother-in-law. They brought her home early and she went quietly to bed, but when she got up the next morning she was filled with determination to break away. She went to Memphis, found Tommy Peck, and told him how restless she was. Tommy said he was bored, too. Within minutes they decided to go to the West Coast on Tommy's motorcycle. They pooled their money and found that they had almost exactly a hundred dollars.

The preparations were easy. Mary went home, crammed her best clothes into her only suitcase, and told her mother that she was going to Memphis to stay with Uncle Edward and look for a job. She put the suitcase on a Greyhound bus bound for Modesto, expecting that she would be waiting at the depot there by the time the bus arrived. Then she and Tommy started off, Mary wearing only a sleeveless blouse and a pair of shorts, and they got as far as Albuquerque before she became so sick with sunburn that they had to stop. Mary got on a bus headed back to Tennessee and Tommy rode the Honda home alone. She never recovered her suitcase and never again saw the West.

Uncle Edward, when Mary's sunburn had healed, found her a job as nurse-companion in the home of an aged woman in Memphis. It didn't pay much but it was easy work: Mary's only duties were to dust the old woman's furniture and keep

her fed and comfortable. Her employers, the woman's children, were generous people of comfortable circumstances,
and after only a few weeks they began to encourage Mary to
continue her education. When she said she had no money
they offered to help, and so late in July she enrolled in a
work-study nurse's training program at Baptist Memorial
Hospital and moved into an inexpensive one-room apartment. She was at the hospital Monday through Friday each
week, and on weekends she worked as a nurse's aide at a
rehabilitation center. She enjoyed all of it and took it seriously. In thirteen months, if she stayed with it, she would be
a licensed practical nurse with a skill that would get her a
job anywhere when, as she intended, she started traveling
again. She settled into a routine of working every day and
studying almost every night and found it surprisingly satisfying.

At the end of the summer Clifford was paroled and returned to Memphis from prison. He got another hospital job
and began seeing Mary regularly. Sometimes they drove out
to Sarah, and Mary's parents were clearly delighted to see
them together. Annie was still very fond of Clifford; she believed that he was entitled to two mistakes, apparently. As
before, Clifford was pleasant company—the more so now,
since Mary had lost her appetite for wild times. He took her
bowling and to movies and night clubs, spent his money as
quickly as he earned it, and was always agreeable when they
were alone together. He did not like parties, however, and in
groups he became sullen and withdrawn. That was one of
the things Mary could not like or understand about him.
The other was his intense jealousy. He resented seeing her
talk to any other man, and sometimes he would telephone an
hour after bringing her home from a date to see if she had
gone out again with someone else. That made her angry.

Generally, however, the relationship was an easy and increasingly intimate one. It fit in well with Mary's life as a
busy working girl on her own, gave her a social life without

the distractions of finding and selecting new boyfriends. Clifford wanted to get married, and to keep from disappointing him she said maybe. Maybe someday, but not now. She didn't mean it, because she still didn't want to marry anyone, but even so there were times when the idea was less than repulsive. Perhaps she would do it, she sometimes thought, after she'd finished the nursing course and had seen the country. Clifford was quite handsome in an undramatic way—much like a very young Alan Ladd—and marrying him was the surest way Mary knew of pleasing her mother. Annie had never liked a boy half so well as she liked Clifford.

Mary's sister, less enthusiastic about Clifford, sensed what was happening and cautioned her against getting married simply to make their mother happy. Don't get caught, she said; finish your training and make something of yourself. Mary promised that she would, and she meant it.

But it was already too late. Less than two weeks after her talk with her sister, Mary learned that she was pregnant.

3

Leila Jackson

I T H A P P E N E D A G A I N on August 25, eleven days after the bodies of Roy and Bernalyn Dumas were found in their apartment. Another murder as mysterious and frightening as the first two. The victim this time was an eighty-year-old widow.

August 25 was a Monday much like the Thursday on which the Dumases were killed. Again it was hot and sunny, and again Memphis was unusually quiet. The Dumas case had lost much of its impact by now. People had stopped talking about it and were forgetting the fear that it had temporarily aroused. The rush to buy guard dogs was over. The police continued to say little about the case, but it was obvious even to casual newspaper readers that a solution was not at hand. Dutifully but with an increasing sense of boredom, reporters from the *Commercial Appeal* and *Press-Scimitar* continued their daily efforts to learn the contents of the autopsy reports, and every few days both papers ran brief items stating again that they still had not been disclosed. The intervals between these items grew progressively longer, and each new version was a bit shorter than its predecessor and buried a bit deeper under more interesting news. Soon, following the natural course of such things, the items could be expected to disappear altogether. It is part of the process by which headlines shrivel and die.

Monday's *Commercial Appeal*, reflecting the city's return to a state of torpor, again had no local news on its front page. Even the world news was tiresome. Northern Ireland was quiet, the icebreaker *Manhattan* had left Pennsylvania to find a northwest passage to the Alaskan oil fields, a battle was in process near Saigon, and American scientists were exclaiming about their "incredibly old moon rocks." The Dumas reward fund, offering cash to anyone who could provide information leading to the arrest and conviction of the killer or killers, was not mentioned. The fund had been created with an offer of $300 from the Shelby County chapter of the Disabled American Veterans, Roy Dumas's brother and sister had added another $150, and finally a few nurses at Baptist Memorial Hospital had pledged smaller amounts. But those were the only offers, and no one came forward with useful information. Like the murders themselves, like the Dumas family's appeal for the killer to turn himself in, the reward was already half forgotten.

On North Somerville Street in the medical center section of midtown Memphis, Monday was a thoroughly ordinary day. Once a quiet street of middle-sized frame houses, North Somerville had become almost unpleasantly busy by the summer of 1969. Most of the original houses had been torn down and replaced with garish apartment buildings, parking meters had been installed along both curbs, and people came and went at all hours of the day and night. Leila Jackson's old house, the white paint peeling from its clapboard siding, remained as a kind of relic of the past in the midst of all the new activity. Hundreds of persons, conceivably a thousand persons, saw the house on Monday. They drove past it, parked near it, crossed its tidy lawn, even stepped onto its wooden porch. Not one of them noticed anything unusual. But at some time during the day, inside her home, Mrs.

Jackson was strangled. Her body lay on a bed in a room at the back of the house, undiscovered for hours.

The Jackson call reached police headquarters at 7:33 P.M. Mrs. Betty Rogers, on duty at the switchboard, heard a young man say that his grandmother had been murdered. She transferred the call to the dispatcher, Warrant Officer D. O. Callarno, who took the address, told the young man to wait there but not to touch anything, and sent out a radio call directing four cars to go immediately to the scene. Then he dialed the homicide bureau upstairs. It was still 7:33 when Bob Cochran answered.

Cochran, just finishing his tenth consecutive twelve-hour working day, was conducting the usual evening review of the Dumas case. Five of his men were with him, including Captain Robert Williams, "Frosty" as he was called, the homicide bureau's deputy commander. Again, no one had any real progress to report. More leads had been explored and discarded, nothing new had been learned, and the list of things remaining to be done was growing steadily shorter. The FBI labs had found nothing helpful among the things sent to Washington from the Dumas apartment, the one unidentified fingerprint found in the apartment remained a mystery, and no skeletons had been found in the Dumas family closet. If things continued this way much longer the bureau would have to return to a normal schedule and hope for a break.

Monday night's review was beginning to devolve into small talk when Cochran picked up his phone. "Captain," Callarno told him, "a boy just called and said he found his grandmother dead at 21 North Somerville, just off Madison. He says she was murdered. I've got two squad cars and two uniformed lieutenants on the way, but I thought you guys would want to know right away."

"Right," said Cochran. "Thanks." He hung up the phone and passed the news to his men.

"Good God," Williams said tiredly, stretching in his chair and yawning. "That's all we need. But we better take a look." Cochran told two of the detectives to stay in the office, and he and the others got slowly to their feet and went in an unexcited procession down to the parking lot at the rear of the building. Cochran got behind the wheel of his car and Frosty Williams got in beside him. On the way to North Somerville they talked more about the Dumas case—and about how pleasant a day off would be—than about what might lie ahead. The two captains were old friends who had joined the police force at about the same time almost twenty years before, and they communicated with each other easily.

The drive from headquarters to North Somerville took only four minutes, and as he drove Cochran felt neither expectation nor apprehension. Many murder reports prove false, and most of the genuine ones are not particularly difficult from a detective's point of view. This new one was not likely to prove extraordinary, and at another time Cochran would not have investigated it personally until after detectives had visited the scene and reported back. His decision to respond immediately was a half-conscious reflex action caused by a growing sense that the Dumas case might be hopeless. Without quite realizing it, he was beginning to clutch at straws.

Earlier that month, he had read reports of a series of unexplained murders in Michigan. Most of the victims had been college coeds, and the killer was still at large. Seeing the reports, Cochran had reflected that such episodes seemed to be growing increasingly commonplace. "One of these days were going to have to deal with that kind of thing here in Memphis," he had told his wife, Bobbie. The possibility preyed on his mind during a vacation trip to Panama City, Florida, a trip that ended the day of the Dumas murders. He was especially afraid, always had been for some reason, of the possibility that someone might begin murdering children in Memphis. Infanticide was his personal, secret terror, a fear so deep that he rarely spoke of it. But such things were not on his mind as he drove to the reported murder scene on North Somerville Monday night. The Dumas case was a tough one, and the chances that it would ever be solved were diminishing daily. There was no reason to think that it might be the beginning of a series of killings, however, and Cochran had not begun to think of it in such terms.

Cochran stopped outside the house at 21 North Somerville, and he and Frosty went up to the front porch. They were met at the door by Lieutenant Johnny Williams, a former homicide investigator now assigned to uniform duty. Cochran and Frosty Williams, no relation, knew him to be an intelligent officer.

"Is it a homicide?" Cochran asked.

"Is it ever," the lieutenant answered, smiling in a way that expressed no amusement. "Wait till you see."

"Anyone inside?"

"Nobody. We found the body and cleared out. Bibbs and Smith have the kid who called in their car."

"Good," said Cochran. "That's the way to do it." He ordered two patrolmen to stand guard at the front and back doors and admit no one without his permission—not even Chief Lux. Then he and Frosty followed Johnny Williams into the house. Walking carefully and in single file, stepping around rugs where possible to avoid disturbing anything, they went through a small living room and a hall lined with bookcases and knickknacks to a bedroom. The body of an obviously very old woman lay face up on a double bed. Her eyes were open slightly and reflected the light from an overhead bulb.

"Who turned the light on?"

"The kid, I guess. I don't know. It was on when I got here."

"Good. You touch anything?"

"Nothing."

"Good." Cochran stepped into the bedroom. The floor was

littered with purses and clothing and assorted household junk, and he walked gingerly so as not to destroy any possible clues.

The lower part of the body was covered with a bedspread, but the knees were raised and spread apart exactly like Bernalyn Dumas's. The old woman's clothing, a simple housecoat and slip, had been pulled apart to expose her torso as Mrs. Dumas's had been exposed. She was not gagged or bound, but a nylon stocking was wound around her neck and knotted tightly at the side. A big butcher knife was on the bedspread between the woman's knees, the spread was smeared with what appeared to be a small quantity of blood, and an ordinary table knife lay beside the body at the edge of the bed. A reading lamp attached to the headboard was turned sideways, parallel to the floor, and instantly Cochran remembered that a lamp on Mrs. Dumas's bed had been turned in exactly the same way. He turned to look at Frosty Williams, and Frosty looked back. Neither man spoke, but each knew what the other was thinking. Cochran would remember it as the most terrible single moment of his entire professional life.

"When I saw that body," he recalled afterward, "I was the loneliest bastard that ever lived. I knew it was the same one." Whoever had killed Roy and Bernalyn Dumas had killed this woman, too. Cochran was certain of that. He—assuming that the killer was male—was probably a lunatic. But lunacy would not necessarily make him easy to find.

"Let's go," Cochran said. He and the others filed out to the porch, and within minutes dozens of additional policemen and crime scene specialists arrived. Most were sent out to the surrounding neighborhood to question persons living nearby. They were told not to say anything to anyone about the details of the killing—if they knew any. The necessary specialists were admitted to the house to begin taking pictures, tape recording descriptions of the scene, and preparing to dust for prints. Emphatically, Cochran told them not to smoke and not to touch anything without specific permission. Still annoyed by the early blundering at the Dumas apartment, he was determined to handle this case as perfectly as possible. Almost as an afterthought, he announced that something could be touched: the window shades. He ordered them lowered so that newsmen could not look in.

The inevitable crowd began to gather outside the house, teenagers and a few old people and young couples with small children. Tennis players in white shorts came with their rackets and ball cans from nearby public courts and leaned against parked cars to talk and sweat and watch the detectives come and go. Residents of a big apartment building on the other side of North Somerville stood in clusters on their balconies, some of the women hugging themselves as if suddenly chilled in the evening heat, most of the men watching the excitement and shouting and waving when they recognized friends under the street lamps below. Then the television crews arrived, hurrying because they still had time to get a minute or two of film on the ten o'clock news. Their eye-stinging lights put a glow on the old house and completed the carnival scene.

Inside, in the comparative quiet of the back bedroom, the dead woman was formally identified as Leila Jackson. According to her grandson, she didn't have much money but was the owner of the house in which she now lay dead. She had lived alone for many years and had not been in good health.

She seemed an improbable target for either a sex killer or a thief.

Mrs. Jackson's murder, like those of Roy and Bernalyn Dumas, was discovered hours after the last copy of the afternoon *Press-Scimitar* had reached the street. Thus the *Commercial Appeal*'s reporters and editors again had the opportunity to get the story first and the problem of assembling it in time for the next morning's first edition. Again they had to hurry. Some reporters tried without success to get into the Jackson house, others tried with only a bit more success to get information from officers working on the case, and still others began moving though the neighborhood searching for people who knew something about Leila Jackson. The result, as often happens, was unfriendly competition between the newspapers and the police department despite the fact that the two organizations were trying to reach different goals. The police were looking for clues, hopefully a big clue that would lead quickly to a solution. The *Commercial Appeal* was looking for Tuesday's top story. Such objectives can be mutually exclusive.

The initial search for information about Leila Jackson was not easy. It quickly became apparent, as newsmen and detectives stumbled over one another in a series of brief and unsatisfying interviews with the dead woman's nearest neighbors, that she had been a sickly recluse who seldom left her home. Few of the people living on North Somerville in 1969 had known her. Only a small number could remember ever having seen her. Mrs. Jackson had lived in the same house for a quarter of a century and at one time she had been quite active. But age and illness and recent changes in the neighborhood, the demolition of most of the houses in which her closest friends had lived, had left her isolated. The friends had moved away to be replaced by apartment dwellers, restless and mobile young people with little interest in the existence of an elderly neighbor. Mrs. Jackson had become a survivor, an anachronism, the occupant of an old-fashioned house on a newfangled thoroughfare, but the distinction had not won her much attention.

The reporters learned little that night, but Chief of Detectives Joe Gagliano told them that Mrs. Jackson's murder bore "striking similarities to the Dumas case." That quote alone was enough to assure the story a place at the top of page one beside news that ISRAEL AND ARABS GIRD FOR BATTLE AS TENSIONS RISE. By noon on Tuesday, inflamed by the latest killing, tensions in Memphis would be rising too.

When the reporters had completed their interviews and telephoned their information to rewrite men and gone home to bed, police were still at work at Mrs. Jackson's house. They worked all night and into the next morning, using all the techniques employed in the Dumas case but with even greater care. For the first time, they had a sense of direction: the top priority was to look for links between the two crimes. Painstakingly, even delicately, Mrs. Jackson's home was photographed and inventoried and dusted and finally examined piece by piece in a search for clues. Even the rugs were rolled up and carried away for laboratory analysis, and the list of everything removed from the house for examination filled three and a half pages with single-spaced type. Later many of these things would be sent to the FBI labs for further study.

Director Holloman and Chief Lux, when they visited the scene Monday night, again offered Cochran more men. This time he accepted, but he asked for permission to select personally the additions to his staff. He wanted only men with homicide bureau experience and good records as investigators. The request was immediately granted, and by early Tuesday more than three dozen experienced detectives were assigned to the Dumas and Jackson cases. One of their first new chores was to run checks on Leila Jackson's background and learn everything possible about what she had done and what had happened around her on the day she was murdered.

Leila Jackson had lived in the house in which she was murdered since the nineteen-forties. Her husband, an optometrist, had died in 1961, and since then she had lived on a small Social Security allotment and income from renting rooms. She had one child, a married son named Reagan who also lived in Memphis and had two grown sons of his own.

Mrs. Jackson's house was not large but it included four bedrooms, three of which she rented out. She had tried to be careful about choosing tenants, even intending at first to accept only women, but things didn't work out exactly as she had hoped. The only applicants were men, and once Mrs. Jackson decided to accept a few of them the chances of attracting respectable women practically disappeared. The accommodations were too confining for perfect privacy, and though the bedrooms were nicely furnished and were kept scrupulously clean, bathrooms had to be shared. In any case, the all-male arrangement proved satisfactory. Mrs. Jackson bought a small "Rooms" sign at a hardware store, and whenever a tenant moved out she placed the sign on her lawn. It was the only advertising she needed, since North Somerville had become such a busy street and was near the city's expanding medical center. She relied largely upon intuition to decide about men who responded to the sign, and when she didn't like a man's looks she had her ways of turning him away. So far as anyone knew or would tell the police, she had never had serious problems with an applicant or tenant. So far as could be determined, in fact, she had never had serious trouble with anyone.

Mrs. Jackson's sign had not been on display the day she was killed. Though one bedroom was unoccupied, it was a room adjacent to her own living room, and its tenant had to share both her front door and her bathroom. For those reasons, apparently, she had not been eager to rent it. Her other rental rooms were occupied by a cab driver named Robert Jones and a bartender named Richard Smith, and they had a separate bathroom and separate entrance at the back of the house. The door connecting their rooms with Mrs. Jackson's quarters had been kept locked on both sides. Mrs. Jackson usually had been careful to lock all her doors, though police found no evidence of forcible entry to her home.

She had been in hospitals several times in recent years, at one point spending seven months in Baptist Memorial recovering from a stroke which sharply limited her mobility. After returning home she had few visitors and did not often go out. Her one regular excursion was a weekly visit to her son's home. He picked her up at midday every Sunday and brought her back to her house every Sunday night. Almost her only luxuries were cigarettes and the care of her gray hair. She smoked Winstons and had been a fairly frequent customer up to the time of her death at Denton's Beauty Salon, a block from her home. Rufus Denton, the proprietor, knew her as a personable and obviously lonely old woman who arrived early for her appointments to have an opportunity to talk with other customers. A burglar had broken into Denton's establishment not long ago, and when he told Mrs. Jackson about it she said confidently that she could never be robbed because she never kept money at home. She always paid Denton by check; certainly she had never drawn attention to herself by displaying large amounts of cash.

On the day before she was murdered, Mrs. Jackson had Sunday dinner as usual with her son and daughter-in-law, Beulah Mae, at their house on Vinton Street. Reagan Jackson, fifty-three years old, was a remarkably devoted son, and he and his wife had devised an elaborate system for helping the old woman cope with her weeks alone. They kept her medicine at their home, for example, and every Sunday afternoon they wrote the names of the days of the week on seven envelopes into which they put the pills and capsules that she was to take each day. Even the times at which each dose was to be taken were written on the envelopes, so that when they were placed on Mrs. Jackson's bathroom shelf they provided her with a complete medical guide for the week ahead. Reagan Jackson knew his mother's routine and habits intimately, and he and his wife telephoned her frequently to assure themselves that she was getting along satisfactorily.

At the end of her last visit to their home, Reagan and Beulah Mae took Mrs. Jackson to a store and helped her buy food for the coming week. Then they took her to 21 North Somerville, put the groceries away, and set the medicine envelopes in their usual place. Reagan checked his mother's money supply and found that she had $85 in a billfold in her bedroom closet. Then he and Beulah Mae said goodnight and started for home, but before getting there Reagan remembered that he had not given his mother the Sunday paper, a small gift but an established part of their weekend routine. So he drove back to North Somerville, knocked on Leila Jackson's tightly locked door, and gave her the paper when she answered. She locked up again when he went home.

The police found it surprisingly easy, considering the isolation and plainness of Leila Jackson's life, to reconstruct most of her last day. They found it possible, by questioning many people and using clues found in her house, to determine what she had done on a nearly minute-to-minute basis almost to the moment of her death. That central moment, however, was concealed and impenetrable. The known chronology of Mrs. Jackson's last morning stopped abruptly not long before she was killed, much as everything known about the Dumases' last day had ended with Bernalyn Dumas's arrival home from work.

When her alarm clock awoke Mrs. Jackson at 7:30 Monday morning, her tenant Jones had been gone for two and a half hours, driving his taxi. Smith the bartender was still asleep in his room. Mrs. Jackson ate breakfast about eight o'clock, took a pill and capsule from her Monday envelope, and made her bed. Then she took a plastic garbage can from beside the kitchen sink, removed the lid and set it on the table, and was about to carry the can outside when the telephone in the bedroom rang. It was Reagan, calling to tell her that he had to go to Shreveport, Louisiana, on business and would not be back for a few days. While Mrs. Jackson was telling her son goodbye the garbage collectors arrived and departed, so after hanging up she decided not to bother taking the can outside. It was only a third full, anyway. She left the lid on the table, the can in the middle of the kitchen floor, and went on to other work.

The first chore of the day was the laundry. Mrs. Jackson's regular laundry man was scheduled to make a pickup that morning, so she wrapped her own bedding and towels and those of her tenants in a sheet which she placed in the living room by the front door. Twelve hours later a newsman would get a peek in that door, mistake the bundled laundry for a body, and report that Leila Jackson had been found dead in her living room.

Mrs. Jackson remembered that the previous week the laundry had failed to return four of her towels, and at 8:45 Monday morning she telephoned to demand that they be replaced. A young woman told Mrs. Jackson that a check for the value of the towels would be mailed to her home; Mrs. Jackson thanked her, said goodbye, and hung up. While she was on the phone Smith's boss, the owner of the bar where he worked, had knocked on his door and told him that he was needed because the regular morning bartender had not shown up. Smith dressed hurriedly and left the house about 8:50 A.M. From that point Mrs. Jackson was completely alone.

Robert Williams, a twenty-one-year-old mailman whose route included North Somerville Street, arrived at Mrs. Jackson's house shortly after ten o'clock. Her front door was open but the screen door was firmly closed, and Mrs. Jackson was seated in a green easy chair just inside smoking a cigarette.

"Morning," Williams said as she rose unsteadily from her chair and began unlatching the screen door. "Looks like you're mighty eager for your mail this morning." He was only joking. He knew that Mrs. Jackson often sat near her door in the morning, waiting not for mail but for a bit of conversation. Though he hadn't had his job long, Williams already was well acquainted with Leila Jackson.

"It's not the mail I'm looking for this morning," Mrs. Jackson said as she took a single letter from Williams's hand. "I'm waiting for that laundry man. I'm fixing to tell him just what I think about the way he loses my towels." This time Mrs. Jackson was doing the joking. Williams knew that she and the old man who drove the laundry truck were good friends.

"Say," Mrs. Jackson exclaimed in a mock-stern voice as she

carefully refastened each of the three locks on the screen door. "I ought to give you a piece of my mind today, too. I'll bet you got plenty wet last Monday."

"Yes, ma'am, I did. I got good and wet."

"Maybe the next time I tell you it's going to rain and offer you an umbrella, you'll listen to me."

"You can bet I will," Williams laughed. "Next time you forecast the weather I'll listen." Mrs. Jackson gave him a little wave as he turned to go. It was approximately 10:15 now, and there was a good deal of pedestrian and motor traffic up and down the street. Williams, accustomed to it, paid little attention and noticed nothing unusual. But Mrs. Jackson was only minutes from being murdered.

About 11:15, no more than an hour after the mailman's departure, W. B. Byrd parked his laundry truck at a meter directly in front of Mrs. Jackson's house and walked to the porch. The screen was unlatched, Bryd discovered when he pulled on it, but the front door was closed. He knocked and rang the bell but no one inside responded, so he left a card to prove that he had been there and went away. Byrd, sixty-five years old, also had noticed nothing unusual and saw no reason to be concerned about the fact that Mrs. Jackson did not appear to be at home. He had been stopping at her home for fifteen years now, and she seemed less a customer than an old friend. He assumed that she had gone to see her doctor or was visiting her son's family.

Jones, the cab driver, returned to his room shortly after four o'clock Monday afternoon and began to cook his supper. Often at this time of day he heard Mrs. Jackson cooking in her kitchen on the other side of his wall, but today he heard nothing. He did not give the silence much thought, however. He thought she had probably gone to see her doctor.

At five o'clock Beulah Mae Jackson attempted to telephone her mother-in-law but got no answer. She waited an hour and a half and then tried again, but again she got no answer.

This was not particularly upsetting, because Leila Jackson often sat on her front porch swing early in the evening and could not hear the telephone from there. When a third call at 7:25 also was not answered, however, Beulah Mae became concerned. She knew that her mother-in-law never remained outdoors that late. Usually she was in bed by seven o'clock, and even when she stayed up later than that she remained inside with the doors locked and was able to hear the telephone. Beulah Mae gave her son Don a key to his grandmother's front door and told him to drive over and see if anything were wrong.

Don Jackson, a tall and strongly built eighteen-year-old, reached 21 North Somerville within a few minutes. He parked his Mustang convertible in Leila Jackson's driveway, and noticed when he went up to the porch that the afternoon paper, still folded, lay beside the front door. He was surprised—and alarmed—that his grandmother had not yet taken the paper inside. He knocked very hard, and when no one answered he pulled at the screen door and found that it was not latched. That too was unusual and therefore frightening.

When he got inside, he discovered that the only light on in the house was in the front bedroom just off the living room. That seemed odd, since the room was presently not being rented and was never used by Mrs. Jackson. It was in good order, though, the bed carefully made and the furniture arranged neatly as usual. In the half light of sunset, young Jackson went through the living room and hall past the bathroom to his grandmother's bedroom. Its door was closed. He pushed it open and switched on the light. Leila Jackson was on her bed. Thinking she was asleep, he stepped to the side of the bed and shook her knee. She did not respond, so he shook her harder and saw the butcher knife on the bedspread between her legs. Pulling his hand back, he moved his eyes hesitantly along her body toward the face, stopping when he saw the stocking knotted at the throat. Then he dialed the operator from the telephone near the bed, was connected with the police, and reported what he had found. After hanging up he ran out the front door. He was on the lawn waving frantically when the first police car arrived a minute later.

These were the things known to have happened at Leila Jackson's home shortly before and shortly after her death. Somewhere between them, within them, the murder had occurred. It was a reasonably ordinary and complete record until the hour between the mailman's departure and the laundry man's arrival. Nothing was known about the eight hours between the laundry man's brief stop and Don Jackson's arrival; the mailman was the last person to have seen Mrs. Jackson alive or to have talked with her. If the killer had entered the house after the mailman's visit but before the laundry man's—and that seemed most probable—he had not been seen and was very lucky or very clever or both. The facts were as simple as they were mystifying. They were far too simple, in fact, utterly lacking in the kinds of complications that might have pointed to a motive or a convincing suspect.

Bob Cochran was not especially disappointed by the brevity and barrenness of Leila Jackson's biography, though he assigned men to continue exploring her life. He was looking for one person now, or one set of persons, responsible for two crimes separated by eleven days. A specific and personal motive was likely only if the Dumases and Mrs. Jackson had something specific and personal in common, which they did not. They had all been quiet, respectable white Memphians, but that was far from specific enough to be suggestive. Bernalyn Dumas had been a longtime employee of Baptist Memorial Hospital and had spent eight hours there the day she was killed; Leila Jackson had lived two blocks from the same hospital and had been a patient there for a long period. That was an obvious connection and one worth exploring, but it was also impersonal since so far as anyone knew the two women had never met. The way to explore it was not to dissect Mrs. Jackson's life story but to send detectives to the hospital. They were sent quickly to question employees and begin a slow search through the personnel files.

All of the obvious possibilities had to be examined. Mrs. Jackson's mailman and laundry man were checked out thoroughly and questioned at length. So were her relatives, her tenants, garbage collectors, meter readers, everyone known to have been at her house recently, including a man who had been hired to do a small repair job on her roof. Everyone who had been regarded as even the most remotely possible suspect in the Dumas case was looked at anew. All of their stories were carefully verified, and when the job was done everyone looked innocent. All reports of stolen cars taken from or recovered in Mrs. Jackson's neighborhood were investigated for possible links to the killing. Recent burglaries and reports of suspicious activities were similarly investigated, and the neighborhood was combed house by house for information about residents. Everyone who had received a parking ticket in Mrs. Jackson's neighborhood on the day of the killing was investigated. All of it produced nothing.

No later inquiries added anything to what detectives had already learned about Leila Jackson's last day. A fourteen-year-old boy caused brief excitement by reporting that he had gone to the back door of Mrs. Jackson's house about 2:20 P.M. Monday and talked with her there. This would have meant that she was still alive long after the laundry man's stop—except that, as it turned out, the boy had not been there the day of the murder but the week before. His information did solve one minor mystery, however. The crime scene investigation unit had found a strangely coarse hair on the railing of Mrs. Jackson's back stairs. It was a hair from the boy's dog. The boy, inevitably, was checked out thoroughly and finally cleared.

Because his hopes of tracing the killer through the discovery of a comprehensible motive had declined so sharply, Cochran took particular interest in the results of the physical examination of Mrs. Jackson's home. They proved disappointing. Color film had been used in photographing the murder scene—a first for the Memphis police department— but though the pictures provided an excellent record of what had been found they revealed absolutely nothing about the identity of the killer. With the help of Reagan Jackson's unusually detailed knowledge of his mother's life, detectives were able to determine that everything found in the house had belonged to Mrs. Jackson. Her billfold, the one in which Reagan had found eighty-five dollars Sunday night, was the only thing known to be missing. The knives found on the bed had been taken from Mrs. Jackson's kitchen. Like everything else, they proved nothing.

The things found scattered on the bedroom floor seemed as meaningless as hieroglyphics. Most were articles of clothing taken from Mrs. Jackson's drawers, and others were things taken from the purses in her closet. Some were a bit odder than that but no more revealing. Near the bed, for example, detectives had found a torn dish towel. It was difficult to understand why such a thing would be on anyone's bedroom floor, even after a murder and ransacking. No one gave it much thought, however, because there were too many other, potentially more productive things to wonder about. All were examined. The traps were removed from under Mrs. Jackson's bathroom and kitchen sinks and tested for traces of blood or hair. Nothing useful was found.

The investigation spread, more detectives were assigned to the homicide bureau, and space became almost as precious as time. Cochran's office was converted into "the Dumas room," headquarters for a team of detectives concentrating on the Dumas case under the direction of Lieutenant Barry Linville. The bureau's reception area was locked off and used as "the Jackson room" by a second team of investigators headed by Lieutenant Gordon Ferguson. New maps and charts went up, and reporters were forbidden to enter. A common file was established for cards bearing the names of every person who had any connection with either case. The Jackson names were put on blue cards, the Dumas names on salmon-colored cards. The file was checked daily to see if any name appeared on cards of different colors, which would have indicated that someone had been linked however indirectly with both cases. The number of cards increased daily, but no such duplication occurred.

The press room was next door to the homicide bureau's day room on the second floor of the headquarters building, and Cochran asked for it. He wanted to use it as an office for some of his additional men. His request was refused, but he was offered a conference room on the first floor. Disgustedly, he said no thanks: the conference room had no phones. Phones were installed. Cochran accepted then but remained disgusted about the power of the press.

As the investigation proceeded without results, Cochran saved his last hopes for the fingerprint search and the autopsy. The first yielded nothing. The knives and purses and furniture and almost everything else in the Jackson house were clean. Mrs. Jackson's prints were found in several places, of course, but her eight-decades-old fingertips had been worn so smooth by age that their mark was only barely visible even on the best surfaces. As for the killer or killers, he or she or they had either worn gloves or had wiped everything clean before leaving the house.

The fingerprints of every suspect in the Jackson case were checked against the one unidentified print found in the Dumas apartment. None matched.

The autopsy confirmed that Mrs. Jackson had been strangled with the nylon stocking found around her neck. The stocking was hers, probably taken from a drawer in her bedroom, and the knot was not unusual. Medical examiners and laboratory tests were unable to determine whether Mrs. Jackson had been raped, but it was found in the course of the autopsy that the walls of her vagina had been lacerated by a sharp instrument, probably the butcher knife found on the bed. Small bloodstains on the spread covering Mrs. Jackson's legs indicated that the knife had been wiped clean before being dropped by the killer.

Marks were found on Mrs. Jackson's neck just above the stocking. They had been made shortly before her death and suggested an unsuccessful attempt to strangle her by other means.

Undigested fragments of a capsule found in Mrs. Jackson's stomach indicated that she had taken her morning medication between two and a half and three hours before being killed. Thus if she had taken the capsule at the prescribed time, eight o'clock, her death had occurred not long after her talk with mailman Robert Williams.

The undersides of Mrs. Jackson's fingernails were examined for traces of foreign tissue, particularly the skin of anyone she might have scratched during a struggle. The results were negative. Similar tests in the Dumas case had been similarly fruitless.

For Cochran, the discovery of vaginal lacerations was the most important result of the entire investigation. It gave him new reason to be glad that details about the Dumas case had not been given to reporters. Disclosure of Mrs. Dumas's lacerations might have inspired some latent psychopath in Memphis to commit a similar crime in imitation of the first. But now it was most improbable that such a thing could have happened. The small cuts inside Leila Jackson's body confirmed Cochran's belief that she and Bernalyn Dumas had been victims of the same murderer.

Beyond that, however, the police could safely believe very little. The murderer was still as undefined as a vapor. Age, sex, appearance, habits and past records were all wide-open questions. No one knew whether the killer carried a weapon, or how the victims had been selected. The homicide bureau's only course was to continue checking everyone with past arrests involving burglary, robbery or sex. Soon almost everyone arrested in Memphis on any charge was being routinely questioned about the Dumas and Jackson cases. Because there was still nowhere in particular to look, the detectives had to continue searching everywhere. All of them continued to work at least twelve hours a day seven days a week in the slow and cool, methodically careful, sometimes dull and repetitious way essential to good investigation.

Outside the stone walls of police headquarters, Memphis was in turmoil as new stories and rumors were churned up in the wake of the new murder. The newspapers and television stations had reported everything that they could learn about Mrs. Jackson and her death—that she was old, helpless and innocent, that there was no known reason for her death. They had reported everything possible in that vein, but everything possible turned out to be not very much because Mrs. Jackson had not been a colorful person and the police were saying almost nothing; soon, therefore, the newspapers turned their attention to other things. One of the most accessible things was fear, which quickly became a recurrent theme. Within a few days after the discovery of Mrs. Jackson's body, the *Press-Scimitar* was proclaiming in bold headlines that all of central Memphis had been "terrified" by the Dumas and Jackson killings. Then the same paper quoted police—without naming any policemen—as saying that all three victims apparently were murdered by "deranged thrill killers." The effect of these stories was to make the city increasingly afraid. The escalation by stages from fear to panic was fully under way.

Gradually, the newspaper stories became bolder and more graphically detailed. The *Press-Scimitar* printed a story given to one of its reporters by a twenty-two-year-old secretary, Sue Matthews, who recalled that on the Saturday night before Leila Jackson's death she had seen the outline of a man silhouetted against the front window of her apartment. When she screamed the man ran away. Other women living near the Jackson house began, if a bit belatedly, to tell reporters about suspicious men they had observed on North Somerville Street.

Three days after Mrs. Jackson's death, a woman named Rachel Moore told police that a white man had attempted to assault her at one o'clock in the morning as she was getting out of her car in front of her home on Range Line Road. The man put a nylon stocking around her neck, Mrs. Moore said, but fled when she jabbed at him with a fingernail file. That story was prominently displayed in Thursday's *Commercial Appeal* along with a report that police had arrested a suspect in the Dumas and Jackson killings. The suspect was a young man believed to have committed numerous burglaries in the medical center area, and when taken into custody he had women's undergarments in his lunch bag. Undressed at police headquarters, he was found to be wearing a slip, bra and panties under his shirt and trousers. Amused and astounded, detectives began to think that they had found the killer. But they hadn't; the man soon provided solid alibis. He was a burglar but not a murderer.

News that this suspect had been cleared after nine hours of questioning, and that the attack on Rachel Moore was not regarded by police as connected to the murders, did nothing to calm the city. Tens of thousands of people were becoming intensely afraid.

Glenda Sue Harden was afraid. She was also glad that she still lived with her parents instead of alone in an apartment like many of her friends.

Mary Christine Pickens was afraid. She lived in an apartment alone, and she bought new locks for her doors.

Mary Bulimore Putt was so afraid that she found it difficult to sleep. She told her husband she wanted to leave the city for a while.

4

Holy Matrimony

ALL THE WAY to Tupelo Mary kept herself pressed against the door, staying as far away from Clifford as possible. She didn't say a word, and Clifford drove glumly without taking his eyes off the road. He spoke once or twice in a grudgingly conciliatory way, but Mary didn't answer. She hated him. She was sure that he must have done something, tricked her somehow, to get her pregnant. It couldn't have been an accident, and no matter what happened to her she would not marry him. Even keeping her promise to go with him to this family reunion was an absurd mistake. She couldn't bear being in the same car with him.

It was mid-November, 1967. Mary had first suspected she might be pregnant in October, but when she went to see a doctor the test results came back negative. Ecstatic over what seemed to have been a narrow escape, she resolved again to break up with Clifford and waited anxiously for her period. When it still didn't come she went to see the doctor again, and the second test was positive. It was the most terrifying thing that had ever happened to her, and at first she thought wildly about killing herself. When she calmed down she began looking for a way to get an abortion.

She didn't ask her doctor for help, didn't even really think about asking him, because she was certain somehow that he would not do anything for her. Instead she went back to work at the hospital and tried to decide who on the staff might tell her what to do. She made her first choice at lunch time, when she went into the fountain room and saw a group of black nurses sitting together at a table. Mary scarcely knew any of them, but their being both black and nurses made her hope that they must know about abortions, so she surprised them by sitting down at their table and then amazed them by quickly explaining her problem. It was a humiliating thing for a white teenager from Mississippi to do and she did it awkwardly, her tongue stumbling over her words, but she was too desperate not to do it. The women listened in cold silence, and it was not until several seconds after Mary had stopped talking that the oldest of them asked her why she had not been using the pill. When Mary replied that she hadn't known she could get the pill, the woman smiled gently and shook her head. Another member of the group, a plump light-skinned woman sitting to Mary's right, suggested that she try taking quinine sulfate. "I heard that works," the woman said. "I don't know for sure." Her manner was stiff, distrustful. Mary muttered a combination of thanks and apologies and hurried out of the room.

She managed to get some quinine sulfate, and in her apartment that night she swallowed as much of it as she dared. It made her very sick, which she took as an encouraging sign and went to bed to wait for a miscarriage. When the sun came up the next morning she was feeling better but was still pregnant.

A few days later she mustered the courage to ask a student nurse at the hospital if she knew how to induce a miscarriage. "Sure," the girl said. "It's easy. Drink a pint of straight whiskey and take a long bath as hot as you can stand it." Mary hated whiskey and had never been able to drink it without becoming nauseated, but she bought a pint of Old Crow after work and went home to do as she had been told.

She spent the night vomiting in her bathtub, and in the morning she was still pregnant. She began to think that the whole episode must be a nightmare. It seemed too horrible to be real.

At the hospital she became timid and withdrawn, separated from her friends by her secret and fearful that people were talking about what she had confessed when asking for advice. Clifford became the sole outlet for her rage. She damned him and accused him and demanded that he admit to having tricked her, and when he insisted that he really hadn't wanted to get her pregnant but did still want to marry her she lost all control. "I don't want to be married," she screamed. "I don't want anything from you." She lashed out at him in every way she could, but Clifford, obviously bewildered, kept coming back to try to talk. He wanted her to go to Tupelo to meet his family, and he asked so many times that finally Mary said she would. She didn't understand herself why she said it. Perhaps to shut him up. Perhaps because a trip, even a trip with Clifford, seemed preferable to staying in her apartment all weekend and crying. Perhaps because she knew, despite her protests, that she was trapped. So after work on Friday evening Clifford picked her up and they started off to Tupelo. As soon as she got into the car, of course, she regretted it.

Clifford's family was large and pleasant—surprisingly so, since he had told her strange and terrible stories about how hard and unhappy his childhood had been. The reunion was at the home of the grandparents, Mr. and Mrs. George Alva Putt, two very old and white-haired people. Mr. Putt seemed to have little to say, but he was friendly to Mary. His wife had some of the flinty toughness of Mary's own mother, but she too was friendly and her home was far nicer than what Mary was accustomed to. Clifford had so many brothers that Mary couldn't keep them straight in her mind at first, and a pretty younger sister who was a student somewhere. The sister's name was Betty Ruth, and Clifford made a big point of telling everyone that Mary's middle name was Ruth too. Everyone clucked happily over that, and suddenly Mary realized that the whole family was receiving her as Clifford's future wife. That embarrassed her and made her angrier than ever with Clifford. When they were alone in a hallway for a moment she snarled that he should not have given his people such an impression. Clifford gave her a quick look of disgust and walked away. For the rest of the visit he ignored her totally, which compounded her embarrassment. She had wanted to ask him why his parents weren't at the reunion, but she decided that she had better not. No one in the family, she noticed, said anything about the fact that one generation was missing.

One of the Putt brothers was almost exactly the same age as Clifford, and the two were identical in size and coloring. Mary thought they might be twins until she learned that Clifford was older by one year. The almost-twin was introduced to her as George Howard Putt, but everyone in the family called him Buster. He had Clifford's blond and boyish good looks, though Mary couldn't see his eyes because he was wearing sunglasses. She found that interesting, since it was nighttime and Grandmother Putt's home was not brightly lighted, and she was impressed by Buster's poise. He was amiable enough, smiling and polite when he spoke in his soft voice, but he had a kind of elegant reserve in his bearing that made Mary think of a priest. She had never known a priest, in fact, but Buster Putt was what she thought a priest must be like. Next to him Clifford seemed adolescent to Mary, and the oldest Putt brother, Johnny, seemed coarse. There were still other brothers around the house, but they were children and Mary paid them no attention. It disappointed her to discover that, of all the Putts, Buster and Clifford were the most delighted about seeing one another. She would have preferred to see Buster condescend to Clifford. She became even more disappointed when the two went off to sit together in a corner and were still talking and laughing when everyone else went to bed. She felt a twinge of jealousy.

When she got up the next morning she found Clifford and Buster talking in the kitchen. Clifford walked out of the room when he saw her, but Buster simply stood up and greeted her in a courtly, smiling way. Mary, eager to seem friendly and talkative, asked him why he was wearing sunglasses. "I have to," he said. "A doctor prescribed them." He smiled again and offered her a chair. He was quite handsome. His arms, though almost as slender as Clifford's, were as tautly muscular as an athlete's.

Early Saturday afternoon Clifford went off to visit some old friends without asking Mary if she wanted to come along. Most of the other Putts seemed to be away for one reason or another and the house was quiet, so Mary went into the living room and sat down alone. A few minutes later Buster came in and sat in an easy chair. For a long time he didn't say anything, but his silence didn't seem unfriendly. He was just a quiet person, Mary had observed, with everyone except Clifford. It wasn't shyness; Buster seemed anything but shy. It was poise, and Mary liked it. Buster seemed very sophisticated.

After leafing through a magazine for a few minutes Buster turned his sunglasses to Mary and asked, in a confiding way, what was wrong between her and Clifford. He seemed to want to help, and Mary told him they were having a fight. "Those things will happen," Buster said softly. He didn't ask for details, but Mary started talking and soon she was telling him that the fight was about getting married. "I'm the one who doesn't want to," she said. She wondered if Buster would believe her.

"No problem, then," said Buster. "Don't get married. There's no law says you have to." He was not taunting her.

"I'm pregnant," Mary blurted. "I don't know what I can do. I don't want to get married, but I can't get an abortion and I'm afraid to tell my parents. I don't know what I'm going to do." She hadn't expected to say all this, and when she heard herself she blushed with shame. Buster didn't seem at all shocked, though, and he gave no sign of being amused by her predicament. He sat in his chair and looked at her without moving or speaking, and Mary got the impression that he was thinking very hard about something, trying to remember something. She felt herself growing anxious, hoping that Buster had an answer. Maybe he knew how to get an abortion.

"If I were you," Buster said at last, "I'd tell my parents. They won't love you any less because of this. I'll bet they'll do everything they can to help you. You should give them a chance to help."

The next day Mary said goodbye to Buster and his sister, thanked their grandparents, and without saying anything to Clifford took the bus back to Memphis. Then, instead of returning to her apartment, she got on another bus and rode to Sarah to see her mother and father. It was late when she arrived, and Richard Bulimore was asleep. Annie, who suffered from chronic insomnia and seldom went to bed before midnight, was still up and brimming with questions about Clifford and the visit to Tupelo. Hurrying to get to the point before her courage left her, Mary took her mother into the kitchen and told her everything. She was relieved when Annie did not explode.

"I do think you should marry Clifford," Annie said, tapping a forefinger on the table. "If only so your baby will have a name." The possibility of an abortion, or of having the baby and giving it up for adoption, did not occur to her. Mary didn't dare suggest such things. She knew that her parents could not accept them.

Mary tried to explain that she could not marry Clifford because she loathed him, but Annie found that incomprehensible and urged her to go back to work and wait a week before making any kind of decision. Mary agreed to that readily, having no other course of action in mind, and she asked Annie not to tell her father about the situation. She spent the night on the rollaway bed in the living room before starting off to Memphis in the morning. As she was leaving,

Annie stepped out onto the porch to say goodbye. "Whatever you decide to do," she told Mary in a low voice that her husband could not overhear, "you know you can count on me to help in any way I can." Mary smiled gratefully and squeezed her mother's hand. Buster Putt had been right.

At first Mary felt incapable of going back to the hospital. She stayed in her apartment, doing nothing, lying in bed most of the time and waiting hopelessly for an idea to come. When the head nurse telephoned, Mary said she was not feeling well but expected to back on the job in a few days. And a few days later she did go back, not to work but to see a man with whom she had become casually friendly during the summer. Being careful to avoid corridors where her supervisors might see her, Mary found the man and bluntly told him that she needed an abortion. She had told so many people by now that it was becoming almost easy. The man was not a doctor—he did not even have much contact with doctors in his job—but he promised to make inquiries and asked her to come back later. The next morning she reported for duty, and when she had a chance she slipped away to see the man again. He looked around to be certain that no one was watching, reached into a desk drawer, and quickly handed her two small packages wrapped in cellophane. Thinking that they must be something very special, Mary slipped them secretively into the pocket of her white skirt.

"What do I do?" she asked, whispering but trying to seem casual in case anyone had seen. "Are there instructions?"

"They're birth control pills," the man whispered back. He too was trying to appear nonchalant. Mary looked at him with what she hoped was an expression of wrathful incredulity.

"Are you joking me? Birth control pills?" Her whisper was harsh now, a suppressed shout.

"Sssst!" the man said to cut her off. "It's the only thing I could come up with, but it's been known to work. Take one whole package, then take a real hot bath, and then take the second package." Mary followed the instructions that evening, but the pills had no effect. They didn't even make her sick.

Two days later she was sitting alone at a table in the fountain room, nursing the dregs of a coke, when Clifford and Buster walked in together and joined her. She had not seen either of them since leaving Tupelo, and seeing them now, so unexpectedly, confused her. Clifford, who became sullen as soon as he was seated, was dressed in his wrinkled and loose-fitting orderly clothes, and they made him look skinny and small. Buster, still in his sunglasses and wearing a trim knit shirt with a turtleneck collar, was as cool and handsome as before. He had taken some time off from his job, he said, to come to Memphis and see the sights. When Clifford got up and went off to work, Buster stayed to talk with Mary. He asked her if she had decided what to do, and she said no. He asked if he could give her a ride home after work, and she said yes. She began to feel better; Buster liked her.

From then on Buster was with Mary every day. They went for rides through the city together, to movies, to her apartment. Mary liked to cook, and Buster praised everything she served him. He was interesting, too. He told her long stories about how he and Clifford had been abandoned by their parents when they were small and had been raised in institutions where they were abused and sometimes beaten. He said he had been in a home for boys in Texas until his twenty-first birthday a few months ago, had gone then to Tupelo because his grandparents were there, and had found a job at a gas station. It wasn't much of a job, he said, but he had hopes of getting something better soon. "I've got training in computers," he said. He seemed very intelligent and very mature.

On Friday, December 8, Buster surprised Mary by suddenly insisting that she decide what to do about the pregnancy. His vehemence annoyed her, because she had become quite successful at pretending that her problem didn't exist. She intended to keep pretending until her belly got big. Clifford and her mother were waiting for her to do something, but she had done nothing except stop going to the hospital and start spending all of her time with Buster. Now Buster was trying to shake her out of her trance.

"You can't just drift along like this," he said. "Not unless you want to ruin your whole life."

"There isn't anything I *can* do. Nothing except marry Clifford, and you know I'm not going to do that."

"You can marry me. I'll be good to you. I'll be good to the baby. Marry me." Buster was not making a magnanimous gesture. His voice was pleading. Mary had broken his reserve, and the realization made her feel triumphant. She told him to come back in three hours and she would give him her decision. He drove off in his seven-year-old white Impala, and when he returned after two and a half hours Mary said yes. She got into the car with him and they drove to Sarah to announce the joyous news.

Mary's mother was not overjoyed, but she did not object. Her father was visibly unhappy, perhaps more because of the pregnancy than because of the wedding plans. Though as usual he expressed no opinion, he seemed almost actively hostile to Buster. Both of her parents still wished that she would marry Clifford, but neither attempted to dissuade her. An expectant daughter needed a husband, after all, and if it couldn't be Clifford then Clifford's brother was perhaps the next best thing. Annie asked Mary and Buster if they had decided on a date, and when Buster answered that it would be as soon as he had found a job in Memphis she told him there was no need to wait that long.

"If you two really have made up your minds," Annie said, "I'll loan you the money to go to Tupelo. You can go right back to your job there and get off to a good start." She went into her bedroom and came back with twenty-five dollars, which she pressed into Buster's hands. Then she returned to the bedroom to put on her Sunday dress, and minutes later she was riding towards Memphis with Buster and Mary. Her husband stayed at home.

The wedding took place that night in the Memphis home

of Brother Stanfield, an old friend of the Bulimores who had once been the preacher at a small church in Sarah and was now, though still an accredited minister of the gospel, working like Clifford and Mary at Baptist Hospital. The ceremony was brief and singularly nonfestive. A darkly silent Clifford was there with a young woman from Arkansas who had been a patient in his ward at the hospital and now, apparently, was his new girl. Mary ignored both of them, but was annoyed that they had come. Only Buster seemed happy or excited.

Afterwards all of them went to a night club for a celebratory drink, but Mary was turned away at the door because she was under the legal age. So they gave up on trying to celebrate, and Buster and Mary took Annie home to Sarah and prepared to start for Tupelo. Buster telephoned his grandparents' home there to announce that he was married and that he and his bride would be arriving in a few hours and would need some money. They reached Tupelo at two o'clock Saturday morning, and Betty Putt gave them another twenty-five dollars. Then they went to the Hotel Tupelo and rented a room with a television—Buster was very careful not to get a room without a television—and settled down to married life. The next day Buster returned to his job at the service station, and on Monday Mary was hired as a waitress at the hotel.

Being married surprised Mary. It was even worse than she had feared. She and Buster lived at the hotel for two weeks, until they received their first paychecks and were able to rent a one-bedroom apartment. The apartment was clean but small and cold and cheaply furnished. Its closest approximation to luxury was an ancient electric heater in the bathroom.

But the problem with being married was not the small apartment and not the fact that Mary and Buster together were not making much money. The problem was Buster, who quickly became strange and troublesome and boring instead of sophisticated as Mary had thought in Memphis. He was not merely reserved, he was as silent as a spider, and sometimes whole days would pass without his uttering a single word except in monosyllabic response to Mary's questions. His silence was not hostile but emotionally neutral; most of the time he did not seem aware that Mary was in the apartment with him. When they were still living at the hotel he consented once in a while to play gin rummy with her, but usually he sat in front of the television without taking his eyes off the screen. He even watched the commercials, all of them, and when Mary put food in front of him he ate it without paying attention to what it was. His favorite shows were horror movies and mysteries, but when none was on he watched whatever came along—game shows, kiddie shows, pottery lessons and geography lectures. He watched from the moment he got home from work until going to bed, and he always watched in his sunglasses. Mary asked him how he could see through them late at night, but he didn't answer. For a while she asked him to go out to the movies and he always agreed to that—so long as the movie was a thriller or a sex film. He took her to lots of movies, until she couldn't stand the blood and skin any more, and then she stopped asking him to go. He returned to the television.

Jealousy appeared to be Buster's only emotion. Like his brother, he became upset whenever Mary spoke to other men. One afternoon, while walking home together from the service station, they passed a man who worked with Mary at the hotel. He smiled and said hello, and Mary returned the courtesy. Buster said nothing. When they got inside their apartment, however, he pulled her down over his knee, spanked her hard, and told her firmly that she was not to talk to men on the street.

"But I work with the guy!" Mary protested. "What do you expect me to do, for God's sake? Ignore people I know when they say hello?"

He struck her again across the buttocks, even more forcefully than before. Three times, and each blow stung.

"It doesn't make any difference whether you work with them or not," he said angrily. "My wife doesn't talk to men on the street." He hit her once more and let her go.

Mary didn't argue. She had never seen Buster so angry, and she had no desire to provoke him further. Soon he was back at the television, as silent and detached as before.

In bed Buster was a perpetual motion machine. He wanted intercourse six, sometimes eight times a night, apparently because it was almost impossible for him to achieve climax. He would labor over Mary until he was exhausted, then she would sleep for an hour, and then he would want to try again. Mary tried for a while to be patient about it, but after a few weeks she told Buster that she simply could not bear that much nocturnal exercise. Buster was surprisingly understanding, and he apologized before getting out of bed and turning on the television. After that he was not so demanding. He was not at all violent or aggressive so long as Mary was careful to avoid other men when he was around. But life with him was inexpressibly dreary.

In February, two months after the wedding, they left Tupelo for Houston, Mississippi. Mary's brother-in-law, her sister's husband, was in business there and gave Buster a job. They rented a kitchen and bedroom in an old house, and Buster squeezed their budget to buy a second-hand television since one did not come with their new quarters. He told Mary that he enjoyed his new job, but things were slow because it was winter and he was making even less money now than before. One day, given an order in what he thought was too sharp a tone, Buster walked off the job without explanation. He went to the local hospital and was hired as an orderly. Not long after that Clifford showed up in Houston and Buster helped him get a job at the hospital. What was worse, for Mary, Clifford moved in with them, and when she insisted that the three of them couldn't live in two rooms

Buster arranged for all of them to move together to another part of the house where they had two bedrooms and a kitchen. Mary tried to ignore Clifford, and he demonstrated no interest in her, but they found it difficult to avoid one another in such crowded rooms. When Clifford was away Mary tried to talk with Buster, to persuade him that Clifford shouldn't be staying with them, but Buster refused to discuss it. "He's my brother and he needs a place to stay," said Buster, and that was that. One of the most frustrating things about Buster was that almost nothing could get him to argue.

From the day that Clifford arrived, Buster's interest in television subsided. The brothers went off together often, not telling Mary where they were going and not telling her where they had been when they returned. Sometimes money was short and when Mary complained that she couldn't buy food they would come home with odd assortments of canned goods, half a bag of flour, three heads of cabbage or two dozen green apples. Once they brought home a huge supply of fresh eggs, cases of them, so many that Mary filled the refrigerator and still had dozens left over. "Where is this stuff coming from?" she asked, and Clifford and Buster looked at each other and snickered like schoolboys. Eventually she gave up and stopped asking. She felt half like the Putt brothers' prisoner, half like their den mother, and her belly, cause and symbol of her bondage to them, was beginning to grow. Feeling unable to control anything, Mary became as passive as she had been in her childhood and early teens. At times she thought Buster and Clifford must be conspiring to destroy her nerves.

When they were all still living in Houston, Mary came inside one day after hanging out laundry and began housecleaning. She was approaching the end of her pregnancy now, spring was becoming summer, and housework was difficult for her in the gathering heat. After about an hour, as she was in her bedroom picking up clothes, she heard a noise and looked up to see the knob on the closet door turn. She wanted to scream but couldn't, and she stood frozen in the middle of the room as the door swung slowly open and Buster stepped out. Mary was too shaken to speak and Buster, incredibly, tried to act as though he had done nothing unusual. When she recovered her voice and asked him why he had been hiding in the closet, he said he hadn't. Later, after she badgered him, Buster admitted that he had come home from work early and had been surprised to find her gone. Suspicious, not knowing that she was in the back yard, he had gone into the closet to wait and find out what she was doing. Mary regarded that as a strange explanation but could not coax a better one out of him.

When Mary was within a month of having her baby, Johnny Putt showed up in Houston and invited his younger brothers to join him on a job-hunting expedition to Florida. Clifford declined, but Buster liked the idea and quit his hospital job. He took Mary to his grandparents' home in Tupelo, said he'd try to send for her before the baby arrived, and left for Florida in Johnny's car. He hitch-hiked back about a week later, alone and broke and hungry, and he and Mary drove to Memphis and moved into the upper floor at Uncle Edward's house. Buster got a job at the Rosewood Convalescent Home, but the baby came before he received his first pay. When her labor began, Mary went to Baptist Hospital but was refused admittance because she had no money and no insurance. Indigents were required to go to City Hospital, which Mary feared because of stories she had heard while in nurses training. Weeping, she telephoned her mother and said she needed two hundred dollars. Mrs. Bulimore called her son, who arrived with the money just as Mary was entering the last stages of labor. Minutes later George Richard Putt, a healthy baby with blond hair and blue eyes, was born. The date was July 13, 1968—exactly one month before the day on which Mary had expected to get her nursing diploma.

By the time Mary and the baby were released from the

hospital Buster had quit his new job, complaining that the pay was too low. He took them directly from the hospital to Tupelo and they moved in with his grandparents, who paid Buster to paint their house, do some repairs, and work in their big garden. After several weeks of that Buster again packed Mary and the baby and their belongings into the car and drove to Houston, where Buster was again hired at the hospital. They moved into a house trailer, and when Mary recovered her strength she took a job as a nurse's aide. Buster worked from seven in the morning until three in the afternoon, Mary worked from three to eleven, and they took turns caring for the baby. Buster was a model father, willing to get up in the middle of the night for feedings and diaper changing, happy to play with the baby for hours. He nicknamed the baby "Pip."

The return to work lifted Mary's spirits. So did the fact that for the first time she and Buster had more than a subsistence income. They were able to trade their aging car in on a 1964 Chevrolet, rent a small but pleasant house, and buy furniture on credit. The hospital had a Licensed Practical Nurse training program, and when Mary was invited to join it and offered advanced placement she happily accepted. She had been thinking of leaving Buster, almost planning on doing so in the months just before Pip was born, but now things seemed to be working out. Buster was still silent, but he was working and staying in one place and keeping out of trouble. Mary got birth control pills at the hospital and determined to take them regularly. She found it hard, though, and sometimes she forgot. She blamed her forgetfulness on her childhood hatred of taking medicine.

Though things went fairly smoothly for a while there were ups and downs, and the over-all direction proved to be relentlessly downward. Early one afternoon, when Buster had a day off from the hospital and Mary was cooking lunch, he called out from the shower that the baby was crying and should be changed. Mary continued with her cooking, thinking that Buster could take care of the baby after his shower, but after a few minutes he burst into the kitchen with an enraged expression on his face and, without saying anything, began hitting her. When she tried to protect herself he shoved her to the floor and slapped her hard and repeatedly in the face. Then, just as suddenly, he got up and ran out of the house. Hours later he returned and apologized for striking her, but he accused her of neglecting the baby and failing to obey his orders. Mary had a black eye, and because of it she did not go to work that afternoon. Her husband, she had learned again, was not to be trifled with.

A few weeks after that incident, Clifford telephoned to announce that he was getting married and wanted Buster and Mary to attend the ceremony. He was marrying, of all people, Retha Redd, the old high school friend whom Mary had introduced to him two years before, and the wedding would be in Blue Goose, Retha's home town. Old friend or not, however, Mary wanted nothing to do with Clifford and refused to go. Buster went alone, stayed away longer than expected, and said when he returned that he had been arrested for fighting with a Negro at the wedding reception and Clifford had bailed him out. He refused to explain.

Things returned to what passed for normal for a while, with Mary continuing to enjoy her work at the hospital, until Buster announced that Clifford and Retha were coming to live with them and that Clifford would be working as an orderly at the hospital. Mary didn't like the idea, but as usual Buster wouldn't discuss it, and she decided that Retha's presence might make the situation bearable. It didn't. Retha, tall and angular and a good deal less than beautiful, was as quiet and submissive in married life as she had been in her maiden days, and when Clifford ordered her not to talk she obeyed. When Mary tried to talk with Retha, Clifford became angry with both of them. Mary regarded the situation as outrageous, and fought Clifford bitterly. Buster and Retha both stayed out of it. Buster seemed not to care, and Retha seemed afraid.

Buster and Clifford renewed their old bond, dressing alike in tight pants and flashy shirts, behaving alike, both wearing sunglasses, often going away on unexplained adventures and not returning until late at night. Annie Bulimore, the first time she saw them together, said jokingly but aptly that they looked "like a couple of outlaws." One night they did not come home at all, and in the morning an administrator at the Houston hospital called Mary to tell her that both of them had been arrested in Memphis on a charge of possessing stolen goods.

"I'm afraid we're going to have to let both of them go," the man said. "I'm sorry about it in a way, but that's how it has to be. George is an excellent worker, but we just can't have this sort of thing happening."

When Mary went to work that evening the head nurse, Mrs. Kriddle, took her aside and assured her that the firing of Buster and Clifford was not held against her in any way. "We still want you here," Mrs. Kriddle said, "and I for one hope you won't give up your plans to finish the LPN program." As far as Mary was concerned, there was nothing to decide. She would stay at the hospital and finish her training. What she did after that would depend on several things —Buster's behavior, mainly, and whether he was in serious trouble in Memphis. Maybe she would divorce him after all.

But a few days later, on Saturday, Buster and Clifford surprised her by roaring up the driveway at the front of the house in Clifford's old car and screeching violently to a stop. Mary, stepping out onto the porch as they came up the stairs, thought they must have escaped.

"Of course we didn't escape, for God's damn sakes," said Buster disgustedly as he walked past her and went inside. "They turned us loose because they didn't have no evidence. We didn't have any stolen goods." He and Clifford already knew that they had lost their jobs, and they were angry about it. They told Mary and Retha to get ready to move to Jackson immediately. Their younger brothers, Lance and Lester, were in a home for boys there, and Clifford and Buster wanted to be near them. On Monday morning they picked up the pay that the hospital owed them, crammed as many belongings as possible into their cars, and left Houston. Mary, unable to see how she could afford rent and furniture payments and a nightly babysitter on her small salary, went along. The landlord said he would move their new furniture into a back room and hold it for them. He did as he promised, but they never returned for it and in time it was repossessed.

In Jackson, Clifford and Retha and Buster and Mary and the baby all moved into a decrepit, dirty, badly furnished two-bedroom apartment and Clifford and Buster got jobs at a hospital. Soon both were discharged because they had given the Houston hospital as a reference and their new employers, in making routine inquiries, learned of the Memphis arrest. They then went to work at a gas station, and Mary was hired as a cashier at a drug store where within a few days she was assigned to the beauty aids counter as a "cosmetics consultant." She joked about her new title but was secretly a little proud of it, and she enjoyed the work. She told Buster emphatically that if she lost another job because of anything he did their marriage would be finished, and she clung to two hopes: that Clifford would go away, and that Buster would stay in one place and keep out of trouble.

A dominoes game in their crowded apartment unexpectedly fulfilled Mary's first hope. Clifford became angry over losing, jumped up from the kitchen table, and began shouting furiously. Buster laughed at him, Mary joined in, and Clifford grew even angrier. The incident evolved into a lacerating quarrel between Buster and Clifford and ended with Buster, Mary and Pip moving out. They found an apartment, soon were saving a little money, and after a few

weeks moved again into a two-bedroom cottage on the outskirts of Jackson. Mary was happy but distrustful.

"Remember," she warned Buster again, "if you get into
trouble I'm leaving." Buster said he would behave himself,
and he did. Mary had no complaints aside from the fact that
since the fight with Clifford he had begun spending a lot of
time with a local man reputed to be a homosexual. "We
drink beer and talk," said Buster. "That's all. He's interesting, and a pretty nice guy." Mary didn't like it but she tried
not to nag.

She worked days and Buster worked nights, arriving home
shortly after midnight and expecting her to have a hot meal
ready. She always did, up to the night that Buster didn't
come home. She notified the police and waited up past dawn,
but Buster didn't return. When he finally got home at ten
o'clock in the morning and refused to explain himself, Mary
became convinced that he must have stayed with his homosexual friend. Fed up, almost nauseated by what she believed, she got the baby out of his crib, took the next bus to
Sarah, and moved in with her parents. Her mother cared for
the baby while she worked first as a waitress in Tunica,
and then on a factory assembly line in Memphis. For $2.10 an
hour she put small pieces of machinery into small cardboard
boxes, and though it wasn't as interesting as hospital work
she found it an absorbing enough way to pass the time. Buster
telephoned repeatedly and asked her to return to Jackson, and
she always flatly refused. Even her mother agreed with her
on this. "That Buster Putt," Annie Bulimore conceded, "just
ain't dependable. The nicest boy in the world to meet, but no
kind of husband."

Then Mary learned that she was pregnant. The blow was
as painful as the confirmation of her first pregnancy, and she
beat her hands against her bedroom wall, weeping and curs-
ing herself for not being more careful about the pill. Again
she tried some folklore abortion techniques which did not
work. Buster was told about the pregnancy by Mrs. Buli-

more, and when he drove to Sarah and asked Mary to come back to Jackson with him she agreed to give it a try. She knew she couldn't keep her job at the factory, and the prospect of asking her parents to support her and Pip was repulsive.

Jackson was repulsive, too, when Mary arrived. Buster had wrecked the cottage. The front door was smashed in, the floor was littered with decaying food and rags and assorted junk, everything was filthy, and several articles of women's clothing were hanging in the bathroom. Her camera and stereo were gone.

"What happened here?" she demanded. "What have you done to this place?"

Buster just shrugged guiltily and opened his hands in a gesture of resignation.

"Where's my stereo? Whose underwear is that in the bathroom?"

Buster had nothing to say, so Mary grabbed his car keys, put what remained of her belongings into the Chevrolet, and started back to Sarah. As she was leaving Buster tried to apologize and said he wanted to come with her. She told him to go to hell and floored the accelerator. She knew she was through with Buster no matter what.

5

Glenda Sue Harden

GLENDA SUE HARDEN was stabbed fourteen times with a long, sharp knife. Each time the blade was driven into her body up to the hilt, and each time it penetrated some vital place. She was stabbed once in the heart, once in the neck, twice in the head, twice in the chest, four times in the side and four times in the back. Any one of her wounds would have been fatal.

She died in a public place but did not cry out. She saw her killer raise the knife the first time but did not resist because she could not: her hands had been bound behind her back.

She died in Memphis on August 29, only four days after the murder of Leila Jackson. Her death transformed fear into panic and sent the entire city into a helpless state of collective hysteria.

She was twenty-one years old in the summer of 1969, a tall and slender girl with long auburn hair, dark eyes and a smooth thin face that broadened and became beautiful when she smiled, a popular girl whose bright personality and striking appearance had won her more than the usual share of suitors. A 1965 graduate of Kingsbury High School in Memphis, she had worked for three and a half years as a directory assistance operator for the South Central Bell Telephone Company and then had taken a job in the downtown office of the Jackson Life Insurance Company. Early in June she had accepted a proposal of marriage from Ronia Sandlin, a twenty-two-year-old paper salesman from Ripley, Tennessee. They planned to announce their engagement formally on September 7 and be married in January.

August 29 was a Friday, the last working day of the month and payday for most of the office workers in downtown Memphis. It was a hot but pleasant day charged with anticipation —the long Labor Day weekend was at hand. Glenda Sue, as eager as anyone for the holiday to arrive, overslept and had to hurry when she finally got out of bed at seven o'clock. She dressed quickly, telephoned her fiance as usual to awaken him, left home without stopping to eat breakfast and drove downtown a little too fast. Sometimes when she was very late, Glenda Sue parked in the Allright Garage at Court and Front Streets next door to her office, but the garage cost more than the Promenade lot on the riverbank and today she decided not to spend the extra money. She pulled off Riverside Drive onto the Promenade, locked her car after rolling up both windows, and started hurriedly off on foot. After crossing Riverside and a set of railroad tracks, she climbed thirty-nine stone steps to Confederate Park and walked past a statue of Jefferson Davis to Front Street and the entrance to the Falls Building.

The Falls Building, eleven stories high, was an ugly old structure with grotesque ornamental shields on its white brick exterior and air-conditioning units protruding from many of its windows. The headquarters of the Jackson Life Insurance Company, an austere suite of offices with tile floors and standard gray metal furniture, was on the top floor. Glenda Sue crossed the building's small lobby, ran for an elevator, and was taken up to her work. She arrived at 7:57, only twelve minutes late. Before settling down at her desk, she talked briefly with her friends Melba Gray and Louise

Morgan and took her last quick look at the newspaper. The morning's *Commercial Appeal* carried on its front page a big picture of Tricia Nixon being driven home from Walter Reed Army Hospital after two days of treatment for a mysterious abdominal pain. Beneath the picture was the latest Dumas-Jackson headline: SIMILARITY OF THREE MURDERS MAY POINT TO THRILL KILLER.

During the morning, in the midst of processing policy applications, Glenda Sue paused to make two entries on her desk calendar with a ballpoint pen. "Went to the drive-in last night," she wrote, and "Ronia Calvin Sandlin, I Love You." This was one of her daily habits, using the flip-over pages of the calendar as a diary. She repeated her declarations of love, or recorded some new event, almost every working day. "Told Everybody We're Getting Married," she had written of June 29. On July 5: "I got my engagement ring, it's beautiful."

Later in the morning she was given her paycheck, and during her lunch break she took it to the Union Planters Bank and cashed it—$100.89 for two weeks of work. On her way back to the office she stopped at the Orsis Hosiery Shop to buy a pair of panty hose and at the Kress variety store, where she bought a cheap imitation topaz ring for her right hand. Her engagement ring, shining with four diamonds, was on her left hand. Then she returned to the office and resumed processing applications. At two o'clock her friend Gertie Wiseman telephoned and said she and her husband wanted Glenda Sue and Ronia to go out with them that night. Glenda Sue said she thought it was a fine idea but had better check with Ronia first, and at 3:10 she tried to call Gertie back but couldn't reach her. At four Ronia called, and Glenda Sue told him to go straight to his apartment after work, change into casual clothes, and pick her up at home. At 4:45 she unplugged her electric typewriter, cleared off her desk, and started for home.

Several of the girls from the Jackson Life office rode together in the elevator to the lobby. On the way down Glenda Sue showed off her new purple ring and said she would not have much time for supper because Ronia was picking her up about six and she wanted to stop at Sears on the way home. The group separated at the building's front door, Glenda Sue crossing Front Street to Confederate Park. At another time of day she might have attracted considerable attention, a long-legged girl in a gold sleeveless minidress, dark reddish hair brushing against her shoulders. But there were scores of attractive young women on the street late Friday afternoon, and Glenda Sue was scarcely noticed. She turned and waved once, when a woman in a parked car honked her horn, then blushed when she realized that the honk had not been for her. She walked past the Jefferson Davis statue, past a stone tablet engraved with the Ten Commandments, past a battery of old cannons pointed harmlessly across the river, and went down the stone steps to Riverside Drive. She was never seen alive again.

Ronia Sandlin telephoned Glenda Sue's home at 6:15 and learned that she was not yet home from work. She was probably shopping, her mother said, and was expected soon. So he drove over to meet her as they had agreed, reaching her home about 6:45 and learning that she still had not arrived. At seven he began calling friends in an effort to locate her, but none of them could guess where she might be. Feeling slightly annoyed, Sandlin sat down in the living room to wait. The wait proved to be a very long one.

By 8:30 Sandlin had long since stopped being annoyed and was very worried. Glenda Sue's mother, Mrs. Louise Lee, was weeping. At 9:10 Sandlin said he would drive downtown and look for Glenda Sue's car. He knew where she usually parked it. While he was gone Mrs. Lee, unable to wait any longer, telephoned police headquarters and reported that her daughter was missing.

The fear caused by Leila Jackson's murder four days before, though mild in comparison with what would soon follow, was still intense that Friday night. Persons in all parts of Memphis, goaded by the newspapers' suggestions that a homicidal maniac must be at large in the city, were calling police headquarters at all hours of the day and night to ask questions and report suspicious activities. The more fearful people became, the more things began to seem suspicious to them, and the volume of incoming calls at the headquarters switchboard reached unmanageable proportions. Thus when Mrs. Lee telephoned at 9:35 P.M., the police had a backlog of eighty calls requiring investigation. Some of them were imperative—traffic accidents, for example—and some were terrified reports of prowlers and attempted burglaries. A report that a young woman had been missing from home for three or four hours was neither unusual nor pressing under the circumstances, and Mrs. Lee's call was given no special priority. Patrolmen Jack Hammonds and Carl Mister were not able to get to the Lee home until 12:36 A.M. Saturday. Mrs. Lee, in giving them the information that they requested, provided a faulty description of her daughter. Glenda Sue, she said, had gone to work that morning in a blue and white dress.

Even after talking with Louise Lee, Hammonds and Mister were not in a position to do much. The flood of calls was continuing, aggravated by all the messy things that happen in any large city on a Friday night, and a full-scale search for one missing girl was out of the question. Young women sometimes stay out without explanation on Friday night, even engaged young women whose mothers and boyfriends are eager to attest to their virtue, and the reasons, if not always innocent, are seldom sinister. Veteran policemen are accustomed to such things and are slow to become concerned over them. Hammonds and Mister took Mrs. Lee's tearful report, and at 12:51 they left on another call, an urgent one. They were not able to radio the description of Glenda Sue Harden and her car to headquarters until 1:30, and it was later than that when detectives were notified. Meanwhile

Ronia Sandlin had returned from downtown. He had driven through the Promenade parking lot, all floors of the Allright Garage, and the area around the Sears store where Glenda Sue had planned to stop. He had found no trace of her or her car. He and Mrs. Lee and Glenda Sue's stepfather sat up and waited for something to happen. Reluctantly, inevitably, they were afraid.

Eventually the missing person report was broadcast to all cars in Memphis and all neighboring jurisdictions, and Detectives Carroll Dunn and Hank Thomas were sent out from the homicide bureau with instructions to look for Glenda Sue's pale blue 1965 Mustang. The calm of early morning made such efforts possible, but essentially the case was still being handled as a routine one. It stopped being routine at 5:15 A.M. when Dunn and Thomas, driving along the river's edge, found the Mustang parked on a cobblestone embankment at the foot of Monroe Street. This was a popular downtown parking area only a few blocks from the Falls Building, but it was several blocks from the Promenade lot where Glenda Sue usually parked. The car was unlocked, the window on the driver's side was down, and the keys were in the ignition. It was covered with dew, indicating that it probably had been parked in the same spot for several hours.

Inside the car the officers found a gold button, a pair of women's shoes, a purse containing a paycheck stub and fifteen cents in change, and a tuft of long reddish hair. Within minutes Dunn drove to the Lee house with a description of what had been discovered. The purse was Glenda Sue's, a horrified Louise Lee said. The low-heeled shoes were Glenda Sue's too, and so was the gold button. She looked in her daughter's closet and confirmed that her original description had been wrong. The blue and white dress was on its hanger. The gold dress was gone.

By sunrise Saturday, finding Glenda Sue Harden was the most urgent problem facing the Memphis police department. It was complicated by the fact that the department, after

more than two weeks of work on the Dumas and Jackson killings, was already overextended. Its men, particularly its detectives, had had little rest since August 14 and were under
increasing strain as the number of calls from frightened
citizens continued to mount. Another complication, a sim-
pler and more normal one, stemmed from the fact that it is
never easy to find a missing person in a city of almost a million citizens. The Memphis police did what they could. They
transmitted a description of the Harden girl to all agencies
in Tennessee, Arkansas and Mississippi, began checking with
her friends and co-workers, and assigned as many men as
could be spared from other duties to begin looking for her.
Because a search of the entire city was not possible—such a
thing is never possible, really, in a city including thousands
of houses and apartment buildings—the available officers
were sent to parks and rail yards and other secluded loca-
tions. President's Island, Mud Island, Overton Park and Riverside Park were all given special attention because they
were big and included many places where a body could easily
be hidden. If Glenda Sue had run away or was hiding somewhere the chances of finding her were virtually nil. They
were not much better if she had been killed. It was purely a
matter of luck.

The search continued all morning and into Saturday afternoon, and as place after place throughout the city was examined without result police were sent to new places and told
to explore them too. By mid-afternoon most of the obvious
possibilities had been written off, and the chances of finding
Glenda Sue had shrunk correspondingly. None of her friends
could guess where she might be; nothing remotely like this,
they all said, had ever happened to her before. Sunset and
the resumption of the city's night life would require a cur-
tailment of the search.

Across the Mississippi River in Crittenden County, Arkansas, sheriff's deputies checked their records and discovered
that a girl matching the description of Glenda Sue Harden

had been found drunk on the riverbank Friday night, arrested, and later released on bond. She had identified herself as Gloria Martin* and had given an address in Memphis. Lieutenant Jim Music went to the address, found the girl, and determined that she was not Glenda Sue. Miss Martin said she was acquainted with the Harden girl but knew nothing about her whereabouts. She insisted that she had not seen Glenda Sue Friday night. Deputies searched the riverbank on the Arkansas side but found nothing.

All day long patrolmen had been looking in Riverside Park, a large and heavily forested recreation area between Interstate Highway 55 and the river. Not far from downtown, thickly overgrown in parts with brush and weeds, the park was both a necessary and an unusually difficult place to search. Officers in squad cars drove around its winding roads and then got out and walked. After several hours they reported that they had found nothing and were told to keep looking.

Shortly after four o'clock, Special Services Patrolmen Frank Irish and Velon Tankersley drove through the park from the McKesson boat ramp to an intersection near the public rest rooms. For no particular reason Irish turned left onto a paved road headed downhill, and after continuing a few hundred yards he noticed a dirt road leading off to the left. He and Tankersley were both tired, and by now they had little real expectation of finding anything. This dirt road was a place that had not yet been checked, however, and it seemed no more futile than the other places they had checked earlier. So Irish pulled onto it, the tailpipe of his squad car crunching against the ground as he drove across a shallow ditch, and soon found himself in dark woods. He followed the road to its dead end and stopped.

"Look there," said Tankersley. He pointed at a yellow and gray plaid sport shirt hanging from the branch of a tree just ahead. "I think I'll check that for blood."

* a pseudonym

The shirt was old and appeared to have been hanging there for a long time. Irish and Tankersley looked it over carefully and satisfied themselves that it was not blood-stained. They were about to go back to their car when Irish noticed a narrow dirt path leading deeper into the woods. The path was worn smooth, but in several places its surface had been gouged open.

"Scuff marks," Tankersley said. "Looks like they're fresh." He and his partner followed the path around a wide-arcing curve until they were out of sight of their car. Seventy-five feet from where they had parked, under a tree at the edge of a small clearing, they found the body of a young woman in a golden-yellow dress.

Within minutes after Irish and Tankersley reported their discovery, dozens of officers converged on the park and sealed off twenty acres around the body. Guards had scarcely been posted when they caught a young man dressed in a suit and necktie moving furtively but clumsily through the brush. Frightened when taken into custody, he said he was a newspaper reporter who had been listening to his police radio and had hurried to get a look at the body as soon as he heard about it. He was taken to headquarters, held until his story was verified, then given a rough warning and set free. More guards were stationed in the woods as the investigation began.

Captain Bob Cochran arrived at the scene at 4:30 P.M. and took charge. Many things had to be done, but two were essential: examining the body and scouring the area nearby for clues. Officers were sent out to get the names of everyone in the park, including ball players and picknickers and idlers, but it was already clear that the chances of finding the killer that way were small. A first look at the body persuaded Cochran that death must have occurred many hours before. Dr. Jerry Francisco, when he arrived, immediately agreed. So did John Carlisle, chief investigator in the attorney general's office.

The body was not moved at first, but even in its original position it revealed several things and suggested others. It lay face down on the grass, long hair spread to both sides, hands tied behind the back and tightly clenched. The upper part of the dress was stained with blood and cut in several places. The holes in the fabric were slit-shaped and very narrow; an amateur investigator could have guessed that they had been made by a knife. The legs were bare, their skin very smooth and white, and the skirt was pulled up high to reveal a white slip and a pair of white panties.

"This has to be the worst one yet," said Cochran, thinking aloud more than talking to anyone. "It really gets to you, a nice-looking young girl like that." A young officer nearby nodded, bent down, and tried to wave away the flies.

At their one-story home on Holliday Street, Glenda Sue Harden's mother and stepfather waited for their part in the Memphis tragedy to reach its climax. Because they lived in an emotional atmosphere contaminated by the earlier murders, they had found it impossible not to begin fearing the worst as soon as Glenda Sue failed to return promptly home from work. Throughout the city, since the killing of Leila Jackson, people had been fearing the worst every time they heard an unexpected knock or were approached by strangers on the street. The fact that fear was everywhere was no help to Harold and Louise Lee, of course; they could not shrug and say, well, everyone is worried these days. They knew that there was no reason for their daughter to have disappeared, that she had not run off to a commune, that no sane person would have kidnapped her for ransom.

The small hopes that they clung to during the night, the agonized stories that they invented in their minds to explain the disappearance, had collapsed with the discovery of Glenda Sue's car and shoes and almost-empty purse. That was the end of the suspense, really, and the only stories that the Lees could invent from that point on were too cumbersome and implausible to offer consolation. By late Saturday afternoon the family was already grieving, and when Lieutenant Billy Wilkie arrived and told them about the body in Riverside Park the news came less as a shock than as a dreadful confirmation. Only one act, an almost anticlimactic one, remained to be played: word must come that the dead girl was indeed Glenda Sue. Her uncle and grandfather were asked to go the the morgue.

The word came shortly after 8:30 Saturday night. By then, many neighbors and friends had gathered at the Lee house to help the family keep vigil, and newspaper reporters had come too in expectation of colorful feature material. Everyone was silent in the moment after the Lees were told that the body had been identified. Then several women began to weep, and some of the faces in the crowd suddenly registered anger.

"She had no enemies," Harold Lee exclaimed bitterly. "It was just some damn nut, some maniac who killed her." The weeping increased. When people began to speak, they did so in whispers.

The city's top police officials, except for Cochran, who remained with the investigation, surprised reporters Saturday night by making themselves available for questioning. Even more surprisingly, they answered some of the questions. For the past two weeks, Fire and Police Director Holloman and Chief Lux had said almost nothing in response to the endless and repetitious questions about the Dumas and Jackson cases. Now they behaved differently, discussing aspects of the new killing that had been handled as secret in the others.

How was the Harden girl killed? Was she strangled?

"The medical examiner will have to determine the exact cause of death," said Henry Lux. "But we know she received several stab wounds from a sharp instrument in her chest and the upper portions of her body." Surprised both because Lux was talking and because the victim apparently had not been strangled, reporters scribbled into their notebooks.

Other than the chest, what upper portions of the body do you mean?

"No comment."

Does this case seem related to the Dumas and Jackson murders?

"There are strong similarities in all the slayings," Lux replied. More scribbling. "But I am not going to tell you what those similarities are." At that the reporters smiled and shook their heads.

Were any clues found at the park? Are there suspects?

"No comment."

Was the girl molested? Strangled?

"No comment." Lux, a round-faced man with thin strands of dark hair combed across his high forehead, was willing to say no more.

"In our opinion we are faced with a cunning sex killer," said Frank Holloman. "We strongly suspect that the individual responsible for this crime was also responsible for the other three slayings."

Amid excited scribbling: Why? "No comment," Holloman replied. But he had already said enough to give the papers their best quote from a policeman speaking on the record since the beginning of the murders. And that was what he had intended to do.

Holloman, who had returned from an out-of-town trip when Glenda Sue Harden's body was found, had chosen his words carefully. He had prepared them in advance, in fact, and late Saturday his office issued typed copies of them as part of a statement to be relayed to the public by the newspapers and television stations. The statement was in equal parts an assurance, a plea, and a warning.

"We are cancelling off days for all men and deploying every available officer to provide maximum security within our capabilities for the citizen, as well as to accelerate the investigation," Holloman told the people of Memphis. That was his assurance, a highly qualified one but the best that he could offer without promising too much. Holloman, a lawyer and a former special agent with the FBI, knew better than to guarantee safety from a killer who left no clues.

"We urge everyone to use every possible effort to preserve security in homes and elsewhere," the statement continued. That was the plea, asking people to protect themselves as much as they could. Specifically, the statement advised all residents of Shelby County to do several things. They were to keep their doors and windows locked at all times—no easy thing for Tennesseeans in September. They were to avoid all strangers, keep their car doors locked both when driving and when parked, not get into their cars before making sure that no one was hiding in the back seat, report all suspicious persons to police, and advise police of any suspicious behavior displayed by friends or fellow workers. No one was to hitchhike or pick up hitch-hikers.

Holloman's warning was implicit in the entire statement: There is a murderer in our midst, and no one in Memphis is safe. The statement was printed in the Sunday *Commercial Appeal* and broadcast by every radio and television station in town. Coming from the city's senior law enforcement officer, it had an explosive impact. That too was intentional.

Holloman drafted and released his statement because the Harden murder convinced him that the city, particularly the city's female population, was in real danger. Two weeks before, he had been skeptical of the propriety of the newspapers' handling of the Dumas killings. Like all policemen, he had ingrained reservations about the value of publicity, and even after the Jackson murder he had limited himself to a few muted and off-the-record warnings. But now still another killing had occurred and the homicide bureau seemed no closer to finding the killer than it had been at the start. More murders could occur at any time, and there was no advantage in pretending otherwise. On the contrary, thoroughly frightened people might be more careful and therefore somewhat safer. Frightened people might be quicker to give the alarm if approached by the killer; that might save a life and could lead to a quick arrest. Over all the situation was an unusual one in which fear, for once, seemed to have its uses.

In the first flush of excitement over the statement, newsmen failed to notice that Hollman had said practically nothing about the Harden killing itself. He had added nothing to Chief Lux's disclosure of the stab wounds, for example, and he had not offered any hints about whether the girl had been killed in the park or simply dumped there afterwards, whether she had been raped or strangled, why he and Lux seemed so certain that this case and the Dumas and Jackson murders must be related. So some of the reporters went back and asked their questions, and once again they found Holloman impenetrable.

A reporter from the *Press-Scimitar* had the imagination to ask Hollman why he had so little to say. Holloman gave three reasons. First, he explained, too much publicity could create legal problems if a suspect were arrested and brought to trial. Second, too many lurid details could have the disastrous effect of causing sex deviates who had not yet killed anyone to try the same thing themselves. Finally, if everyone knew all about the killings it would be extremely difficult for police to question suspects effectively. Some innocent but tortured soul might confess—such occurrences were not rare —and if he had read thorough newspaper descriptions of the killings his confession might seem all too convincing. Secrecy, even more than fear, had its value.

The investigation of the place where Glenda Sue Harden's body had been found provided police with a variety of problems. For one thing, the discovery occurred so late on Saturday afternoon that not enough daylight remained for a full exploration to be organized. For another, the dirt road near which the body lay was popular both as a dumping ground and as a lovers lane, and therefore the whole surrounding area was littered with a bewildering assortment of household refuse, old tires, boxes, cans and dried prophylactics—all of which would make the search for clues extraordinarily difficult. Detectives used the time before sunset to photograph the scene, remove the body, and make a superficial preliminary check of the immediate vicinity. When further work became impossible six patrolmen were assigned to stand guard during the night and the detectives returned to headquarters to begin looking into the Harden girl's background and questioning persons who might be suspects or sources of useful information.

At 5:30 A.M. Sunday, Cochran assembled thirty-six men at the entrance to the dirt road and sent them marching in a slow-moving line through the thick underbrush and the trash. They were like soldiers picking up cigarette butts, and the idea was that if the killer had left anything behind one of them might find it. The searching men picked up enough junk to fill a dump truck, but none of it seemed related to the crime. The discoveries that provoked the most comment were a turtle and a snake.

The homicide bureau had been able during the night to borrow three metal detectors from an Army depot and the Memphis Light, Gas and Water Division, and these were used in a search for hidden objects. They found many, some of which were buried under six inches of dirt. All, when dug up, were worthless. There were tin cans, pieces of scrap, and one large but very old knife so corroded and crusted with filth that it obviously had not been used recently.

The dirt road and footpath, soft from rains, bore the imprints of many tires and shoes. Photographs and plaster castings were taken of these. Puddles were probed, and some were baled dry. A detective discovered bootprints leading from the road downhill into a dark and jungle-like ravine, and when he followed them he discovered a hidden pond. A fire department salvage unit was called in, and its big suction hoses were used to drain the pond. Detectives sifted through the mud with rakes and shovels but found nothing.

Sunday afternoon, when the search was ending and police were preparing to leave the park, Cochran took a shovel and dug up the blood-soaked patch of grass and earth on which the body had been found. He carried every trace of blood into a clump of bushes and buried it there, then returned to the discovery site and covered his shovel marks with branches and leaves. He knew that when his men left the reporters would move in, and he did not want them to be able to tell where the body had been.

The homicide bureau swelled up suddenly to unprecedented dimensions. Cochran was given additional men, desks for them were moved into the bureau's already overcrowded working spaces, and fourteen new telephones were installed to handle the fresh torrent of calls provoked by Holloman's appeal for information. By the end of the Labor Day weekend more than a hundred homicide investigators and thirty-five vice squad officers were working on the killings, and Cochran commanded three times the number of men that had been in his charge a month earlier. On the street, also, police operations were expanded. By eliminating days off and extending the length of each officer's working day by half, Chief Lux managed to double the number of uniformed men on patrol. A special telephone number and a special post office box were advertised for use by persons wishing to volunteer information anonymously. "Rumor lines," established during racial disturbances following the 1968 shooting of Martin Luther King and later dormant, were suddenly in active use again. The terrified and the morbidly curious used them to ask police incredibly imaginative and sometimes nauseating questions about the murders.

Inquiries into Glenda Sue Harden's life turned up nothing surprising. She had been an ordinary girl, well-behaved and well-liked, close to her parents and an enthusiastic member of her Sunday School class at Thrifthaven Baptist Church. She was neither a troublemaker nor a prig; like many Southern girls, she liked to sing on the bandstand at nightclubs, and she sometimes drank a Budweiser or two when out on dates. It appeared unlikely that she had ever given anyone a reason to kill her, and by now the men in the homicide bureau were prepared to accept such appearances as entirely plausible. Any information to the contrary would have clouded the perception, shared by Holloman and Cochran and Chief of Detectives Joe Gagliano, that the Harden girl had been slain by a killer whose victims were chosen at random.

Glenda Sue's youth and attractiveness, coupled with her essentially innocent nature ("She was the sort of trusting person who would leave her car unlocked and give a ride to someone who needed help," said a friend), made her an ideal newspaper subject. Statements by her relatives and acquaintances were printed in the newspapers and intensified the effect of her murder.

"She was a wonderful girl who deeply loved her parents and everyone around her," said her stepfather. "Whenever she wasn't at home or at work she was at church."

Her mother described her as "a sweet, outgoing, lovable Christian girl" and said that she had "loved people and didn't know what it was to be unkind to others."

"It is such a shock to think that something like this could happen to a person who was so good, someone who loved life as much as she did," said Mrs. Elbert Bell, who lived across the street from Glenda Sue's home. "We don't believe it possible that the killer knew her. I just can't believe that anyone who was a friend of hers would have a mind like that."

Holloman could not have hoped for more. These quotes, when published, were far more effective than his cautiously worded warning in persuading the people of Memphis that they were in danger. The quotes carried a message that was as clear as a syllogism: Glenda Sue Harden was an innocent; Glenda Sue Harden was murdered; therefore anyone could be murdered. The city began to draw into itself. People stayed at home and kept their doors locked. Managers of apartment buildings bought new locks and hired guards. Working women, particularly waitresses and telephone operators and others on night shifts, became afraid to go to work and afraid to go home afterwards. By eight-thirty on the Monday night after Glenda Sue's murder there were no people on Main Street downtown. Previously the street had never been so deserted until the middle of the night.

On Labor Day police in Tunica, Mississippi, telephoned the Memphis homicide bureau to report that they had arrested two sixteen-year-old Negro youths on suspicion of kidnapping, robbing and murdering an elderly man. The boys were from Memphis, and under questioning they had confessed to killing Glenda Sue Harden. Detective Roy Davis and Patrolman Rooster McWhirter drove to Tunica to question them and were quickly satisfied that they knew nothing about the Harden case. They had confessed in the hope that they might elude Mississippi authorities by being extradited to Tennessee.

The same day police in Greenville, Mississippi, reported arresting a twenty-two-year-old white man with scratches on his arms and a very confused story about where he had been the preceding Friday. Davis and McWhirter drove from Tunica to Greenville to question the man and found that he had an explanation for the scratches and an alibi for Friday. His story held up solidly when checked.

On Tuesday the police department announced that a citizen who wished to remain anonymous—"a friend of law enforcement," Holloman called him—was offering a five thousand dollar reward for information leading to capture and conviction of the killer. The Memphis City Council met the same day and voted to add another five thousand to that amount. Other offers followed quickly, and Mayor Henry Loeb became custodian of the funds.

Even with their extended working hours and the increased number of telephones, the police found it impossible to cope with the number of incoming calls. People called to ask questions and to volunteer what they thought might be helpful information. They called to report strange noises and frightening shadows and to say that their neighbor or brother-in-law or plumber had been acting strangely. All of the calls had to be handled carefully, and many of them had to be investigated. At the same time the city was continuing to have its usual fights and accidents and petty crimes, and run-of-the-mill and therefore nonfrightening homicides were occurring at the usual rate of one about every two days. These things too had to be dealt with. The overload soon became so great that dispatchers found it difficult to get squad cars to the scenes of auto accidents in less than half an hour.

Business was hurt also. Women reduced their shopping to the minimum necessary level, venturing out only to buy groceries and other essentials and then buying as much as possible so as not to have to go out again for several days. Merchandise remained on the shelves of stores throughout the city and began to grow old. The most conspicuous exceptions were locks and guns. Hardware stores quickly sold all their locks and had to compete with one another to order more. Men and women stood in line to buy guns only to learn that Tennessee law required a waiting period before delivery. Frustrated and angry, many drove to gun shops in Mississippi and Arkansas.

Door-to-door salesmen found it impossible to make a living; women would not talk to them. One insurance salesman announced that he was going out of business until the killer was found.

At the center of the turmoil, Bob Cochran stayed at his desk in the homicide bureau's crowded offices fifteen and sixteen hours a day to direct the investigation. As before, he knew far more than he was willing to tell the newspapers but far less than he needed to know to solve the killings. The bureau was a nest of telephones by now, but though the ringing was incessant little came of any of it. Almost everything that Cochran knew and regarded as worth knowing would have been learned if no one had called at all.

He knew that Glenda Sue Harden had died Friday evening not long after leaving work and that the cause of death was fourteen deep knife wounds in her chest, neck, head and back. He knew that she had not been strangled or sexually mutilated. Jerry Francisco had relayed all of this information to him after completing the autopsy. Cochran was certain that she had been killed in the park where her body was found, that she had not been killed elsewhere and then taken to the park, because a huge quantity of blood had been found under the body and when opened the hands were found to contain tufts of grass. To Cochran, the grass indicated that the girl must have been on her back when first stabbed and had clutched at the ground in a death grip.

He knew that Glenda Sue had been almost fully dressed when found, with only her shoes and panty hose missing. Oddly, part of her slip had been tucked into her panties at the back. Her hands had been bound behind her back with a pair of panty hose—almost certainly her own—so tightly knotted that big blood blisters were found on her wrists. She was still wearing her diamond engagement ring and the imitation topaz she had bought Friday.

He did not know how she had come to be in the park Friday evening. Presumably—what else could Cochran think?—she had been forced to go there by someone who abducted her after she left the Falls Building. He did not know how her Mustang had come to be parked at the place on the riverfront where it was found Saturday, but it was impossible to believe that she had left it there willingly. She had customarily parked on the Promenade, and detectives had found a man who remembered seeing a red-haired young woman in a gold dress walking across Riverside Drive toward the Promenade about five o'clock Friday. After that no one had noticed her, but she and her car had been moved to other places, presumably together. There was no way of knowing how. Imprints of Glenda Sue's tires did not match the plaster impressions made on the dirt road at Riverside Park.

A blue girdle discovered at the water's edge near the spot where the Mustang had been found could not be traced. Louise Lee said she was certain her daughter had never owned or worn such a thing.

If the Harden girl had been accosted by the killer at the Promenade, she must not have offered much resistance. Many people were on the lot when she reached it, and someone would have noticed screams or a fight. In order to get the Mustang off the lot, she or whoever was driving it had to deposit fifty cents at the automatic toll gate. This too suggested that the car had been removed from the lot rather quietly.

If Glenda Sue had been alone in her car when she left the lot, it became necessary to assume that she had been abducted elsewhere. But where? She had said she was going to Sears, but no one at the store remembered having seen her there and no purchases had been found in the car. That did not prove she had not gone to the store, of course. But perhaps someone pretending to be in trouble had waved to her from the side of the road and she had stopped to help. It was possible; she had been that kind of person. But for whom might she have stopped? Someone very young or very old or very harmless-looking, perhaps. A well-groomed young gentleman in a coat and tie. A woman. The autopsy had failed to establish that Glenda Sue was raped.

This was a too-familiar line of thought for Bob Cochran. It was precisely the same as wondering what kind of person Leila Jackson might have unlocked her screen door for, what kind of person the Dumases might have admitted to their apartment. A person with type A blood: hardly a helpful description. The captain leaned back in his leather chair and stared blankly across the room. He and Holloman and Lux and Joe Gagliano had been discussing all these possibilities daily for weeks, and none of it had done them any good. It was futile, really. There was nothing to prove that Glenda Sue Harden had been accosted in the parking lot or had stopped at Sears or had tried to help anyone along the road. Nothing proved anything except that she had been stabbed to death in a park. Conceivably she went to the park alone and first encountered the killer there. That was very hard to believe, unless some part of her life had been very, very secret. And if that was the case she could have been going to the park to meet the person who killed her. And that would mean she had known the killer, which in turn resurrected the old question of whether the killer had known the Dumases and Mrs. Jackson.

Cochran shook his head tiredly. It was useless to think these things. His men had spent hundreds of hours searching for any tiny indication that the Dumases and Mrs. Jackson and Glenda Sue Harden had an acquaintance in common anywhere in the world, or that any suspect in any of the killings could be linked in even an indirect way to the others. No such indication had been found, and there was nothing to do but to get back to work.

Part of the work at hand was the dismantling of Glenda Sue's Mustang. It had been towed to police headquarters, examined for fingerprints, and slowly searched piece by piece. The seats, accessories—any part that might conceal a fingerprint or something dropped by the killer was removed. But nothing was found.

On Tuesday afternoon the Jackson Life Insurance office was closed for Glenda Sue Harden's funeral. More than two hundred persons attended the service—including Lieutenant Tommy Smith, looking for faces seen at the Dumas and Jackson funerals—but for most people who worked in downtown

Memphis Tuesday meant a return to business as usual. They parked their cars along the riverfront in the morning, and late in the afternoon they returned to their cars to go home just as the Harden girl had four days before. Many of them thought of the murder as they approached the Promenade, the women walking in groups now, and the ones who had forgotten were reminded by the sight of two city policemen standing guard. The officers had been assigned to the Promenade both to provide security and to watch for suspicious activity, but it turned out to be a dull assignment. They stopped three small boys from swimming in the river, told an old man that he could not sleep under a tree, and had little else to do all day.

Other policemen spent several hours that day writing down the license numbers of cars parked along the riverfront. Later the owners of these cars would be questioned to see if they had been parked in the same area on Friday and, if so, whether they had noticed anything out of the ordinary. This exercise also gave police an opportunity to determine whether the Promenade was regularly used as a parking place by anyone with a criminal record.

Detectives also checked the Memphis public library's list of persons who had taken out copies of Gerold Frank's book *The Boston Strangler*. Word about that got into the newspapers and caused no small consternation among some elements of the city's reading public, but the inquiry turned up no suspects. As an afterthought, Cochran told Detective Hank Thomas to read the book and write a report on its contents. Thomas found the assignment absorbing but not specifically helpful in the search for Memphis's murderer. His report noted that the Boston slayings had been similar to those in Memphis and, worse, that the presumed strangler was found only because he bragged to his cellmates about his exploits after being arrested on a relatively minor charge. Frank's book offered no encouragement.

Joe Gagliano questioned Los Angeles police officials by telephone about the Sharon Tate murders and learned that they bore little resemblance to what had been happening in Memphis. Assistant Chief Routt flew to Boston for a closer look at the strangler case and returned with bad news. Boston police, Routt learned, were not unanimously convinced that they had in fact caught the strangler. There was some suspicion that the man officially identified as the strangler, the man Gerold Frank had written his book about, was an innocent psychopath who had confessed to murders he hadn't committed.

The Memphis police had suspects in the Harden case, a steady stream of them in fact, but most were quickly cleared. Some were men and women whose lives had intersected Glenda Sue Harden's, while others were ex-convicts and hoodlums accustomed to being picked up whenever a major crime occurred, or men who had done something to inspire reports about "suspicious" behavior. Some had been questioned after the Dumas and Jackson killings and others were new. Of the new ones, two interested Cochran particularly.

The first was a young man reported to be a transvestite. Detectives questioned him, verified his alibis, and were satisfied that he could not have committed any of the killings. When Cochran read the interrogation report, however, he decided that he wanted to know more and ordered the man brought to his office for further questioning. The man came willingly, even bringing photographs of himself in women's clothing, and he talked freely for a very long time. Calmly and articulately, with what appeared to be genuine interest in helping the police, he explained his own sexual peculiarities and told what he knew about transvestitism generally. Cochran listened with growing interest, not only because the subject was bizarre but also because it opened new possibilities for the investigation. It suggested possible answers to several mysteries—the virtual invisibility of the killer, the apparent ease with which the killer had gained entrance to the Dumas and Jackson homes, the fact that no one had seen anything unusual the afternoon that Glenda Sue Harden disappeared. A man convincingly dressed as a woman—and Cochran's young informant assured him that transvestites were often highly convincing—might find it very easy to win the confidence of an intended victim. Women seldom arouse as much suspicion as men. By the end of the interview Cochran had decided that his bureau must make new efforts to learn everything possible about transvestites in Memphis.

The second interesting suspect was a professional man whose office was not far from Glenda Sue Harden's. He became a suspect because he had on several occasions been reported for frightening young women downtown. He would follow girls on foot, or persuade them to stop their cars by telling them they had flat tires, and then make brutally frank advances. Detectives questioned him and were not satisfied by his explanations for his behavior or his account of where he had been the evening Glenda Sue Harden was killed. He was put under twenty-four-hour surveillance and followed everywhere he went.

Public reaction continued to mount and created increasing problems. On Tuesday afternoon a woman reported that she had been attacked by a white man on the basement stairs of the J. C. Penney Store at Poplar Plaza Shopping Center. The man pushed her to the ground and attempted to strangle her with a stocking, the woman said, but when she screamed he ran away. The story was in Wednesday's *Commercial Appeal,* and others like it followed so quickly that they became staple features of Memphis's daily news. In a discouraging number of instances, investigating officers found that reported assaults were the inventions of women desperate for attention. In others, it was impossible to tell. Reports of prowlers—and of men shooting at what they believed to be prowlers—became so numerous that the street patrols were constantly behind schedule.

One day in the week following the Harden murder the homicide bureau received a call from a woman who stated

that her husband was the killer. The call was sufficiently unusual to be transferred to Cochran's phone, and the woman
told him her story.

"I know my husband is the nut," she insisted. "I'm absolutely sure of it, and it's got me scared to death."

"What makes you say that, ma'am?"

"I can't find out where he was when any of these killings
happened," the woman replied. "He wasn't at home and I
know he wasn't at work because I checked that myself. And
he's been acting real funny."

"Well," said Cochran, "that doesn't make him a murderer.
I mean, a lot of people around here are acting funny these
days."

"Not funny like my husband. I'm telling you, he's the nut.
A lady was killed in Atlanta when he was there not very long
ago, and now he's got bloodstains on his shirt."

The husband, a frightened and confused middle-aged man
with dark red stains on his work shirt, was picked up and
brought to headquarters for questioning. The shirt was
taken away for laboratory tests while he was interrogated,
and as he stammered his alibi it was checked by telephone
and confirmed. He was not, could not have been, the killer.
The shirt came back from the lab. It was stained, as the terrified man had vowed, with rust.

Things went on and on that way, the panic growing steadily worse instead of lessening, the newspapers larding one
edition after another with dubious accounts of new murder
attempts. The police, exhausted and making no headway,
found themselves in the acutely uncomfortable position of
feeling quite certain that another murder was likely to occur
soon but not knowing where or when or how.

"The thing that scares me," Cochran told Joe Gagliano,
"is that this son of a bitch seems to be experimenting with
murder. First he kills a middle-aged couple, then a real old
lady, and then a pretty young girl. What's next? I'm afraid
it's going to be a child."

The best hope, not a very satisfying one, was that next time the murderer would not get away quite so cleanly. Nothing else seemed to be working. The offer of a ten thousand dollar reward for the killer's arrest and conviction had done no good. Early in September Tennessee Governor Buford Ellington, drawing upon state funds, doubled it to more than twenty thousand dollars.

Detective Jo Ann Moore was working the phone desk in the vice bureau on September 9 when a call came in from a woman who would not give her name but said she worked at Baptist Hospital.

"Go to 2084 Carr and find Clifford Putt," the woman said. "Clifford Putt, P-U-T-T. He's got a rust-colored car and he's the man you're looking for. He's the murderer."

Detective Moore checked the department files and found an arrest record and a mug shot of a smiling blond young man under the name Clifford Putt. She went to the Carr Street address but could find no trace of him. No one living nearby had ever heard of him, and he was not in the phone book. She put the arrest record and the photograph and a memo about the anonymous call into a file folder and sent it to her boss, Lieutenant Bill Wallace. The next day Wallace reviewed it, marked it for forwarding to the homicide bureau, and dropped it into his out box. It didn't reach the homicide bureau until after the next murder had occurred.

6

Living with Fear

EARLY IN 1969 Mary Putt gave up. Pregnant, sick, broke and unable to work, she agreed to a reconciliation with Buster and abandoned her last hopes for a free life. She decided that she was firmly trapped and could only try to make the best of her entrapment. Nineteen years old now, she blamed herself for the destruction of her future.

"I'm sorry about everything I did," Buster told her when he arrived in Sarah from Jackson. "If you'll come back I won't do it again. You know how important you are to me—you and the baby. You know I'll be good to the baby."

Mary found the entire appeal disgusting, but she especially resented the part about the baby because she knew it was true. Buster was always good to the baby, and in telling her so he was taking advantage of her need for help. Everything else, including the promise to stay out of trouble, was comfortably unbelievable. Buster himself, childlike in his begging for forgiveness, aroused only contempt. But Mary would soon have two babies to worry about, and no money. Her situation was worse than it had been thirteen months before, when she had agreed to marry Buster. "Okay," she said without enthusiasm. "Let's try again."

Buster, it turned out, had distorted the facts when he

asked her to come back. There was nothing to come back to. He had lost his job and the cottage in Jackson and was almost as penniless as Mary. He promised to get a job as quickly as possible, however, and they moved into the Bulimores' house in Sarah. He and Mary slept on the old rollaway bed, moving it into the kitchen every night because the woodburning stove in the living room made the front half of the house too hot for sleeping, and life became excruciatingly unpleasant. Mary's parents had not wanted her to see Buster again, and her mother had agreed that doing so might be a good thing only after learning of the new pregnancy. Her father, confirmed in his original dislike for Buster, became unfriendlier than ever. Buster only made things worse for everyone by displaying his most ingratiating behavior, addressing Mr. and Mrs. Bulimore as "Dad" and "Mom," talking with them in an exaggeratedly meek and polite way, studiously playing a role that no one in the house found credible. He looked for a job but couldn't find one, and at night he upset the family by walking and crying out in his sleep. He had had nightmares before, but never as frequently or as violently as this. Disturbances became an almost nightly occurrence.

In February Annie Bulimore took Buster to the Jagline Garment Company plant in Sledge and, through an old friend, got him a job as a mechanic. Then she helped Buster find and rent an old house in Crenshaw, a hamlet on the highway between Sarah and Sledge, and furnished it by begging and borrowing odds and ends from neighbors. Buster, Mary and Pip settled into the house, and things were fine until, with maddening inevitability, Clifford and Retha arrived. They had no money, Clifford was out of work, and Buster invited them to move in.

"You can't do this!" Mary hissed. "You can't let them live with us again!"

"Clifford is my brother," Buster answered. "He needs help, and I'm not going to turn him away." He walked out of the house to help Clifford and Retha unload their car, and the subject was closed.

Next, and for the first time in her life, Mary discovered that she had a rival. This was Eileen King,* a tall and attractive brunette who lived nearby with her husband and small children and worked at a factory not far from Sarah. Mary had known her all her life and had always disliked her as a haughty, snobbish girl, one who somehow regarded herself as superior to her neighbors. Now, however, Eileen suddenly became very friendly, driving to Crenshaw one Saturday afternoon and inviting Mary and Buster to join the church in which she was a conspicuously active member. Mary, who had been forced to listen to long, dull sermons every Sunday of her childhood, wanted nothing to do with church or with Eileen King. Buster, though, was charmed by the smiling Eileen and her proposal. The next morning he put on his best clothes and went off to church alone. Soon Eileen was coming to Crenshaw regularly, and to Mary it seemed clear that she was flirting with Buster. One night she knocked on the door after midnight and woke Buster to show him her new hairdo. Buster enrolled in Sunday School and never failed to attend.

Early in April Eileen insisted that Mary and Buster come with her and her husband Dean* to a dance. Buster, who had never before demonstrated any liking for such affairs, happily agreed. Mary, who had always enjoyed night clubs, went along only to see what would happen. Buster and Eileen danced together all evening, stopping occasionally for a glass of beer and then returning to the dance floor. Dean King sat at a table across from Mary, staring at a glass of bourbon and seldom saying anything. Obviously he was as suspicious as Mary and at least as unhappy. Mary drank nothing for a long time, but late in the evening she reached impulsively for Dean's bottle and half-filled a glass with

* a pseudonym

bourbon which she topped off with Seven-Up. It tasted terrible to her, but she choked it down and filled the glass again. By the time the dance ended she was drunker than she had ever been in her life. Eileen laughed about it and suggested that Buster and Mary spend the night at her house in Sarah rather than driving back to Crenshaw. Buster laughed too and said it was a good idea. "That way we'll be closer to church in the morning," he said, and he and Eileen burst into fresh laughter together. Mary, in her angry stupor, couldn't understand what was so funny.

Very late that night, some time in the silent hours before Sunday's dawn, Mary awoke to find herself in a strange bedroom with Buster deep in sleep beside her. The back of his head was buried deep in a pillow, but his blond hair glistened in the light from a hall outside the door and his face was strong and handsomely suntanned against the white bedding. Mary stared at him for a long moment and then, without conscious motive, without thinking about what she was doing, she picked up her pillow and pressed it down on his face. When he began to struggle she pressed harder, raising herself onto her knees for leverage, trying to keep his head pinned against the mattress. He was too strong for her, but as soon as he forced the pillow aside she let it go and clutched his throat with both hands. She squeezed as tightly as she could, lunging to put the full weight of her body behind her wrists, but Buster broke her grip and rolled over backwards out of bed to get away from her. "God damn!" he shouted. "What are you trying to do?" Mary, as confused as Buster, lay back on the bed and looked at the doorway as Eileen and her husband came running into the room. Suddenly overwhelmed with nausea, she got out of bed and stumbled into the hall looking for the bathroom, reaching it just in time to vomit. She was sick for a long time, and afterwards she sat on the bathroom floor with her elbow on the edge of the commode and pressed her fingers against her aching forehead.

After a while Buster, shirtless but wearing his trousers, came in and leaned against the wall with his hands in his pockets.

"You all right?" he asked.

"Um. Yeah."

"You tried to kill me, do you know that?" Buster was silhouetted against the doorway, and Mary could not see his face. His voice was soft, not angry but interested, amazed. He might have used the same tone to ask her if she realized she had just jumped a seven-foot fence.

"You were really trying to kill me." A touch of amusement was in his voice now. Mary waved him away and he went back to bed. The next morning no one mentioned what had happened, and Buster took Mary home without waiting to go to church.

A few weeks later, on April 28, Buster left the car at home and rode to work with a neighbor. That morning Mary made her regular Monday visit to a doctor for prenatal care and treatment of a kidney infection, and when she got home she discovered that Buster had forgotten to take his lunch. It was almost noon, so she put Pip back into his car bed and started for Sledge. She was almost there when she noticed a familiar dark car approaching from the other direction, and as it drew nearer she saw that it was Dean and Eileen King's Ford and that two people were in the front seat. She almost put her hand out to wave but decided not to be so friendly, and as the Ford swept past she looked over and saw that Buster was driving. Eileen was beside him, looking at Mary with wide eyes and then ducking down too late. Mary put on the brakes and pulled onto the dirt shoulder at the edge of the highway, then spun around in a U-turn and tried to follow the Ford. She couldn't catch it—Buster was driving at breakneck speed and went through Crenshaw without slowing down—so she returned home to wait. When Buster didn't come home that night she reported him missing to the sheriff's office and learned that Eileen was missing too. Her family knew nothing except that she had taken a roast out of the freezer before leaving for work that morning and had not returned to cook it that evening. Her husband and grandfather had both been worried, but when they learned of Buster's disappearance they became furious and said they were going to kill him. By Tuesday the story that Buster and Eileen had run off together was the leading gossip at every crossroads from Sarah to Sledge. On Wednesday a sheriff's deputy told Mary that a warrant had been issued charging Buster with stealing a television from the home of his homosexual friend in Jackson. There was some talk of organizing a search party but nothing came of it. Most people treated the whole affair as a joke.

Thursday afternoon a man from the finance company came to see Buster about overdue payments on the Chevrolet. Mary told him that Buster was away and she had no money, so the man took the keys, locked the car, and said he would send someone to pick it up in the morning. But in the morning the car was gone and Dean King's Ford, its engine burned out and its seats and floors littered with empty meat cans, was found in an alley a hundred yards away. Mary joined a group of men gathered around the Ford. "Your husband must have hot-wired that Chevy of yours to get away with it like that," a smiling man in bib overalls told her. "Just like damn Bonnie and Clyde!" an admiring teenager exclaimed.

It was Friday, payday, and the occasion for a kind of strange carnival down the highway in Sledge. People at the Jagline factory learned that Buster had come for his car in the night and they waited and watched all day, wondering if he would return in daylight to get his pay. Eileen's grandfather arrived with a revolver, saying that he had persuaded Dean King to stay home by promising that if he saw Buster he would shoot him without asking questions. He sat in his car outside the factory for hours, and finally he drove off to get a sandwich. When he returned half an hour later a laughing man shouted out the window that Eileen and Buster had just left. The old man telephoned the sheriff's office, and minutes later Buster and Eileen were stopped in Sardis near the county line. Buster was arrested and put in the Sardis jail's only cell.

Mary got a ride to Sardis late in the afternoon, and when she walked into the jail she saw Buster and Eileen holding hands through the bars of Buster's cell. Eileen looked almost as beautiful as usual despite her week on the run, and she smiled and said "Hi" in such an outrageously cheerful way that Mary lost her temper. She hit Eileen in the chest with both hands and knocked her down, then grabbed her by the hair and began dragging her back and forth across the floor. Both of them were screaming. A deputy jumped in and forced Mary to let go.

"You want to be in jail with your husband?" he barked.

"Yeah, sure," Mary shouted, closing her hands into tight fists. "Go ahead and put me in. I'll tear him apart too." The deputy took her by the arm and pushed her outside, and when she calmed down she discovered that her hands were filled with long dark strands of Eileen's hair. She dropped the hair into the dirt and rubbed her palms together. She could hear Eileen crying inside.

"You go on get away from here now," the deputy said. He was red-faced and very upset.

"I don't have to go away. That bitch ran off with my husband and left me without a dime in the world. She's got a beating coming to her."

"Not here," the deputy puffed. "You get on home. She gives you any trouble at home you can hit her with a board or do anything you please. But you ain't gonna do it here."

Mary got the Chevy from behind the jailhouse and returned to Crenshaw. That night Clifford and Retha moved out, and later Mary learned that they had gone to Richmond, Virginia. Grandmother and Grandfather Putt had moved to Richmond during the winter, and Clifford

wanted to see them. Mary tried to stay in the house in Crenshaw, but too many men in town came around at night to see
if she were lonely. One night a drunken neighbor with a six-
pack of beer under his arm tried to force his way in, and the
next morning Mary moved back to her parents' house in
Sarah. She applied for welfare and learned that Mississippi
would give her only twenty-six dollars a month. In Tennessee she could get ninety-seven dollars, so she moved with Pip
into her Uncle Edward's house in Memphis. The finance
company let her keep the car when she promised to resume
payments after her baby was born. It was not an act of kind-
ness; she owed more on the car than it was worth.

Buster was transferred from Sardis to Jackson to stand
trial on a charge of burglary, but on May 5, after pleading
guilty to a lesser charge of possessing stolen property, he was
sentenced to six months at the Hinds County Penal Farm
and fined five hundred dollars. "It might as well be five million, for all we can pay it," said Mary when she heard.

At the end of June, almost two months after Buster's arrest
and the departure of Clifford and Retha, Mary's mother telephoned her with more family news. "Buster escaped last
Thursday," Annie Bulimore said. "He just ran off, and nobody knows where he is. Did he come to see you?"

"No. I haven't heard from him at all." She felt almost
hurt.

"That's what I told the police," said Annie. "Your daddy
asked me to tell you that if Buster comes around you
shouldn't have anything to do with him. Your daddy says if
he sees Buster around here he'll either turn him in or shoot
him."

Mary was not really surprised when, on July 25, Buster
showed up in Memphis. She had been expecting him for
weeks, ever since learning of his escape, and as time passed
and her first welfare check did not come she found herself

very nearly hoping for his arrival. She was in her seventh month of pregnancy, her kidney infection had grown worse, and the events of the past year and a half had affected her nerves severely. Pip, just beginning to walk, was sometimes almost too much for her to handle. She needed help and she needed money, and the runaway Buster was the only possible source of either unless she continued to borrow from her parents and her uncle. She did not want to do that.

The surprise was that Buster did not arrive alone. Clifford and Retha came with him, drove him to Memphis in fact, and they acted as though they expected Mary to be glad to see them. She wasn't, and she made her feelings clear. They had all been in Richmond together, Clifford said, staying with Grandfather and Grandmother Putt, and Buster hastened to assure Mary that the idea of returning to Memphis had been his. He was blonder and browner than ever, as trim and attractive as the night Mary had met him, and he and Clifford were dressed alike in sunglasses and bright turtle-neck shirts. The four of them talked quietly and self-consciously for a while and then Clifford and Retha drove off to find a hotel room. Mary went upstairs to her rooms on the second floor of Uncle Edward's house with Buster on her heels. He had been self-assured enough in his brother's presence, but with Clifford gone he reverted to the penitent child role that had always been part of his campaigns to effect a reconciliation. Predictably, he made a great fuss over the sleeping Pip, and then he began offering explanations for his misadventures. That too could have been foreseen; Buster could be talkative when he wanted to win Mary over.

"Do you want a divorce?" he asked. The question was transparently rhetorical, Mary's cue to declare her undying love. It almost made her laugh, but she smothered the impulse by clenching her teeth.

"I don't know," she said solemnly. "I thought you'd be the one to want a divorce."

"Me? Why me?" Buster's surprise seemed genuine.

"You're the one who ran off with Eileen King. I didn't run off with anybody."

"I didn't either. I didn't run off with Eileen. She was scared and I tried to help her."

This time Mary did laugh. "Bull," she said. "That's a lot of bull."

"You listen," Buster said urgently. "It wasn't what you think. Eileen and me were driving home for lunch that day, and when she saw you see us she got scared and said she was afraid to go home. She said Dean would beat hell out of her if you told him we were riding together. I figured if she wasn't going home I'd better not either, so we took off."

"Took off for where?"

"For Memphis. Here. We slept in the car and I sold blood so we could get some money to eat. When the car started to go bad we came back to Sarah to get the Chevy. That was all. I wasn't being smart, but nothing bad happened."

Buster put his arms around Mary. "Listen, Mary Ruth," he said tenderly, trying to be seductive, "I'm really sorry about all that. It was dumb, but it won't happen again. Let's forget it. Let's be happy and look after our babies."

"No."

"No? You mean you do want a divorce?" Buster dropped his arms to his side. "You don't want to live with me any more?"

"You should have been an actor."

"That's not fair. Anybody can make a mistake. I won't do it again."

"You always do it again," said Mary. She was not seducible, but she was capable of being mercenary now that she had Buster on the defensive. "I don't want anything to do with you," she said, "but if you can get a job and make some money maybe I'll think about changing my mind."

"Well, heck, I was going to get a job anyway. You know that. When I do can we live together again?"

"Maybe. You make some money and we'll talk about it

then." Mary experienced a sense of triumph, realizing that she should have handled Buster this way long ago. She let him have the car keys and he went off to find Clifford and Retha, promising to return the next day in time to take her to her doctor's appointment. He kept his promise, and afterwards he went home with Mary and Pip and settled down possessively in an easy chair. He was in a pleasant, open mood, and he said he had found a nice room at the Terrace Hotel on Madison Street. Later, when Mary asked him how he had escaped from prison, he told her a long and amusing story the point of which was to illustrate his own cleverness and daring. He had behaved himself perfectly at first, he said, in order to be made a trusty, and then he became a model trusty to get an assignment as a truck driver. His opportunity came on June 26, when he was sent into Jackson to pick up a group of prisoners on a work detail at the jail. He picked them up as instructed, and on his way back to the farm he stopped at the side of the Natchez Trace Highway and announced to his passengers that he was escaping. He invited them to join him but they all said no—like Buster, they were serving short sentences for petty crimes—and so he put the ignition keys in his pocket and walked off. He followed the Natchez Trace northeast for several days and nights, keeping to the woods to avoid being seen, and when he got to Tupelo he borrowed clothes from a friend of his grandparents and hitch-hiked to Richmond. He stayed at his grandparents' home there with Clifford and Retha, worked briefly at a hospital, and then decided to return to Memphis.

"How's that for smart?" he asked. "They never came close to catching me."

"It was dumb," Mary laughed. "The dumbest thing I ever heard. You could have stayed on the farm, and you'd be almost out by now. But now you're a wanted man."

"Sure," said Buster. "Sure. And how was I gonna pay them that five hundred dollars? How'd you like to pay it for me?" He reached out for her hand but she backed away. She didn't scold him, though, and he leaned back contentedly in his chair.

From then on Buster came to see Mary every day, and sometimes she and Pip went for rides with him or to the hotel to visit Clifford and Retha. Clifford, more subdued than Mary had ever seen him, was almost cordial. It was all fairly pleasant, though Mary still was not feeling well and Buster never failed to make a daily appeal for sex or, failing that, permission to move in with her on what he promised would be a "brotherly" basis. Mary was never tempted to say yes, but the pleas didn't offend her because they offered proof that Buster, properly controlled, might still prove useful. He didn't get a job, but he had brought a little money from Richmond and he shared it with her.

On July 29 Buster took Mary to the Terrace Hotel to say goodbye to Clifford and Retha. They were going across the border to live with Retha's family in Blue Goose and look for work. When they were gone, Mary went up to Buster's room and put the baby on the bed to nap. Buster whispered to her that he had to move out because he hadn't paid his bill. "You better find something quick then," Mary said sharply. "You're not moving in with me."

That afternoon they went for a walk along the streets surrounding the hotel, checking at several houses advertising rooms for rent. All the rooms they saw were very inexpensive, but they were also very dingy and Buster said he didn't like them. Mary thought he was stalling, hoping to force her to take him in. At 21 North Somerville, about a block and a half from the hotel, they saw a rental sign on the lawn in front of an old white house, and when Buster knocked on the door an old woman answered. She introduced herself as Mrs. Jackson and showed them an attractive bedroom in the back of the house, but when she learned that the pregnant Mary was Buster's wife and Pip was their son she wanted to know why he wanted a room only for himself. Buster fumbled clumsily for an answer, failed to devise one, and Mrs. Jackson became suspicious. She said the room would be seven dollars a day, thirty-five dollars a week, payable in advance every Sunday.

"That's more than I'm paying for a bigger room at the Terrace," Buster protested.

"I'm sorry," Mrs. Jackson said without a trace of sorrow. "That's what I charge." Buster left angrily, leaving Mary behind to carry the baby and catch up with him on the sidewalk. He said he was sure the old woman had hiked the rent to get rid of him.

Buster moved to the Tennessee Hotel, and when he was asked to pay there he moved to the Rex. When Clifford and Retha came to Memphis to visit, Buster told his brother about his trouble with the old woman on North Somerville and the difficulty he was having in finding a job and a place to stay. Clifford didn't seem interested in Mrs. Jackson, but he said the job situation was just as bad in Mississippi and Buster might as well stay where he was and keep trying. Blue Goose was not a long drive from Memphis, and Clifford and Retha made the trip several times a week. Clifford continued to be unusually quiet, and he and Buster did not go off together or get into trouble.

On August 7 Buster stopped by in the morning to tell Mary that he had been hired at a Star Service Station on South Third Street downtown and would be working from noon to eight in the evening six days a week for $1.60 an hour. "Can I move in now?" he asked. "Not yet," said Mary, trying to play him carefully. "Ask me when you get paid." The next morning Buster returned and told Mary he had quit the job. The station was near police headquarters, he said, and many officers parked their personal cars on an adjacent lot before going on duty. He was afraid that one of them would discover that he was an escaped convict. Mary had to admit that it seemed a reasonable fear.

On August 10 Mary finally got her first welfare check—ninety-seven dollars for the month of July. Two days later another check came—another ninety-seven dollars for August. It was the most money she'd had in a long time, and she bought a newspaper and went through the list of furnished apartments. She wanted her own place; Uncle Edward never interfered in her affairs, but he knew by now that she was seeing Buster and had advised her to keep away from him. An inexpensive three-room place was available on Bethel Street, and when Mary went to see it she found that it was in an attractive white stucco building on a quiet street. The apartment itself was ugly and shabbily furnished, and to get to it she had to climb a steep and dark staircase to the second floor. The landlord required only $32.50 for the first two weeks, though, and Mary gave him the money immediately. That night, after Buster had helped her move in, he asked how she expected to pay sixty-five dollars a month in rent when her total income was only thirty-two dollars more than that. "That's up to you," she answered. "If you get a job I'll let you move in."

On August 15 the Dumas murders made headlines. Buster, with his usual interest in horrible events, visited Mary every evening to watch the news on television, and he began to buy and read newspapers. He became obsessed by the case, full of theories and eager to explain them. When Michael Dumas appealed for the killer to surrender Buster said confidently that the plea was a police trick, a "come-on."

On August 19 Buster announced that he had been hired at the Hudson Service Station on North Bellevue near the outskirts of the city. He would be working a rotating shift at all hours of the day and night, but the pay was $1.70 an hour, a dime better than the first job had paid. He would get his first check, he said, before Mary's welfare money ran out. That night Clifford and Retha came to visit, and Clifford said he was starting work the next day at the Chromecraft furniture factory in Senatobia, Mississippi. Buster wanted to talk about the murders, but the subject seemed to make Clifford uncomfortable so they celebrated their new jobs.

Buster moved into the apartment on Bethel. He and Mary drove to Sarah to see her mother, being careful to arrive after her father was asleep. Buster honked his horn once and they waited outside in the dark until Annie came out of the house. She did not seem surprised to see Buster and she greeted him affectionately, reaching out to pat him on the arm. "Stay out of trouble and the police won't even look for you," she assured him. "They've got worse people than you to look for."

"That's for sure!" said Buster with a laugh. "Especially these days."

August 26 was Buster's day off. He went out late in the morning and returned in the middle of the afternoon, very excited and waving two newspapers. "Remember the old lady I tried to rent the room from over near the Terrace Hotel?" he asked. "That Mrs. Jackson, remember her? Somebody killed her just like that Dumas couple! There must be some kind of really bad nut loose in this town!" Mary read the story in the *Commercial Appeal* but didn't want to talk about it. Buster, rebuffed, became withdrawn. He read the papers and watched the evening news, and then Clifford and Retha arrived on one of their visits. Mary left Pip with neighbors across the hall, as she often did, and they went out to play miniature golf. It was not an enjoyable evening. The weather was hot, Mary felt heavy and nauseated, and Buster kept talking to Clifford about the murders and about how the new victim was the same crabby old woman he had mentioned before. Clifford was unresponsive, and after a while Buster again became silent. It seemed to Mary that the relationship between the two brothers had changed somehow since their return from Virginia, that something beyond her understanding had passed between them. Their conversations were strange, filled with great expanses of silence, and it was impossible for her to tell whether they had lost the ability to communicate with each other or were communicating in some newly intimate way. Clifford particularly was interesting to watch. He remained less assertive than Mary had ever seen him in the past. He didn't appear to enjoy his visits to Memphis, but he continued to make them and to bring his passive wife.

After the trip to the miniature golf course Buster stopped talking about the murders and withdrew behind his sunglasses. Everyone else was talking about the murders, however, and Mary found the subject so frightening that she became unable to sleep at night or relax during the day. Her doctor prescribed tranquilizers and advised her to keep as calm as possible. He said he was concerned about her condition, and he wanted to see her almost every day. Buster read the papers morning and afternoon, watched television whenever he was not working, and never missed a news broadcast. Whenever he went out alone he warned Mary to keep the doors locked. "You don't have to worry about that," she told him. "I'm not letting *anybody* in here when you're not here." She seldom left home except to see the doctor, and no one came to see her when Buster was away except the housewife who lived across the hall, a small woman named Mandy* who was as afraid as Mary. Mandy would knock on Mary's door, call out to identify herself, and run back into her own apartment if Mary didn't open up almost immediately. The landing between the two apartments was big and dark, and Mandy was afraid to stand in it for more than half a minute. When she came to visit she talked too much about the murders, but nevertheless Mary usually was grateful to have some company.

Early one afternoon not many days after the Jackson murder, Mary was sitting on the sofa in her living room and watching television when she looked over her shoulder to check on the baby and saw the figure of a man out of the corner of her eye. He was standing directly behind her, not moving. She jumped to her feet, spun around, and was trying to get enough breath to scream when she realized that the

* a pseudonym

man was Buster. She had thought he was at work. Motionless as a figure in a photograph, he was standing in the doorway between the living room and the bedroom, watching her from behind the dark lenses covering his eyes. Without speaking he walked over to her, grabbed her upper arm with his hand, and began to shake her violently. He shook her until she fell to the floor and began to weep, and then he bent down and put his knee on her chest. When he spoke, it was in a low voice taut with constricted anger.

"The door was unlocked," he said. "The goddamned door was unlocked. Don't you know there's a nut running around killing people? He could have come in here and killed you. Didn't I tell you to lock the doors?"

Mary had locked both doors early that morning when Buster left for work and had checked them later to be sure. But Pip had been toddling from room to room while she watched television, and she assumed that somehow he must have turned the key in the door between the bedroom and the landing. She hadn't guessed he was strong enough to do that—or, for that matter, that anyone could have come up the bare wooden stairs without being heard. She tried to explain all this to Buster but he cut her off with a sweep of his hand and did not say another word all day. When Mary called him to supper, he ignored her. Buster had a big appetite, and this was the first time in Mary's memory that he had willingly missed a meal. His nightmares that night were more violent than usual, and Mary got very little sleep.

The day after that, while Buster was at work, someone knocked on the living room door. It was locked. "Who's there?" Mary asked. "Mandy?"

"It's the Red Man exterminator," a man's voice answered.

"I don't know no damned Red Man."

"The landlord says you have roaches."

"You'll have to wait till my husband gets home."

The man left. Mary heard his feet thumping down the stairs and ran to the bedroom to look out the front window.

No truck was parked outside, and though Mary watched for several minutes she saw no one leave the house. That night she told Buster about the incident and said she was certain the caller must have been the murderer. "I can't stand one more day of this," she said. "I'm afraid I'll lose my mind." The next day, Friday August 29, Buster took her and Pip to Sarah for the long holiday weekend. They left Memphis early in the afternoon, and on the way out of town Buster stopped at the Hudson station and got permission to start work at four o'clock that day instead of three as scheduled. He dropped Mary and the baby off at the Bulimores' house and started back to Memphis immediately.

On the morning of Monday September 1, Labor Day, Buster returned to Sarah to get Mary and Pip and took them home to Bethel Street. The apartment was a mess, newspapers strewn about and sandwich wrappers all over the floor. Buster explained that Clifford and Retha had spent the entire weekend with him, arriving Friday evening and staying until early Monday, and that they had eaten carry-out food instead of cooking. "They made the mess," he said, "not me. I was at work every day you were gone." Then he left for work, again on the three-to-midnight shift, and Mary cleaned. The Harden murder was in the news now, and Mary was afraid to be back in Memphis. She had returned only because she had to be near her doctor and the hospital.

That night, while Buster was still at work, Clifford and Retha returned to Memphis with their belongings. Clifford said he had quit his job at Chromecraft and planned to get a job in the city. He was tired of driving back and forth all the time, he said, and he wanted to be near Buster. Because Buster was not home, Mary was able to tell Clifford and Retha that she had no room for them. They went to a hotel.

The next day, Tuesday, September 2, Buster announced that he had bought a 1961 Buick station wagon. Mary was enraged. They were short of money, they already had one car that was not paid for, and after Buster brought the station wagon home he could not get it started again. He worked on it for hours but couldn't make it run, and he was unable to explain why he had bought it. Mary became afraid that she was losing control of him. Her sole remaining source of leverage, now that Buster had moved in, was sex. He asked for it every day and was always refused.

On Sunday, September 7, Mary was feeling sick and complaining of the heat, so in the afternoon Buster took her for a drive. Riding along Union Street, enjoying the breeze coming in her window, Mary saw a woman walking alone. It had become unusual for women to walk alone in Memphis. "My God, she doesn't look like she's very worried," Mary said. "I guess some fools never learn." Buster burst out laughing and couldn't stop. He said it was the funniest thing he'd heard in months. Mary told him that she hadn't been joking, and he laughed again uproariously.

His laughter stopped minutes later when a policeman pulled him over for rolling through a stop sign. Buster sat tensely behind the wheel while the officer walked slowly around the car checking the license plates, and when he was asked to get out of the car and show his driver's license he hurried to obey. He had no license, but Clifford had given him an expired one, and as he pulled it out of his billfold several other identification cards fell to the ground. He stooped quickly to pick them up. Mary could see that he was frightened.

"Clifford Putt?" the policeman asked, reading from the license.

"Yes."

"This permit is expired."

"I know. I forgot to renew it."

The officer took the other cards out of Buster's hands and examined them. "George Putt," he read aloud. "What *is* your name, anyway—Clifford or George?"

Buster told him the truth. Then, lying, he said he'd lost his license and had borrowed one temporarily from his brother. The policeman watched him quizzically for a moment, then looked inside the car at Mary and Pip. He was young and had an agreeable face.

"This your husband?" he asked.

"Yes it is."

"How is he? A good boy?" This jokingly.

"Oh, most of the time he's pretty good," Mary answered with a forced laugh. "He's okay."

Buster was warned to replace his lost license and allowed to go. He got behind the wheel and drove slowly, carefully home. "Oh, God," he said tensely, leaning forward against the steering wheel. "That was so close. If that guy had called in to check my name I'd be on my way back to Hinds County. Thank God for dumb cops."

On Monday, Buster's day off, he went with Mandy's husband Ray* to a factory in Memphis to apply for a job. The company was hiring, Ray said, and it paid half again as much as Buster was making at the gas station. Late in the afternoon Buster returned home and told Mary that Ray had been right: he'd been given a job. He said it was dirty work, though, and he began to talk about moving to Texas after the baby was born. "Good jobs are easy to find in Texas," he said, "and the police aren't likely to be looking for me there."

On Tuesday Buster got home from work late in the afternoon and told Mary that Clifford had been hired at a gas station and had rented an apartment at 144 North Bellevue Street. He and Retha wanted them to see their new place, Buster said, so after supper he and Mary drove along Madison Street to Bellevue, turned left, and began looking for the address. She pointed to a large and attractive building with a sign in front that said LaBlanche Apartments. 'Wrong place," Buster said after a quick look. "That's 41 North Bellevue. Clifford's at 144." Clifford and Retha were not, of course, living in a large and attractive apartment building.

* a pseudonym

They had two dingy rooms on the second floor of a collapsing old frame house. The visit was strange. Nobody said much of anything. They watched television most of the evening, talking occasionally about jobs and apartments and the heat, and Clifford became increasingly nervous for no reason that Mary could determine. By the time she and Buster left, Mary was wondering if something might be seriously wrong with Clifford.

One Wednesday night, at supper, Mary asked Buster if he had heard that the reward for the killer had been raised to twenty thousand dollars. He swallowed quickly and looked at her.

"*Twenty thousand dollars?*" he asked. "God, that's a lot of money. For twenty thousand dollars, you ought to turn *me* in."

"How would they believe me?"

"They'd believe you. I've got a record and I'm a wanted man. I'm probably on the FBI list. Don't worry—they'd believe you."

"I'll think about it," Mary said with a smile. She wanted Buster to smile, too, but his lips were a straight line. His eyes were concealed behind the sunglasses. He finished his meal and then started at her again.

"Twenty thousand dollars, Mary Ruth," he said. "Why don't you turn me in?" Again he failed to smile.

"You shut up, Buster!" Mary snapped, feeling her nerves unravel. "I don't think you're funny one bit. Things like that are nothing to joke about."

7
Another Murder

MRS. GRACE OLDHAM, sixty-eight years old, lived on the third floor of the LaBlanche apartment building at 41 North Bellevue Street. On Thursday September 11, a few minutes after one o'clock in the afternoon, she heard a knock at her front door.

"Who's there?" she called. Mrs. Oldham knew what had been happening in the city, and she was in no hurry to unlock her door.

"I'm here to collect a bad check on Oldham," a man's voice half shouted from the landing outside.

That sounded most improbable to Mrs. Oldham. "What Oldham?" she called back.

For several seconds there was no answer. "Johnny Oldham," the voice answered at last.

Improbable indeed. Mrs. Oldham had no relative named Johnny. Her husband, dead thirty-five years, had been named James, and anyone could have found her last name on the mailbox on the first floor. "Go away," she said sharply. After a moment she heard footsteps going down the stairs. When they were most of the way down she opened the door without unfastening the chain and peeked out in time to see a young man stumble as he reached the landing below.

The man did not appear to have heard Mrs. Oldham open her door. As she watched, he stopped on the landing and looked out through a set of glass doors to the porch and courtyard below. He seemed an attractive young man, fair-haired and trimly dressed in a short-sleeved white shirt and dark trousers, barely out of his teens. Suddenly he stiffened, turned, and went down to the first floor. Mrs. Oldham heard the screen door swing open and slam shut. She closed her door and went to her front window in time to catch a glimpse of the young man striding across the grass toward the apartments at the other end of the building. She wondered if she had been wrong to turn him away so rudely.

It was twelve days since Glenda Sue Harden's body had been discovered, and Mrs. Oldham's fearful response to the knock at her door was typical of how most women in Memphis would have behaved under the same circumstances. In the time since the Harden murder, reports of strange men attempting to break into houses and apartments had mounted steadily until now they were at a bewildering, nerve rending, days-old crescendo. Morning and afternoon, the newspapers presented new and ominous stories about attempted assaults and prowlers who somehow always escaped. The city seemed on the verge of collapse. The murders were on everyone's mind and intruded into almost every casual conversation, and it was everywhere expected that another killing could occur at any moment. Daytime was no less frightening than the middle of the night, and a locked apartment or a crowded street seemed not much safer than a back alley in the slums.

The killings had penetrated even the editorial pages of the Memphis papers. "The Faceless Killer" had been the title of one editorial. Another: "Never Mind the Cost, Get the Man."

The police department was not minding the cost. Every squad car in working order was on the street, patrolling constantly and ready to close in quickly when the killer struck again. It had been twenty-nine days since the Dumas murders, and the men in the cars were nervous, frustrated, extremely tired. They gathered at the scene of every new alarm, then dispersed again when nothing, as usual, was found. A hundred and thirty-five detectives did little except sleep when necessary, eat when possible, and hunt the killer. It was the biggest manhunt in Memphis history and one of the longest; still the police knew almost nothing about the killer.

By now the homicide bureau had almost finished going through the files of every person arrested in Memphis in recent years and had got nothing out of them. By now the evidence from the Harden killing had been sent to Washington, where the FBI examined it and found nothing helpful. By now, too, the department's top officers had agreed that the Dumas, Jackson and Harden cases together confronted them with the most difficult problem they had ever encountered— one infinitely more baffling, by comparison, than the shooting of Martin Luther King a year before.

The top officers were, in a way, resigned to the mystery. Either there would be another murder or there would not. If none occurred, the city would eventually return to normal. If someone else were killed, the murderer would be caught or would get away again. If he got away, he would leave clues or he would not. With clues, the police would hunt him down. Without clues, they would be forced to wait again. Whatever happened, the situation was at least temporarily out of control.

At times it seemed improbable that there would be any more murders. If the killer had a shred of sanity, he knew that he had already stretched his luck beyond the normal breaking point. Perhaps he had left Memphis, though that was nothing to count on.

At about the same time that Mrs. Oldham heard the knock at her door, fifty-nine-year old Henry Clay Currie came out of the basement of the LaBlanche building carrying a slingshot. It had been dark in the basement, and the sun outside was so painfully bright that Currie had to squint at first as he looked about for a place to do his shooting. The lawn in front, spacious and shaded by big trees, would be pleasant. It might also be safest. The bushes and white stone benches at the edge of the grass would make good targets, and a wild shot would be unlikely to break anything. Staying in the shade at the side of the building, Currie started toward the lawn. But after half a dozen steps he stopped and looked around again.

The lawn would not do, he decided. Someone might see him and complain. The front entrances to all forty-seven apartments faced the courtyard that opened onto the lawn, and people were always coming and going. Someone might see him shooting and not like it. The parking lot would be better, if he took care not to hit any car windows. He would be less conspicuous there.

The parking lot was at the east side of the horseshoe-shaped LaBlanche building. Only the back windows of fewer than half of the apartments looked out onto it, and now, at one o'clock, most of those apartments were empty. A cyclone fence stood at the back of the lot, and Currie chose it as his target. If the slingshot worked at all, he would give it a real test by trying to hit one of the little holes formed by the wire.

There was no danger. The only car parked near the fence was Currie's own 1958 Ford, and a few more dents wouldn't change its appearance. There was nothing on the other side of the fence but a patch of weeds and, beyond that, the dirt roadbed for a freeway still in the early stages of construction. Satisfied, Currie knelt on a low tree stump at the edge of the sidewalk and picked up a small stone. Pinching the stone into the sling, he pushed his left hand forward and drew his right hand back, took aim, and let go.

The stone hit the pavement ten feet short of the fence. Currie bent down to get another one.

Henry Clay Currie, a short and stocky black man with graying hair, was not in his second childhood. He was custodian at the LaBlanche building, and he took his duties seriously. He had made the slingshot as a gift for his nine-year-old grandson, Billy, and he wanted to be sure that it worked properly before giving it to the boy. Then he would get back to work.

He took aim and fired again. The stone chinked against the wire only three feet to the right of the fencepost Currie had tried to hit. Not bad. He was picking up his third stone when the screaming began.

It was a woman screaming, obviously, but Currie had never heard anyone scream this way before. The voice was out of control, unbelievably loud, more like a terrified animal than a human being. At first it was a pure scream, a cry without words, but as Currie dropped his slingshot and turned toward the building it changed.

"Oh," Currie heard. "Oh, you don't have to do that. Don't kill me. Don't kill me." Then the scream changed again and became unintelligible.

Currie was at the side of the building now, looking up. The scream was coming from just above him, from an apartment on the second or third floor. He just about had it pinpointed when the screaming stopped and everything was silent. Dumbfounded, he continued to stand there, still looking up, waiting for something more to happen. Then he heard footsteps pounding on stairs.

By one o'clock, the first edition of the afternoon's *Press-Scimitar* was off the presses. The last edition would not begin its run until more than an hour later. In the newsroom on the fifth floor of the building shared by the *Press-Scimitar* and the *Commercial Appeal*, editors and reporters were relaxing as the end of their workday approached. Unless something shattering happened, only a few routine adjustments remained to be made for the final press run. Two floors below, in the *Commerical Appeal*'s city room, things were equally quiet as the early crew went through the preliminary motions of getting ready to produce Friday morning's first edition.

The two papers were competing to keep their readers abreast of the terror. Wednesday's *Press-Scimitar* had carried on its front page a banner headline proclaiming POLICE ARE SEEKING ARMED PROWLER. The story underneath explained that two women had told police about a tall, thin man who tried to get into their homes by claiming to be a meter reader and then threatened them with a gun. The man wore bell-bottom pants and was "a hippie-type," according to the story. The explanation of how the women had escaped harm was vague.

Thursday morning's *Commercial Appeal* had topped that story with a longer and more detailed one about a prowler who did not claim to be a meter reader but seemed equally menacing. In this newest addition to the growing list of such incidents, a young divorcee named Mary Coleman related that at noon on the previous day, while preparing to go to bed after a night of work at the telephone company, she had heard a knock at her front door. Mrs. Coleman had been a friend of Glenda Sue Harden, she said, and she was very much afraid of being killed herself, so instead of opening the door she looked out a window. No one was there. An instant later she heard her kitchen door rattling, pulled back the curtains of another window, and saw the hands of a white man trying to turn the knob. Screaming, she ran to get a can of chemical mace that she had bought for protection. Unable to find the mace, she telephoned police, and though officers arrived promptly they could find no trace of a prowler. They did find Eddie Lee Webb, a youth in his late teens who said he had been painting a bathroom in the apartment next to Mrs. Coleman's when he heard her scream. He had looked out and seen a man running away, Webb said. The man was tall. He wore a white shirt and black gloves, was carrying a pistol, and had long flowing brown hair. The *Commerical*

Appeal ran the story with a large, artfully posed picture of a pretty girl peering fearfully out of a slightly ajar but chain-locked door. A separate story told of how other prowlers had been seen in several parts of the city, and of how a man on Rembert Street had fired his pistol at a Peeping Tom who got away.

In its first edition Thursday, the edition that was on sale when Henry Clay Currie heard the screams, the *Press-Scimitar* carried the competition one step farther. It presented on its front page not only a new story about a prowler who had attempted to attack a woman in her home, but a drawing of the prowler's face as well. The woman in this incident, a housewife who lived on South Greer Street, said the man had come to her home after dark and tried to force his way in. He was young and thin, she said, and he wore dark glasses and a very thin leather belt. His face, drawn from details given to an artist by the woman, was dominated by one feature: an unnaturally large and bulbous nose. On the same page with the drawing was the announcement that Governor Ellington had doubled the reward for the capture of the killer. It was good coverage, all in all, good enough to carry the *Press-Scimitar* once again past the *Commercial Appeal* in their daily game of leapfrog. The *Press-Scimitar*'s editors could not have foreseen that before their last edition went to press all of it—the reward increase, the prowler story, and especially that misshapen nose—would be totally obsolete.

Mrs. Emma Gross, an immigrant who had served as a nurse with the German Army in the Second World War and now worked at Baptist Memorial Hospital, was in her kitchen fixing a sandwich when she heard the same screams that interrupted Currie's slingshot test. She was dressed in her white uniform and planned to leave for the hospital immediately after lunch. The screams came from almost directly below her third-floor apartment, and she recognized the voice at once.

"Murder!" she heard. "No, no, no, don't! Don't kill me!"

Mrs. Gross dropped her sandwich and ran into her living room. Without stopping to think she unlocked the door and pulled it open, hurried down two flights of stairs, and had to stop abruptly to avoid bumping into a young man on the second floor landing. The man, crouching at first, turned his face toward her and stood up while reaching out with both hands. He held a purse in one hand and a long-bladed knife in the other. The blade was covered with thick, dripping blood, and when he jabbed it at her two fat drops fell on Mrs. Gross's white skirt. She backed quickly up the stairs, then turned and ran. She did not realize that she was screaming now. The man threw the purse at her before running downstairs. His trail was marked by circular drops of blood.

Uptown, the *Commerical Appeal's* early staff continued with the leisurely job of beginning to block out the next morning's paper. The police reporter would be on duty soon, and if any new assaults or prowlers were reported he would have plenty of time to get the necessary information. The news editors weren't particularly worried about whether anything new happened today, however, as long as it didn't happen to their wives. Prowler stories were becoming tiresome, and anyway the *Commerical Appeal* had something much better for tomorrow, a kind of journalistic trump card to be dropped triumphantly on top of the *Press-Scimitar's* drawing of a big-nosed man. Reporter James Chisum had interviewed psychiatrists in the Memphis area and, by combining their speculations, had put together a hypothetical profile of the murderer. It was a fascinating, persuasive story, and Chisum had done a good job of writing it. Displayed on page one under a two-column headline, it would leave the *Press-Scimitar* far behind. According to the psychiatrists who agreed to talk with Chisum, the killer probably hated and feared women as a result of "abnormal early experiences." The doctors guessed that the killer must be white because the victims were white and probably were identified in the killer's mind with the women, possibly relatives, who had traumatized him early in life. One psychiatrist said he was surprised by the frequency of the murders, and added that he would not be surprised to learn that the killer had come to Memphis recently after murdering other women in other places. If the killer is caught, the same doctor said, "you'll probably find that nobody knows him real well." Another said that the killer, though possibly very withdrawn, probably would seem quite normal to most people and was probably "rational enough, except in the moment of passion, to change cities and get a job as a hospital orderly, a gasoline station attendant or a watchman." It was a remarkable article, the most intelligent written about the murders, and the *Commercial Appeal*'s editors were understandably pleased about it. By early Thursday afternoon they had sent it to the composing room to be set in type. They could not know that long before their first deadline the story, though suddenly more absorbing and suggestive than ever, would be knocked off the front page by a rush of new events.

The screams in the LaBlanche building awoke Wayne Armstrong, a gray-haired liquor store clerk whose apartment was below Emma Gross's. The sound, as alarming as a siren and almost as loud, seemed to be coming from just outside his front door. He scrambled quickly to his feet, ran to the door, and opened it to see a strange man crouching in the doorway of the apartment on the other side of the landing. The stranger turned and looked up, and when Armstrong saw that he had a bloody knife in his hand he slammed his door shut and ran to his bedroom to get the pistol he kept there. When he got back to the landing the stranger was gone, so Armstrong turned around and ran through his apartment and down the back stairs, thinking that if the fleeing man were trying to get to a car parked on the lot at the side of the building he could cut him off before he reached it.

At the bottom of the stairs Armstrong found Henry Clay

Currie staring blankly at him. The stranger came running out from behind the corner of the building and started up the driveway toward Bellevue Street. "Stop right there," Armstrong shouted, and the stranger stopped and turned around. Armstrong pointed his revolver at him and said, "Come back here." The man took a few steps in Armstrong's direction and stopped. Armstrong could see that he was dressed in a white shirt and dark pants, but the face was a blur. In his hurry to get his pistol Armstrong had forgotten to put on his eyeglasses. He also had not stopped to dress and was wearing only a pair of boxer shorts and a sleeveless undershirt.

The stranger was still holding the knife at his side. "You wouldn't shoot me in the back," he said matter-of-factly.

Armstrong took a step forward and raised the pistol higher. "I'll shoot you in the back or face or anything else if you try to run away," he said. The stranger turned and bolted for the street and Armstrong opened fire. He got off three quick shots and saw the white shirt reel over sideways into a row of hedges at the edge of the drive.

"You got him!" Currie shouted.

But almost immediately the man crawled out of the hedges, put the knife in his belt, and again began running down the driveway. He reached Bellevue and spun to the right, heading toward Madison half a block away. Armstrong ran after him, but Currie ran in the other direction to get his car. He had a .22-caliber pistol in the glove compartment, and he pulled it out and put it on the seat beside him. He started the car, gunned the engine, and went roaring down the driveway. In the street ahead he could see Armstrong stop running long enough to take aim and fire again.

To follow the fleeing man, Currie had to drive the wrong way on a one-way street. Before he could get to the corner of Bellevue and Madison, his path was blocked by a telephone company truck going the right way. Currie honked his horn and put his head out the window.

"Get out of my way!" he yelled. "I'm chasing a killer! Pull over and call the police!"

"Killer my ass!" the man driving the truck shouted back. "I'll call the police, all right, but not about no killer! Back up out of my way!" Currie honked again but the truck didn't budge, so he drove up onto the sidewalk to get around it. The truck driver radioed his dispatcher and asked him to inform the police that something funny was going on around Bellevue and Madison.

By the time Currie reached Madison he was far behind in what was rapidly developing into a very big and very complicated chase. The spectacle of a young man being pursued down the street by an armed man dressed only in underwear had attracted a great deal of attention, and several persons joined the pursuit while others telephoned police.

The first call came from Sherrie Anderson, a young woman who was in a dentist's waiting room at 16 North Bellevue when she heard a gunshot and looked out the front window. She saw a blond man in a white shirt being chased by an older man waving a pistol and ran to the phone to report what she had seen. Officer J. D. Milligan took the call and ordered two cars to investigate.

Seconds later Milligan got another call from an excited man reporting much the same thing. The man said something about underwear and a gun, said he was at Madison and Bellevue, and hung up. Milligan had heard service station sounds in the background, and he relayed what little he knew to Warrant Officer Joe Laurenzi, the senior dispatcher on duty. "It looks like it's probably a gas station holdup," Milligan said. Laurenzi sent four additional cars to the scene and instructed any others in the vicinity to go also.

The fleeing man's route was so complicated that afterwards the police would have great difficulty in trying to reconstruct it. He ran west on Madison until he was cut off by pursuers, then veered off into a parking lot where he was blocked momentarily by a tall fence. He climbed onto the hood of a truck, leaving bloody marks on its white paint, and

from there he pulled himself over the fence and ran downhill onto the freeway's dirt roadbed. He was followed by Ray
Brenner and Melvin Hutcheson, who had been at a Gulf station on Madison when he ran past, and by Roger Meckley, a
technician who worked at Shipman's Optical Dispensary at
1177 Madison. He tried at first to run north on the roadbed,
but when Brenner and Meckley cut him off he turned
around and ran south. Brenner tried to catch him but was
quickly outdistanced. The fleeing man, Brenner insisted
later, was one of the fastest runners he had ever seen.

When Currie finally got his car to the place where the freeway route passed under Madison, he stopped and got out
with his pistol. The air was filled with the sound of sirens
now, and squad cars were converging on the area from all
directions. Looking down from the overpass, Currie could
see the tiny figure of a running man far to the north. When
the figure reached the shadow of the next overpass, it stopped
to strip off its shirt and then resumed running. Currie, still
hopeful of catching up, was returning to his car when a
young policeman wearing sunglasses stopped him.

"Hey, boy," the officer drawled. "Where you going with
that thing?" He pointed at the pistol.

"I'm going after that killer," Currie said excitedly. "I
chased him all the way over from the LaBlanche apartments,
and now he's way down there on the highway. He's getting
away."

"You let us worry about that," said the policeman. "You
go on home. And put that son of a bitch away before you
really get into trouble." Again he pointed at the pistol. Suddenly meek, Currie did as he was told.

Police arrived at the LaBlanche building long before
Currie's return. Emma Gross led them to the second floor
landing where she had encountered the man with the knife
and pointed to an apartment door, closed now, that had been
open at the time of the encounter. Officers tried the door,
and when they found that it was locked they went around

the building to the back door to the same apartment. It was locked too, so Warrant Officer Harry Randle kicked it open and went inside. On the living room floor he found the body of a middle-aged woman, face down with upraised hands against the inside of the front door. The floor was awash with blood, and blood was dripping from great splashes on the wall. Randle looked back inquisitively at Mrs. Gross, who had followed him into the room and now was backing out with her hands against her face. "It's Chris," she said in her thick German accent. "Chris Pickens. Today is her birthday. My God, that blood looks like the Mississippi River."

Mary Christine Pickens, known to her friends as Chris, was a tall and thin woman who looked younger than she was. She had lived in Apartment Twelve at the LaBlanche building for almost five years, and people who knew her well were often amused by the childlike pride with which she cleaned and decorated her three rooms. Every new piece of furniture, every knickknack added to her shelves, became a major subject of conversation for her. She was a prim woman, very nearly prissy, but she was well liked all the same. She had the ability to demonstrate real interest in people, real concern for their problems. She would take soup to an acquaintance who was ill, or sit up all night with a friend who had just undergone surgery.

She called herself Mrs. Pickens, but Pickens was her maiden name and none of her friends knew anything about the man who presumably had once been her husband. She never spoke of him except to say that he had been killed in the Second World War only a month after the wedding. She had been born in Tiptonville, Tennessee, the daughter of a Methodist minister, and had attended Lambuth College in Jackson. In Memphis she was an active member of the Madison Heights Methodist Church.

In the mid-fifties Chris Pickens had worked for Dr. J. Cash King, a radiologist at Methodist Hospital. Then, after five years on the job, she found herself in conflict with another woman in the office and resigned. She left quietly, without complaints or recriminations, trying to remove herself from an unpleasant situation without hurting anyone's feelings. It was her way, and people admired her for it. She took a job as a receptionist in the office of Dr. Robert Armstrong, a dentist, and remained there contentedly for the last ten years of her life. Dr. Armstrong knew Mrs. Pickens to be a conscientious worker whose friendliness made a good impression with patients.

As a woman living alone in a large city, Mrs. Pickens was no stranger to fear. It was a constant part of life, if not for her certainly for many of her women friends. One of them gave her a can of mace on her fifty-eighth birthday in 1968. "Here, Chris," the friend had said. "You may need this some day." When the 1969 murders began, Mrs. Pickens had new locks put on her doors. She would never, she said emphatically, open her door to a stranger.

On Thursday, September 11, she arrived for work at the Sterick Building downtown shortly before 8:30 and eagerly let everyone know it was her birthday. She was fifty-nine now, though when anyone asked she tittered and said "Twenty-five." This year she could look forward to extra hours of celebration, because Dr. Armstrong's office was always closed on Thursday afternoons. At noon, as she was leaving for the day, another woman offered her a ride.

"No, I've got an errand to run," Mrs. Pickens replied. "I don't want to be in a hurry. You go on." She went to a music store and paid $11.50 for a ukelele and two song books, which she planned to use as birthday gifts for the child of a friend, and then she went to a bakery and bought half a coconut cake. When her shopping was completed she got on a bus and went home.

The bus stopped at the corner of Bellevue and Madison at two minutes after one o'clock, almost precisely the same time that a knock sounded on Grace Oldham's door, and Mrs.

Pickens stepped off. She was smartly dressed in black patent leather shoes, a white blouse, a gray woolen suit and, almost as if to advertise the kind of person she was, a pair of spotless white gloves. She crossed Madison through heavy midday traffic, walked along Bellevue for a hundred yards, and turned into the front lawn of the LaBlanche building. It was a beautiful afternoon, bright but deliciously cool after many days of severe heat, and birds were singing in the big oak and magnolia trees. The building, a stucco and brick mock-Spanish structure somewhat past its prime, looked very nice in the sunlight. Mrs. Pickens, holding her packages against her chest, walked briskly into the courtyard and turned to the first entranceway on the left. She opened the screen door and started up the stairs. One minute later she was dead.

It began to seem at least remotely possible that the man with the knife might escape. He had remained ridiculously visible as long as he stayed in the freeway roadbed, and as squad cars pursued him along streets paralleling the freeway on both sides a perfect trap began to take shape. But before the cars were able to close in, he turned east off the roadbed into a residential area and suddenly was out of sight. It became impossible for anyone, least of all dispatchers trying to coordinate the chase from police headquarters downtown, to know exactly where he was. The squad cars were ordered to concentrate east of the freeway and to look everywhere for a young white man who might be running, might be carrying a knife, might not be wearing a shirt. The odds of finding him were still good, but they were far from perfect. He had to be picked up before he got into a hiding place or stole a car and left the area.

The dispatchers waited for a report of a new sighting and counted the seconds since the man had disappeared. The seconds accumulated, and each one was a defeat. When they added up to a full minute the situation began to look very bad.

8

A Long Bad Morning

THURSDAY HAD BEGUN very early for Mary and Buster—before dawn, in fact, because Buster had to be at work at six o'clock. He had been on the six-to-three shift all week now, ever since starting work at the factory, and though it was good to have a regular schedule for a change he and Mary both hated to get up so early. She turned off the alarm, nudged him with her knee, and went back to sleep. A minute later he shook her by the arm, muttered that it was time to get up, and went back to sleep. They went on this way for ten minutes and finally both got out of bed without speaking. Buster stumbled to the bathroom in his shorts and Mary went to the kitchen to make breakfast.

It had been a bad night, not as hot as previous nights but still too hot for comfort. There was no breeze, the electric fan was broken, and the air at midnight was like a damp woolen shroud. Mary felt very tense when she went to bed, and though she took a tranquilizer a long time passed before she was able to relax. At some point in what seemed the middle of the night she began to doze, but before she was fully asleep Buster startled her by rolling over in the bed and crying out. His words were unintelligible, but the choking sound of his voice in the dark made them terrifying. Mary shook him awake, and he sat up but said nothing.

"You were dreaming again," she said after a long moment. Buster did not answer. There was just enough light from the street to make the outline of his head visible. Mary could see him run a hand backward through his hair.

"Are you all right?" she asked. "What were you dreaming?"

"Nothing." Buster's voice was throaty, irritated. "I don't even know. I've never been so hot in my whole life." He fell back against his pillow, turned toward the wall, and after a few minutes was asleep again. He snorted and stirred, then settled back into his agonizing muted snore. Mary became angry, jealous of him for being able to sleep. She went to the bathroom to get another tranquilizer, and when she lay down again the baby began to kick inside her. Another long period passed before her mind finally disengaged itself from her nerves, and when the alarm went off she felt she had been sleeping only a few minutes.

The day began as badly as the night. Mary had a hard time focusing her attention, and as she switched on the bare lightbulb in the tiny kitchen and squintingly groped for a box of Aunt Jemima, her stomach, out in front of her somewhere like the prow of a large and unfamiliar boat, thumped awkwardly against the sink. Her hands were unsteady, not trembling but just barely under control, so that as she measured off a cupful of mix little puffs of yellow powder fell to the floor and made a mess. As she splashed a cup of milk into the mix she heard Buster urinating noisily in the bathroom a few feet away. She began to feel sick. It was cool now, though, and that helped.

Buster ate quickly and without speaking, leaning forward to keep the syrup from spattering his shirt. Mary put two sandwiches into a paper bag and sat down at the dining room table, wanting to make conversation but unable to think of anything to say. She wondered what other couples talked about. A narrow band of light, shining through the curtain that served as a kitchen door, cut across the table and up Buster's chest to his face and yellow hair. The bulb in the

kitchen was reflected in both lenses of his sunglasses. Everything else was in twilight.

Mary cleared her throat. "You forgot to shave," she said.

Buster swallowed and looked up. "I didn't think I had
time," he answered. "I'll be all right till this afternoon." He
finished the pancakes and got to his feet.

"Are you going to get paid soon?" she asked. "We're running out of everything."

"Soon, yeah. Within the next day or two. You need anything from the store today?"

"I can get by another day. But I'd like to go to the laun-
dromat. We're both about out of underwear."

"I can do that tonight," said Buster. "Or this afternoon on
my way home from work. Where's the bag?" Mary went to
the bathroom and returned with a plastic bag filled with
dirty clothes. Buster closed the top with one hand, swung it
over his shoulder, and started for the door. The bag had
many damp diapers in it, and Buster's body leaned under the
weight. Mary unlocked the door for him and handed him his
lunch as he stepped out onto the landing.

"Keep the door locked till I get home," he said. Mary
closed the door and turned the key, and the bolt clicked deci-
sively into place.

"Good," said Buster from outside. "Don't let anybody in."
She heard him going slowly down the dark stairs. A minute
later, when she went into the bedroom to check Pip, she
heard Buster start the Chevy, slam its door, and pull away.
Pip was sleeping comfortably, naked except for his diaper, so
Mary went into the living room, lit a cigarette, and turned
on the television. She almost never smoked so early in the
day, but this morning she was as nervous as she'd been the
night before. She sat down and put an open hand on her
abdomen, probing with her fingertips until she felt something hard. The hard thing moved, and moved again.

The entire morning was boring, like all of Mary's morn-
ings now. She watched the "Today" show for a while, then

got Pip up and fed him and dressed and fixed her hair. Later she took a box of Rit from the kitchen shelf and dyed a stack of diapers pink. The dye didn't quite match the few pink baby clothes she'd been able to buy, but it was close enough and might be closer when it dried. She was sure the new baby would be a girl. It felt like a girl, she wanted a girl, and in eight months of pregnancy she had gained only four and a half pounds. That, she felt, must be a sure sign.

Pip, fourteen months old and already a proficient walker, wandered around the apartment all morning playing with an empty milk carton and a set of mixing spoons. By noon he was tired and crying, so Mary fed and changed him and put him to bed with a bottle.

He was a good baby, she thought with satisfaction. And things were not so bad generally. After the new baby came maybe they could all go to Texas as Buster wanted and things would get better. He would get the paper mill job he'd talked about, and the police wouldn't be looking for him there. She might be able to go back to work, too, or even into another nurse's training program. She could find a good baby sitter if she tried hard enough, and with Buster working in a paper mill there would be money for one.

Things could be worse. They'd been worse before. This apartment was a horror, just bare battered floors and walls and a few pieces of old and ugly furniture, but Buster was working and staying out of trouble. He and Clifford had stopped behaving like children. Perhaps the bad times were ending.

There was no meat left in the refrigerator, so Mary ate a peanut butter sandwich and took a glass of iced tea into the living room. She watched the end of the news, then "As The World Turns," then went to the kitchen for more tea as "The Days Of Our Lives" began.

Many blocks away, at the LaBlanche apartments, Chris Pickens was arriving home from work, walking carefully up the stairs to her apartment door, groping in her purse for her key while struggling to hold onto her parcels, unaware that someone was following her.

Mary returned to the television: to two women discussing some domestic tragedy in a beautiful Early American kitchen bigger than any living room in Sarah, Mississippi. It was an unusually dull installment of a usually dull show, but Mary had nothing else to do so she sat and watched.

Chris Pickens, in her living room, screamed and screamed and grasped blindly at a man she could not stop, a man driving a long blade into her chest and neck again and again and again—six times, a dozen times, nineteen times in all, each time to the hilt. The knife punctured her lungs, her heart, her windpipe, her aorta. Blood splashed to the floor and onto perfect white walls; Mrs. Pickens dropped to her knees, could not scream, fell dead on her face by the door.

In the Early American kitchen, one woman was scolding the other, who put her face in her hands and wept with soundless shakes of her shoulders. I should have such problems, Mary thought, and such time for working them out. But maybe she did. Maybe her life would make a soap opera. She rolled the empty tea glass, still cool, between her palm and her cheek. No, she was not the stuff of television, not interesting and not exciting. She was just dumb, a dumb housewife waiting for the birth of a second unwanted child in a furnished dump in Tennessee. She was twenty years old and already precisely everything she had never wanted to be. She could not imagine a soap opera heroine living in such a place, married to George Howard Putt. She went to the bathroom and to get a cigarette and still another glass of tea—too much tea for bad kidneys, but there was nothing else to do.

"The Days Of Our Lives" was still on when Patrolman Glenn Noblin turned sharply onto Pasadena Place and started north, tires squealing and the light atop his squad car flashing red. Noblin and his partner, Phil Scruggs, had been pulled off patrol to join the hunt for the fleeing killer, and now they were in the neighborhood where he had disappeared after leaving the freeway. They were less than a block from Linden Street when someone came running around the corner onto Pasadena—a man in a hurry, legs rising from the sidewalk and coming down sharply, moving straight towards them. But he stopped when he saw the flashing light, turned, and walked across the street and up the driveway of a large old house. Noblin pulled to a stop at the end of the driveway and Scruggs jumped out, one hand on the butt of his holstered .38. The man continued up the drive, but when Scruggs shouted at him he stopped and looked back. He was young, blond, shirtless, out of breath and panting. Scruggs, stepping closer, thought he might be a painter—his pants were spattered, and his arms looked as if they'd been dipped almost to the elbows in a bucket of bright red paint.

"What's the big hurry?"

"No hurry, officer. Going home."

"You were running."

"I was trying to get away from some dude. He was shooting at me. You'd run too if some dude was shooting at you."

"What's that all over your hands?"

"Oh. Blood, I reckon. I cut myself jumping over a fence."

"Pretty bad cut, I'd say." Scruggs pulled a pair of handcuffs from his belt.

The television screen flickered and turned a bright blank gray, erasing the afternoon movie and then gathering itself into a kind of signboard on which white block letters formed the words "News Bulletin."

"We interrupt our program to bring you a special bulletin. Memphis police have confirmed that a woman was murdered in her midtown apartment in the Medical Center district minutes ago. This is the fifth killing of this kind to occur in Memphis in the past month, but according to preliminary reports a suspect has been apprehended. Stay tuned for further details as they become available."

The signboard vanished, and for an incoherent instant the movie returned. It was replaced by a girl Mary had seen before, a girl who always threw an unbreakable bottle of Prell shampoo down a flight of stairs.

Of course, Mary thought. Another murder. There was bound to be another murder. She glanced over her shoulder at the door, which had not been unlocked since Buster left for work.

"It's just Prell," said the girl, "doing its lather thing." And like a familiar demon fulfilling some foreknown but inescapable destiny she flicked her wrist and dropped the bottle down the stairs. The news about the suspect was not very exciting. The police had found suspects before, but the murders had not stopped.

Minutes later someone knocked on the door in a quick series of light taps. "Anybody home?" a girlish voice cried. "Mary? Are you home?" It was Mandy, the woman who lived across the hall. Mary unlocked the door and let her in.

"Hi!" said Mandy, all smiles and fluttering hands. "Did you hear the news? They caught the nut. He killed another woman and they caught him. I felt so relieved I put the kids down for a nap and came right over to celebrate." She stepped to the middle of the room and lifted her arms in a gesture of profound relief. Then she dropped them to her sides with a contented sigh, trying to be theatrical but not succeeding. There was nothing graceful about her.

Mary smiled almost in spite of herself. "I heard it a few minutes ago on the television," she said. "I was about to go over and tell you." That was a lie, but a friendly one intended to make Mandy feel appreciated.

When Mary reached for the door, Mandy stepped forward. "Don't close it," she laughed, putting a small hand on Mary's forearm. "We don't have to lock the doors any more. They caught the nut, and we're not prisoners any more!" She wagged her head as she talked, and strings of dry blond hair floated stiffly around her face.

"You hope they caught the nut," said Mary. "I'll believe it when I see it." She pushed the door shut and felt a little foolish as the lock snapped into place. The fact that frightened little Mandy had lost her fear made Mary less afraid. If even Mandy wasn't afraid, maybe there wasn't a reason to be afraid any more.

"Well," Mary said, "even if they haven't caught him, I guess he's done his killing for today. We can breathe easy for a while at least. Come on in and I'll make some coffee. But be a little quiet—the baby's sleeping."

She turned the volume dial on the television until there was no sound and sat down, taking another cigarette from her pack of Winstons and lighting it. Mandy sat down too. She had her own pack of Viceroys and was already absorbed in talk.

"This whole thing makes me so happy," she was saying. "It's like Ray said last night—this stuff couldn't go on forever. If the nut kept killing people they were bound to catch him, Ray said. And they did! God, we can go back to living like human beings."

Mandy put a cigarette in her mouth and tried to strike a match. She failed the first four times, and with each try the match got more bent and difficult to handle. Nerves weren't the problem in Mandy's case, just native awkwardness. She was always the same and never self-conscious. Crouching intently over the match, she finally got it to ignite. Then she inhaled deeply on her cigarette. Throughout the whole pantomime she had not stopped talking.

Mary sat slouched in a ruptured old chair near the open window and held an impossibly small tin ashtray in the fingers of her left hand. It was a landlord-special furnished-apartment ashtray—junk. Everything in the place was junk. As Mandy talked, Mary tried to tap an ash from the tip of her cigarette into the ashtray and missed. The ash settled for an instant on her thumb, then fell to the floor. More dirt. It made her angry and depressed to think of all the dirt and junk she'd had to live with since marrying Buster.

Mandy and Ray didn't seem to mind junk. Buster didn't, either.

"You know," Mandy said, "we have to get ourselves a baby

sitter and all go out one of these nights. You and Buster and me and Ray. We could go to a nightclub and really have a good time. That would cheer you up."

Mary puffed on her cigarette and almost choked. She knew that Buster would not take her to a night club, especially not with another couple. Not if the woman wasn't Eileen King. Anyway, Buster had been avoiding Ray since the day he'd gone with him to get a job.

"We could try, if the doctor would let me," she said. "But it's hard for Buster. He has to get up so early, the way the plant opens at six. I hope he can get some better hours later. If he could just start a little later, it would help so much. I don't know how Ray can stand it, or how. . . ."

"Mary!" Mandy interrupted. "What are you saying? Are you trying to tell me you think Buster is at the plant with Ray? You *know* he isn't."

Mary narrowed her eyes. "I don't understand what you mean," she said.

"Oh, come on. You know. The day Ray took Buster to the plant. The way Buster worked a couple of hours and then walked away and didn't come back. He never did tell Ray why, and Ray still talks about it. Didn't Buster like it there? Didn't he tell you what happened?"

Mary didn't dare look up. She tapped her cigarette over the ashtray but nothing fell off. "It was something about a foreman," she said, wishing she were a more agile liar. "It didn't look like it was going to work out, so he thought he'd better leave. Probably just as well—he seems to like his job at the gas station all right. Excuse me a minute."

She pushed herself heavily up out of the chair and hurried through the dining room to the bath, closing the door behind her. It was hard to know what to think, except that Buster apparently was starting to go out of control again. He had told her about getting the factory job, and he'd gone to work there this morning, but now Mandy was telling her that he'd been hired and had quit all in one day. If she was right, Buster had lied. But why? The plant might be crummy, but any plant paid more than any gas station. Nothing Buster did made sense to Mary. She took her bottle of tranquilizers from the medicine cabinet, popped the cap off with her thumb, and swallowed a capsule without water. Whenever you need to relax, the doctor had said. She needed to relax now, and badly. She also needed to call Buster and give him a piece of her mind. Not that it would do any good; he wouldn't talk back. Mary smiled sourly when she realized that she didn't even know where Buster was.

Mandy was so dumb it was pathetic, Mary decided. Twenty-five years old and living in an ugly apartment with linoleum floors and a hick husband who wore white socks and an oily black pompadour. In five years she'd be thirty and have five or six kids, Ray would still have his pompadour and would still be working in some factory for eighty-five dollars a week, and the floors would still be linoleum. Mandy was dead. Nothing would ever happen to her except her kids would grow up and Ray's hair would finally fall out and they'd both be old and poor. She would never learn that Tennessee was not the center of the universe. She would never play on the beach in California or go riding with a Hell's Angel or own one really nice dress.

I'm dead too, Mary told herself as she sat on the edge of the bathtub. I'm deader than Mandy. Ray was a hick, but he would always go to work and he would always come home. Mandy could count on that for the next forty years. Mary could count on Buster to quit every job he got and lie to her and run away with other women or with Clifford and get into trouble and come back and start it all over again. And she was stuck with him. He would run her and the babies through every town in Mississippi and Tennessee and Texas, and when things were going really well they'd live in furnished dumps with linoleum on the floor.

All she had to do was sit and wait. Everything that she had never wanted to happen to her was going to happen automatically. Half of it already had.

She was splashing water on her face when she heard

Mandy calling her. She dried herself quickly and walked back to the living room. Mandy was bent over next to the television, one hand on a dial. The news bulletin signboard was on the screen again, and as Mary saw it Mandy looked up and put a finger across her lips: Quiet.

". . . identified as Mary Christine Pickens, fifty-nine years old. Police confirm that she was stabbed to death in her apartment at 41 North Bellevue early this afternoon. A suspect has been apprehended, and according to police he is believed to have been the same person seen running from the scene of the crime by witnesses who heard Miss Pickens's screams. The suspect has not been identified but is described as a white youth. We'll have a full report on the five o'clock news. Stay tuned for further. . . ."

Triumphantly, Mandy turned the television off. "See!" she yelped. "They caught him! I told you so, sour puss."

"I'm beginning to think you might be right," said Mary. "It sounds real. God, 41 North Bellevue is only a block away from where my brother-in-law lives. I was over there the day before yesterday. I'll make that coffee now." But Pip was snuffling in his crib, so she went to get him up. Mandy unlocked the door and went across the hall to check on her own children. In half a minute she was back.

"Still snoring," she said. "I'll never get them to bed tonight. Let me start the coffee while you get the baby changed." She danced on into the kitchen and left the front door standing open. But that was all right now, Mary decided. It sounded as though the police really had caught the nut. And even if they hadn't, he wouldn't be likely to bother anybody again today.

"I'm really glad it was a white boy," Mandy called from the kitchen. "It would have scared me more if they'd found out it was some nigger." Mary could hear her rinsing the coffee pot at the sink. It was probably full of dust.

"I hope they execute him real slow," Mandy shouted after a moment. "I hope they cut his balls off and stick them in his ears." She giggled loudly at her own naughtiness; it was probably something she had heard Ray say. The coffee pot clanked as Mandy put it on the stove.

Mary and Mandy had just sat down in the living room with their cups of coffee when the screen door downstairs slammed and feet started up the stairs. They were heavy feet, coming up fast. Mandy stiffened in her chair and looked at Mary. Mary set her cup on the floor and tried to stand up. The door was wide open.

Late in the afternoon Annie Bulimore arrived home from shopping. Her husband was in the living room watching television, and when she came in from the kitchen he looked up at her with the bright eyes of a man waiting to reveal a secret.

"Well," he said, smiling at the corners of his mouth, "they caught that guy."

"The nut?"

"That's right, they caught the nut."

"High time, I'd say. Who was it, a colored boy?"

"No." The life went out of Bulimore's face, and he turned to stare out the window. "No, it was a Putt. It was Buster."

He kept looking outside. Annie sat down. She was shocked, but not half so shocked as her husband thought. She knew a thing or two about Buster Putt. She knew things she had never told anyone.

9

"I Killed Them All"

BOB COCHRAN, who had worked all night and gone home at dawn Thursday for a nap and a shower, was driving back to his office at 1:20 P.M. when he heard a detective in one of the homicide bureau's cruisers radio headquarters to report that he was on the scene at 41 North Bellevue. Within seconds two other detectives made identical calls, followed by excited reports from officers apparently involved in a chase. Cochran, still a bit groggy after his short sleep, picked up his handset and pressed the talk switch to find out if something important was happening.

"Dispatcher, this is Captain Cochran," he said. "What's the nature of that call on North Bellevue?"

"Sorry, captain. You'll have to telephone for that information."

"Okay." It was something that could not go out over the radio—something sensitive, perhaps something big. Cochran was not far from headquarters, however, so he decided to drive on in instead of stopping and trying to find a telephone. He had lost twenty-six pounds in the twenty-nine days since the Dumas killing and was too worn out to waste energy.

When he pulled into the headquarters garage he saw that all of the homicide cruisers were gone. That was unusual;

the bureau almost always kept a few cars on hand for emergencies. He hurried upstairs and found when he reached the bureau that it was nearly deserted.

"There's been another murder!" an excited clerk shouted as Cochran stepped in the door.

"On North Bellevue?"

"Right. A woman again. Almost everybody went out there as soon as we got the call."

Cochran picked up a phone and dialed the dispatcher's office. Joe Laurenzi answered and without waiting to be questioned said a woman had been stabbed to death, a man had been seen running away, and a suspect had been arrested several blocks from the murder scene. "Captain Williams and Chief Lux and Mr. Holloman are already there," Laurenzi continued. "So's the crime scene evidence unit. I haven't got a name on the suspect, but they're bringing him downtown now."

Cochran decided not to go to the scene. He could trust Frosty Williams to handle that end, and questioning the suspect seemed more important. He told Detectives Roy Davis and Bubba Willis, the only men left in the bureau, to go to the desk lieutenant's cage at the jail entrance and wait for the suspect to arrive.

"The lieutenant will book him in and let him make a call," he said. "As soon as that's done, bring him straight up here to my office. Whatever he had with him when he was arrested, bring that up too."

Minutes later Cochran's phone rang. It was Davis. "We've got the suspect," he said, "but he's all bloody and sick. He threw up on the way here and passed out while we were booking him in. Lieutenant Paschall sent him up to the jail on the elevator."

"Is he hurt?" Cochran asked.

"Doesn't look like it. I'm pretty sure the blood isn't his. The boys who caught him checked him before they brought him in, and they said he looked okay."

"Who is he?"

"Lemme see." Davis paused. "Putt, he said his name is. George Howard Putt, twenty-three years old. He said he lives at 624 Bethel, has a wife there. That's all I know now."

Cochran hurried to the jail, but it took time to get there. He had to go downstairs to the desk cage, turn in his revolver, and then take an elevator to the fifth floor. When he arrived he found a uniformed guard kneeling inside an unlocked cell beside a shirtless man who was sprawled on the floor with his head and hands in a toilet bowl. "I think he's going to puke," the guard said, but as Cochran stepped closer he saw the shirtless man's hands moving very slightly in the water. The guard seemed not to have noticed that. Angrily, Cochran reached down to grab the man by his upper arm and pulled him to his feet.

"You're Putt?" the captain asked. The man nodded but did not speak. Cochran turned to the guard. "This man isn't any sicker than you are," he said disgustedly. "He's pretending to be sick so he can wash his hands in the goddamn commode while you stand there staring into space. He's washing away evidence." The guard, bewildered and frightened, was sent away to get a box of cotton which Cochran used to wipe what remained of a thin film of blood from Putt's hands and arms. The red-stained cotton was placed in an envelope for possible later use as evidence. Putt sat on the edge of a bunk and stared across the cell with open, empty eyes.

Information was coming in fast and detectives relayed it to Cochran in the jail. The dead woman was named Mary Christine Pickens, and the police had no record on her. A bloody hunting knife had been found near a fence that the fleeing man had jumped in his effort to escape, and a matching scabbard had been found on the freeway roadbed. A blood-spattered white shirt had been found under a bridge crossing the roadbed, and its breast pocket contained a parking ticket issued in Memphis that morning to a 1964 Chevrolet bearing Mississippi license number 9C1137. Mississippi authorities said the license had been issued to George Howard Putt. Putt had a record in Tennessee and Mississippi, and detectives were tracing it to see how far back it went and what it included.

Cochran stood at the cell door listening to the reports and watching Putt. He found it hard to believe, somehow, that this blond and handsome youngster had terrorized almost a million people for more than four weeks. But already the evidence seemed damning. "Have you been advised of your rights?" he asked. Putt did not answer. He appeared to be dazed—or, Cochran thought, to be pretending that he was dazed.

"His rights were read to him when he was arrested," Bubba Willis said. "Phil Scruggs read them to him."

Cochran, taking no chances, took a card from his wallet and read Putt's rights to him again. He had him examined by Doctor Jerry Francisco to be certain that he was not injured and therefore had someone else's blood on his hands, and had him photographed in his bloody clothes. Then he asked questions, but Putt remained silent, picking nervously at his fingernails, trying to clean them of the remaining dried blood.

"I still feel kind of sick," Putt said at last. "Could I wash my face?"

"You can take a shower for all I care," said Cochran. "I've got all I need off you." Putt was led away to the jail shower, and after he had washed he was permitted to walk back and forth in the corridor outside his cell. Cochran and Willis walked with him, and Cochran asked questions.

"Did you kill Roy and Bernalyn Dumas last month?"

"No, I did not. I didn't kill anybody."

"Did you kill Mrs. Leila Jackson?"

"I did not."

"Did you kill Glenda Sue Harden?"

"No."

"Did you kill a woman named Mary Pickens today?"

"No." Putt was sullen, walking quickly and keeping his eyes on the floor. He was put back in the cell, and Willis went with him. Cochran returned to his office to answer phone calls from Holloman and Lux, who wanted statements for the press.

Early in the evening came the show-up, the placing of Putt in a line of other men to see if witnesses brought to police headquarters from the murder scene could identify him. Because Putt's gray cotton pants and the white shirt found on the freeway were stained red across the front, Cochran sent a policeman across the street to the Shelby County Jail to borrow a pair of prisoner's dungarees. The officer returned with an extra-large denim shirt and a pair of enormous jeans which hung on the slightly-built suspect in ridiculous shroudlike folds.

Seven men were used in the show-up, Putt and six other young white men who happened to be in custody Thursday afternoon. They stood side by side in numbered spots on a brightly lighted stage, in a different order for each new witness.

The first witness was Emma Gross, and when she entered the show-up room George Howard Putt was the fourth man from the left. "Number five," said Mrs. Gross, wrong by one. Number five was a twenty-two-year-old man named Campbell who had been arrested on a peace disturbance charge. He was fair-haired, trimly muscular, and wore a light-colored sport shirt.

For the next witness, Wayne Armstrong, Putt was number two and Campbell was number three. "Three," said Armstrong.

Harriet Busby, one of the bystanders who had seen the chase from the LaBlanche Building, was brought in next. Campbell was number one now, Putt number seven. "One," said Mrs. Busby.

The next witness, another bystander, identified neither Putt nor Campbell.

Henry Clay Currie identified Putt.

Sherrie Anderson identified Putt.

Roger Meckley identified Campbell.

Melvin Hutcheson identified Campbell.

Captain Cochran stopped the show-up.

Convinced that he had committed a serious error in permitting his suspect to be displayed in jail dungarees, Cochran sent a patrolman out to buy a white shirt and a pair of gray cotton pants in Putt's size. Before returning to his office, he instructed Detective Willis to stay with Putt in the waiting area behind the show-up room and attempt to get him to talk. The choice was not casual. Willis was a superb interrogator, a man with an uncanny instinct for establishing rapport with people and winning their confidence. If anyone could persuade Putt to open up, Bubba Willis would do it.

The homicide bureau was in a furor when Cochran arrived there after stopping the show-up. Holloman and Lux were still calling, still wanting information for the newspapers. Testily, Cochran said he had no information and might never get any if he weren't left alone and permitted to concentrate on the investigation. His superiors continued to call, however, saying that the papers were demanding to know what was going on. Cochran said the papers would have to wait, but the calls did not stop.

Information was pouring in as detectives worked on the killing and on George Howard Putt's background. The suspect had a wife and child in Memphis and a brother who had a record and lived only a block from the Pickens apartment. A woman's billfold containing $8.55 and believed to have belonged to Mary Christine Pickens had been found at Madison and Bellevue. Investigators had found fingerprints and palm prints at the murder scene, and they appeared to be Putt's. The suspect's record had been traced through Mississippi to Texas and Virginia, and it was far longer and more serious than results of the first inquiries had suggested. Michael Dumas, brought to headquarters, said that the bloody knife found shortly after the killing had once belonged to his father.

Cochran knew that this was important information, but before he could get it ordered in his mind he received a call asking him to go as quickly as possible to the room where Putt was being held. He ran to get there, certain that his suspect either had attempted to escape or had decided to talk.

Only seconds passed before Cochran reached the room, but when he entered nothing at all seemed to be happening. Putt and Willis were sitting quietly in a corner, and the six men being used as dummies in the show-up were clustered together at the other end of the room, seemingly trying to keep as far away from the murder suspect as they could. Putt was still dressed in jail dungarees, and he watched calmly as Cochran approached.

"Mr. Putt here says he would like to talk to you," Willis said in a voice not much louder than a whisper. "He says he committed all the, uh, all the acts we were asking him about."

Putt nodded his head in agreement, then glanced at the group of men at the far side of the room. "I'd like to talk in private," he said. Cochran and Willis took him around a corner to a place where the others couldn't see them.

"Now," Cochran began, "what have you got to say?"

"I did it," said Putt in a low voice, looking down at the floor. He was almost a head shorter than the captain, and he looked almost childlike in his oversized clothes.

"You did what?"

"The murders. All of them. I did them."

"What murders?"

"You know, all those people who were killed. Mr. and Mrs. Dumas and Mrs. Jackson and all those. I killed them." He shifted his weight from one foot to another and, looking briefly up into Cochran's face, seemed to be growing impatient. More than ever he resembled a petulant child.

"Listen," said Cochran, "you're going to have to do better

than that. Tell me the names of all the people you killed, and tell me how you killed them."

"All of them. I killed them all." He was mumbling now, and his words were barely audible.

"I'm afraid that's not good enough. I have to have the names and some dates and some details."

Putt hesitated. Still looking down, he closed his eyes and shook his head sharply as if trying to erase some ugly thought. "I think I better see my wife," he said. "I want to talk to her before I say any more."

"All right," Cochran said. He left the room and returned half a minute later. "I told Lieutenant Linville in my office to have your wife brought in," he told Putt. "Now you tell me who you killed and enough about each killing so I'll know you're telling me the truth—not just something you read in the papers."

10

"I Guess I Don't Understand..."

HOMICIDE DETECTIVE Bill Hylander reached the landing before Mary could get out of her chair, and when he looked in the open door and saw two obviously frightened women he quickly apologized and said he was trying to find Mrs. Putt. Mandy pointed at Mary, who nodded and reluctantly conceded that she was Mrs. Putt. Hylander took a wallet from his coat pocket and was displaying a badge and identification card when Mandy excused herself and left. As she was crossing the landing to her apartment Detective Don Lewis came up the stairs, and he too took a badge from his pocket. Mandy slammed her door and loudly locked it. Mary, still afraid, asked the men what they wanted.

"I don't even know, ma'am," Hylander said. "We were in our car when we got orders to come to this address and find you. If I can use your phone maybe I can find out more." Mary said she didn't have a phone, so he went back down the stairs and out the door to his car, returning a few minutes later and calling Lewis out onto the landing for a brief, whispered conversation that Mary tried to overhear but couldn't. Then he went downstairs again. Lewis stepped into the living room and closed the door.

"I'll have to stay with you till my partner gets back, Mrs.

Putt," he said. "He had to run downtown, but he ought to be back in about fifteen minutes."

"Why? What's going on?"

"I don't know, but I'm sure there's no reason for you to worry yourself. Just go on about your business and don't let me get in your way." He lowered himself gingerly into a chair, taking pains not to wrinkle his crisply pressed dark suit. He was a stocky man with black hair cut close to the scalp and a beefily pleasant face that expressed nothing.

"*Something* must be going on," Mary demanded. This mysterious silence made her angry. "Has something happened to my husband?"

"Not that I know of," Lewis answered in a calm and friendly drawl. He looked at Mary's swollen stomach, then up again at her face. "There's no reason why you should upset yourself, Mrs. Putt, and I don't think you should. Just do whatever you have to do and try to pretend I'm not here. With any luck I'll be out of your way in no time." He looked at his watch and folded his hands in his lap. Mary went to the kitchen and tried to think. She suspected that Buster had been arrested for escaping from the penal farm, but she was afraid to ask. Perhaps he was in some smaller trouble, or had had an accident, or perhaps this had nothing to do with Buster. Whatever it was, questions might be dangerous. They might lead police to the discovery that Buster was a fugitive. She decided that she had better keep quiet.

Hylander did not return in fifteen minutes, half an hour, or an hour. Lewis sat in the living room and slowly wilted in the afternoon heat. First he loosened his tie, then he took off his jacket, and finally in an exasperated voice he asked Mary if she had anything to read. She gave him half a dozen movie magazines and sat down on the sofa. She was hot and nervous, this quiet stranger made her feel awkwardly self-conscious, and as more time passed and Buster did not arrive home from work she became increasingly upset. She went to the bathroom for her bottle of tranquilizers and carried it back to her seat in the living room. When she popped the bottle open Lewis looked up at her, watched as she put a capsule in her mouth and swallowed, and returned to his magazine. Mary went into the dining room and tried to play with Pip, but she found she could not be patient with him and sat down at the table to smoke a cigarette. When a knock sounded on the front door Lewis answered it and stood talking for a short time with someone on the landing. Then he closed the door, turned the key, and came into the dining room.

"That was your landlord," he said. "I told him he'd have to come back later." He went back to the living room and Mary lit another cigarette. A few minutes later there was another knock, and again the detective opened the door and talked quietly with someone outside. He talked longer this time, and after a while he raised his voice so that Mary could understand his words. "That's just too bad," he said. "Go downtown and see if they'll talk to you there." He locked the door and returned to his chair without telling Mary anything. She was beginning to feel sick, almost drunk, and she lowered her head to the table. The room seemed to be spinning, and she thought she was going to throw up. Vaguely, she wondered if she could be in trouble. She had allowed Buster to live with her though she'd known he was wanted. You could go to jail for that. Her mouth filled with saliva. When she swallowed, it filled again. She expected to vomit but didn't.

There were more knocks on the door, so many and so frequently that Lewis moved to the sofa and gave up trying to read. He didn't let anyone in, but Mary heard enough fragments of conversation to realize at last who was knocking. Newspaper reporters, wanting to talk to her. Why? She strained to understand but couldn't. Her mind seemed locked, unable to move.

Still another knock. The detective opened the door and talked in whispers for an unusually long time. Then, instead of closing the door as before, he pulled it all the way open and Mary heard someone come in. She got up from the table, went into the living room, and saw Clifford and Retha.

"These people say they're family," the detective said. He was sweating heavily, and the tail of his white shirt was coming out of his pants.

"Hi," Mary said glumly. "Yeah. This is my brother's husband and his wife."

"Your husband's brother, you mean."

"Yeah. That's what I said."

Clifford, dressed in soiled work clothes, looked warily from Mary to the detective and back again. "We heard there was some kind of trouble," he said. "We thought we'd better come over and see if you were okay."

"I'm fine," Mary answered. "I think I am. I don't know what to think. Have you seen Buster?"

"No," said Clifford, surprised. "I haven't seen him." Again he glanced quickly at the detective. Mary sat on the sofa and Clifford sat beside her, crossing his legs and jiggling one foot nervously. The lanky Retha crossed the room in a few steps and sat down in a chair. Lewis left the room, and a moment later Mary heard him running water in the kitchen. She leaned toward Clifford and whispered as quickly as she could.

"Should I think," she began, stopping and shaking her head in annoyance. Even her tongue was coming unhinged. "Do you think I should tell the police anything about Buster? I mean, if they ask, should I tell them he escaped from prison?"

Clifford shrugged. "What the heck," he said, "if they arrested Buster for anything they know by now that he escaped from prison. That won't be any secret. But listen. . . ." He stopped in mid-sentence and looked up. Lewis, back from the kitchen, was standing in the doorway and studying his watch.

"Past five already," the detective said. "This is the longest fifteen minute wait I ever saw."

Five o'clock. News time. Mary bolted out of her seat and snapped on the television. Her timing was incredible. The first thing that appeared on the screen was a picture of a slender, shirtless man whose face was turned from the camera. His hands were manacled behind him, and his upper arm was tattooed. As Mary screamed he moved his head and was just beginning to expose part of his face when Lewis reached the television and turned it off.

"That's my husband!" Mary cried. "Clifford, that was Buster!" She turned to look at Clifford, but he kept his eyes on the empty screen and it was impossible to tell what he was thinking. "Buster!" she shouted, confused. "Didn't you see? That was Clifford on the television!" She began to cry. Clifford turned toward her, his eyes flashing alarm and confusion.

"Take it easy," said Lewis. "You couldn't see who that was. You couldn't even see the face."

Mary, hunched over on the sofa, saw the detective's dark trousers beside her. She felt him put a hand on her shoulder. "I know," she stammered. "I know who it was. I know those tattoos." She sobbed and began to gag, but after a few minutes she got herself under control and wiped her eyes on the hem of her dress. Lewis returned to his chair, Mary straightened up with Clifford sitting stiffly beside her, and they all looked at each other without saying anything. Mary found the bottle of tranquilizers in the pocket of her skirt, took one out and swallowed it, and rattled the bottle noisily in one hand. Everybody seemed to be looking at her now, and Pip was trying to climb into her lap. She picked him up and set him beside her, and he began to pluck at loose strands of unraveling upholstery. Mary tapped his small hand lightly with her fingers.

"Do don't," she said. "That do." She looked up, surprised by her own words. She concentrated on composing one sentence: I don't think I can take much more of this. But when she spoke, slowly and deliberately, the words came out in an order that even she couldn't understand. She tried again, and the result was even worse. Retha giggled, Mary felt her face flush with anger, and Lewis stood up. He walked to Mary's chair and took the bottle out of her hand.

"What are these things?" he asked.

"Doctors," Mary said. She shook her head. "Pills. Tranquilizer pills, from the doctor."

Lewis put them in his shirt pocket. "I don't think you'd better take any more today," he said.

A few minutes later, after Clifford and Retha left, Mary went to the bedroom and looked out the window. A crowd was gathered on the sidewalk below. People were looking up at her, and a few were pointing. She went to the kitchen, fed Pip and put him to bed early, and sat down in the living room. She had no doubts, now, about why the detectives had come. Buster was the murder suspect. She was certain, however, that it had to be a horrible mistake. She knew Buster, she lived with him, and if he were a killer she would know it. He was a screwed-up petty thief but not a killer. He was a suspect because the police had picked him up and found out that he was an escaped convict. That had to be it: an accident.

"Can't I just look at some television shows?" she asked. "I promise not to watch any news. I can't just sit here all night and do nothing."

"No, ma'am," said the detective, who was quite literally twiddling his thumbs. "I'm sorry, but I'm not enjoying this any more than you."

At nine o'clock Hylander finally returned, bringing two police lieutenants with him. "Sorry to be so long," he said. "This whole deal is more complicated than I expected." One of the lieutenants sat down beside Mary and began speaking to her in a slow and careful voice. She stared at him mutely, so dazed that she was barely aware of her surroundings.

"Mrs. Putt, I don't know if you know what happened today," the lieutenant began, "but your husband is downtown under arrest. He's charged with murder, stealing, and carrying a concealed weapon—a knife. I've got a search warrant here, and these men are going to have to search your home. I'd like you to read it before they start." He unfolded a piece of white paper and handed it to her. She held it for a moment, tried without success to read it, and handed it back.

"It's all right," she said. "Go ahead and search. I'm so mixed up I don't know what to think." The lieutenant folded the paper and slipped it into his pocket.

"There's one other thing," he said. "Your husband wants to see you. He said he won't talk to us until he talks to you. Would you be willing to come downtown to see him? It's pretty important."

"I guess so. Sure. I don't see why not."

The lieutenant nodded and smiled, patting himself on the thigh. "Good," he said. "You go and get ready. The sooner the better."

When she went into the bedroom to get a fresh dress from the closet, several policemen were poking through drawers, looking under the mattress, going through the pockets of Buster's pants. One of them was photographing pages from one of Buster's sex magazines. As Mary left the room, he was aiming his camera at a picture of a woman bent over to expose her anus.

She went to the bathroom, washed slowly with cold water, and changed dresses. When she came out detectives were in the kitchen, emptying cabinets and drawers. One of them held a long butcher knife up to the light with a thumb and one finger, examining it carefully. "Your husband ever borrow any of these knives, take them anywhere?" he asked. Mary shook her head, but he put the knife in a plastic bag. Mary noticed that many of her belongings were being put into plastic bags.

Her mother was on the landing when Mary left the apartment. "Don't worry about a thing," said Annie, looking stricken. "I'll look after Pip." Mary nodded and smiled gratefully, putting a hand on her mother's arm. Annie was let into the apartment, and two policemen took Mary's arms and led her slowly, like a crippled old woman, down the stairs.

The crowd that Mary had seen from her bedroom window

was much larger now, and men with notebooks and cameras ran forward as she stepped outside. Flashbulbs exploded in her eyes and she recoiled, pulling back toward the door. The policemen held her firmly and moved her forward across the porch and down the last steps. The flashbulbs had blinded her, and from all sides men were shouting questions.

"Do you believe your husband did it, Mrs. Putt?"

"How do you feel about all this, Mrs. Putt?"

"Miz Putt! Miz Putt, can you tell us anything about your husband?"

"Do you think he was capable of killing people?"

"No comment!" the officer holding Mary's left arm kept shouting. "Mrs. Putt has no comment!" He led her to the street and put her in the front seat of an unmarked car. Hylander got behind the wheel, started the engine, and pulled away from the curb so rapidly that two young men had to jump frantically out of the way.

"Reporters," he grumbled. "Always in the way."

The night was clear and cool, and the breeze coming in the car window made Mary feel better. She waited for the policeman to say something, but he drove without speaking. It was surprising, she thought, that no one had yet tried to get information from her. She would have expected the police to grill her about Buster, but no one seemed to want to know anything.

"Has my husband confessed anything?" she asked.

"No, I don't think so," Hylander answered. He was silent again for a while, but as he drove into the downtown area and approached police headquarters he said he didn't think Mary should say anything to reporters when they tried to interview her. "Especially not anything unfavorable about your husband," he said. "It wouldn't be good for your children's sake."

Mary was taken upstairs into the homicide bureau and through a narrow corridor to a small room in which Buster sat talking with another man. The man got to his feet when he saw Mary, but Buster merely looked up and smiled faintly. He was slouched over in a wooden chair, his hands clasped between his knees, not handcuffed.

"Here she is, George," Hylander said, "come to see you just like we promised." He left, and the man who had been talking with Buster stepped around a desk and pulled up a chair for Mary.

"Please sit down, Mrs. Putt," he said. "I'm Detective Willis, pleased to meet you. Your husband has been waiting for you. If you'd like to talk in private I can wait outside."

"I guess that would be okay," Mary said. Everything was a surprise today. She'd expected to find Buster handcuffed in a cell, and here he was in an office, wearing a new-looking white shirt. He had a pretty heavy growth of beard now, his hair was tousled, and his sunglasses were gone. His eyes were so red Mary wondered if he'd been crying. He looked no more like a murderer than he had that morning. He was shivering in the air-conditioning, and Mary thought he looked like a small boy who'd been caught doing something bad and was afraid of being spanked.

Detective Willis left the room, but returned almost immediately. "I'll be right down the hall if you need anything, Mrs. Putt," he said jovially. "You want anything, just give a call. This ain't no restaurant, but Buster here can tell you we serve pretty good hamburgers and pop. He's a good hamburger-eater, too." Buster laughed, and Willis waved and left. Mary began to feel confused again. This couldn't be how police handled murder suspects. She looked at Buster. He was watching her with his naughty boy expression. Suddenly, for the first time since she'd met him, she felt afraid to be alone with him.

"Is it true?" she asked, speaking softly so that no one outside could hear. "Did you really kill those four people."

"Five," said Buster. "I killed five, counting the one today." He kept his hands between his legs and rocked slightly back and forth in his chair.

"Why?"

"I don't know. For money, I guess. I guess I'll never see you again."

"Don't say that. You'll see me again." Mary didn't believe Buster. He was too calm, too offhandedly casual in his admission. She didn't believe that anyone could murder five people, get caught, and be so calm. She thought he must be making all this up for some reason beyond her understanding.

"What should I do?" he asked. "Should I confess or what?"

"What about evidence? Is there evidence?"

"Sure there is." He smiled. "The evidence is strong. They caught me stabbing that lady and they chased me. They have the knife."

Mary, beginning to believe him, clutched at the arms of her chair. "Well," she said, "if you did it I don't see why you shouldn't tell them. We sure haven't got any money for a lawyer."

"Okay," said Buster with a pert nod. "I'm going to tell them everything."

"And don't worry. I'll be in to see you."

Neither said anything more. Soon Willis put his head in the door and asked Buster if he was ready for a talk. "Yeah," said Buster, "I'm ready now." He got to his feet, smiled at Mary, and was taken away. Other detectives came into the room and asked Mary if she would consent to be questioned. She too said yes, and she was taken to a larger office and given a chair surrounded by several men.

"We've got an awful lot of ground to cover, Mrs. Putt," Lieutenant Sam McCachran began. "It's liable to take all night, if you're up to it. But the first thing we need to know is what you know about your husband." He paused, gesturing with both hands and seeming to grope for words, and Lieutenant Linville cut in.

"Just talk about your husband," he said. "Off the top of your head, tell us what kind of man he is."

Mary sat without speaking for a long time. "I don't know what I can tell you," she said finally. "It looks to me like I don't know my husband at all."

11

The Confession

THE MEMPHIS MURDERS presented three basic questions: Who, How, Why. Until George Howard Putt was arrested, only the first of these questions had real urgency. Until the arrest and the confession that soon followed, in fact, the second and third questions were considered only insofar as they might help produce answers to the first. The city's terror and the desperate urgency of finding and stopping the killer reduced interest in his methods and his motives to distinctly secondary importance.

The most urgent question was, however, the most easily answered. Almost from the moment of Putt's arrest, Memphis police had no doubt of his guilt and little reason to entertain doubts. From the beginning the evidence was overwhelmingly damning. The suspect, caught literally redhanded, had been taken into custody after a chase from the scene of the Mary Christine Pickens murder; at least some of the witnesses to the beginning of the chase had identified Putt as the man seen running from the LaBlanche Apartments; the shirt discarded by the fleeing man contained a parking ticket issued to Putt's automobile; Putt himself was unable to explain any of these things in a way that even faintly suggested his innocence.

As the police acquired additional information, it continued to point toward Putt's guilt. His record, as it was assembled piece by piece, became increasingly suggestive. Clearly it was the record of at least a potential murderer. The possibility that he might have killed only the Pickens woman and none of the other victims remained tenable for only a few hours after his arrest—until Michael Dumas was brought to police headquarters and identified the bloody knife found near the LaBlanche building as one that had belonged to his father. He had not noticed that the knife was missing from his parents' belongings after their deaths, young Dumas said, but apparently it had been stolen. That identification linked the Pickens case to the Dumas murders and, by simple extension, connected Putt to both. The police needed little imagination to surmise that Putt must also have been involved in the Leila Jackson killing, which had been so similar to the Dumas case, and in the Glenda Sue Harden killing, in which a knife also had been used.

Even such simple guesswork became superfluous when Putt confessed. Not all confessions are valid, but the Memphis detectives knew that and operated accordingly. Thus Captain Cochran rejected his suspect's first vague and general admissions and demanded information that only the killer could have possessed. After talking with Mary, Putt provided such information. He confessed at length and in impressive detail, and with one interesting exception that did not vitiate the confession he was able to give a complete account of all five murders. He knew things that the police had known from the beginning but had carefully kept from the public. He was able to draw accurate floor plans of the Dumas apartment and Mrs. Jackson's house, to describe the contents of both, and to describe the condition in which the Harden girl's body had been found. He was also able to explain most of the secondary mysteries of each case—why a girl living above the Dumases had heard a cry on the afternoon they were killed, for example, and how Glenda Sue Harden had disappeared on her way home from work.

Within eighteen hours after his arrest, in short, Putt gave

an almost complete and thoroughly plausible account of the murders. In doing so he demonstrated his guilt beyond question and made his conviction after trial virtually inevitable. He also answered the second basic question, the question of how he had committed the crimes and had managed, until the end, to escape undetected.

Only the last question remained: Why? That proved to be the most difficult question of all. In time it became clear that George Howard Putt was himself incapable of providing an answer.

"I had never read the book The Boston Strangler, *but years ago I did see the movie, but I forgot what it was about,"* Buster told the detectives who questioned him. *"It didn't have anything to do with this. The only reason I went in there was for money. I only picked the house at random. I had never met Mr. and Mrs. Dumas and I knew nothing about them. I just picked their house."*

On August 14, Buster explained, he had been without money, a job, or a home. That morning he drove into downtown Memphis and went to a blood company outlet at 118 Jefferson Street in a skid-row area on the fringe of the city's commercial center. He knew by now—had learned at least as early as his adventures with Eileen King the previous spring —that it was possible to earn pocket money by selling blood and plasma on Jefferson Street. On a one-time basis blood was a more profitable commodity, but plasma could be sold more frequently and thus provided steadier income. On this day, as he had done before and as he would do repeatedly in the month ahead, Buster sold plasma. An attendant, asking few questions and following routine procedure, removed two pints of Buster's blood and put them into a centrifuge which separated the white cells from the red. The red cells were then returned to Buster's bloodstream, he was paid the usual five dollars, and he left. The principal danger of plasma loss is that it can make the donor incapable of resisting infection.

Buster, by this time, was selling plasma at an almost suicidal rate and was extremely vulnerable to disease.

He returned to his car and drove to the OK Cafe at 1063 Madison Street in central Memphis, where he drank two or three bottles of Budweiser and tried to think of a way to get more money. He was weary of jobhunting by now, and he decided to rob someone though he had neither a weapon nor any idea of whom he might rob or how. He paid for his beer, put what remained of the five dollars in his pocket, and left the cafe. He got into his car again and began driving east on Madison. He was miles from the Dumas apartment when he set out and was not familiar with the neighborhood in which it was located, but though he had no destination in mind his eventual arrival at that apartment was in a way entirely logical.

Going east on Madison away from downtown, Buster found himself on a long and major thoroughfare lined on both sides with stores and busy with cars and pedestrian traffic. It was a distinctly unpromising place for an unarmed man to attempt a robbery—even a simple purse-snatching would have been hazardous—and so he continued driving for more than five minutes until he came to Cooper Street. At Cooper, Madison ceases to be a major boulevard and most traffic turns right; Buster, enmeshed in the traffic and still watching for his first opportunity, followed the flow and found himself southbound on Cooper. For a considerable distance Cooper is much like Madison, commercial and busy, and it does not change until it intersects with Young Street and most traffic turns again to resume an easterly direction. At this intersection, perhaps because he was annoyed by now and realized that he needed to find a quiet area, Buster did not follow the traffic. Instead he stayed on Cooper and continued south.

Cooper Street in the blocks just south of Young is not busy, but for other reasons it is an unpromising place for a robbery. On both sides it is a mixture of church buildings, poor bungalows, and junk shops. None of these suggested ready money, and Buster drove past them without slowing, alert for a place where he might rob someone and escape with a substantial amount of cash.

A seemingly ideal place lay just ahead, and it became visible as Buster approached South Street. The Hermitage apartment complex, its brick walls tall and opulent after blocks of near-poverty, its shaded courtyards secluded after miles of busy sidewalks, caught his attention from a distance of more than a hundred yards. He drove across South Street, slowed as his car passed the front of the Hermitage, and made his decision. He turned off Cooper, circled the apartment buildings, and parked on a lot at the rear of the complex. Seeing no activity around him, confident that no one was watching, he started walking. Slowly, as casually as possible, he went around to the front of the nearest building and went in through the front door. It was 1:50 P.M.

The card on the door of apartment one—"Roy K. Dumas, Notary Public"—was like an invitation. Buster had only the vaguest idea of what it meant, but it suggested to him that an office must be inside. An office, he thought, must have money. He knocked hard enough to be heard above the blare of the television just inside the door, and when Roy Dumas answered Buster needed only a quick look to decide that he could be overpowered as easily as a child. He shoved Dumas backward into the living room, closed the door, and demanded money. Dumas, angry and frightened but too small and frail to have any hope of defending himself, said that he had no money. Buster took him by the arm and pushed him out of the room and down the hall to the back bedroom, where he threw him onto one of the twin beds and warned him to keep silent. Rummaging quickly through a dresser drawer, Buster found elastic suspenders which he used to bind Dumas's hands and feet and a pair of white panty hose which he tied as a gag around Dumas's mouth. Then, with his victim helpless and the need for hurry gone, he searched the dresser more carefully and removed two things—a hunting knife and a pair of brown leather gloves. He put the knife, which had a five-inch blade in a leather sheath, in his pants pocket, but he dropped the gloves onto the top of the dresser and left them there. After a quick glance at the bed to assure himself that Dumas was still securely bound, he left the bedroom and began searching other rooms. He had never lived in, had seldom even seen, such a modern and handsomely furnished apartment, and he became increasingly certain that in such a place money must be hidden somewhere. His life had kept him a stranger to the world of bank accounts and credit cards; in his experience, wealth existed only in the form of cash and the things that cash could buy.

The office next to Roy Dumas's bedroom interested him especially, with its desk and files and incomprehensible business papers. He explored it with particular care, but found only five dollars in a shallow drawer. He put the money in his pocket and continued searching.

During Buster's search, Dumas managed to struggle free of his bindings and pull the nylon gag from his mouth. But then, halfway to safety, he made the second to last mistake of his life. Instead of moving quietly off the bed and locking the door to keep the intruder away, instead of pulling a window open in order to call for help to the people at the swimming pool only a short distance away, he simply sat up and began to scream. Buster came running, silencing Dumas by striking him as hard as he could on the side of the head with his fist.

"Where the hell's your money?"

"I told you," the terrified Dumas replied, shuddering and clutching a bony hand against his now-bloody left ear, "I don't have any." Buster raised his fist, and Dumas cringed. "My wife has the money," he said, making his last mistake. "She'll be home by three-thirty." Buster pushed him face down on the bed and refastened the suspenders around his ankles and wrists more tightly than before. Again he gagged Dumas, this time with a red wool scarf, and for the first time he realized that Dumas must have a wallet. Reaching into Dumas's back pockets, he found a wallet and pulled it out, but after taking it into the living room he opened it and was disappointed to discover that it contained only seven dollars. He put the bills in his pocket with the money he had found in the office and, sitting down in an easy chair near the front door, looked through Dumas's credit cards. He decided that the cards had no possible value to him and put them and the wallet on the floor under the chair. Having committed his robbery and gotten only twelve dollars for it, he decided to wait for the promised arrival of the missing wife. It would be necessary, he decided, to prepare for her arrival.

In a bedroom that clearly appeared to be Mrs. Dumas's—its closet was filled with a woman's clothing—Buster pulled the double bed away from the wall and looked through drawers for binding material. He found plenty, numerous scarves and pairs of hose, and tied the ends of four stockings and one scarf to the bedframe near the head. He pulled the knots until they were hard and tight to be certain that they would hold the woman when she came home and he got her onto the bed.

He decided to wear a mask, and in one of the back bedroom's amply stocked drawers he found a large blue and gold handkerchief that made a very satisfactory one. He folded it in half, drew it across his face, and tied the ends at the back of his neck. It was a good enough fit, but when he looked at himself in a mirror he decided that he didn't like it. Pulling it off without untying the knot, he dropped it to the floor. He looked in the drawer again and found two wool dickeys, one black and the other white. When he drew the black dickey over his head and down to the lower half of his face and looked again into the mirror, he liked what he saw. Satisfied now with what he thought was a very dramatic mask, he took the white dickey into the woman's bedroom and threw it onto the bed.

A moment later, back in the living room, he decided that

the dickey was too hot. He pulled it off, went again to the back bedroom, and selected a handsome rayon handkerchief from the supply in the drawer. It was cooler than the dickey, better-looking than the first handkerchief, and in any case nothing better was available. After inspecting himself in the mirror Buster returned to the living room, turned off the television so he could listen for the woman's arrival, and went into the kitchen where he selected a butcher knife from a cabinet drawer. Forgetting about the hunting knife in his pocket, he decided that this would be his weapon. Big and heavy-bladed, it was as fearsome as a machete.

What had begun as improvised preparations had evolved by now into a complete plan. Buster went to the woman's bedroom and sat down on the floor to wait. He waited there for a long time, the mask around his mouth and the butcher knife in his hand. At last, when he heard a key in the front door, he got to his feet and slipped into the closet to hide. Two rooms away Roy Dumas was completely silent.

Crouching in the closet, holding the knife ready near his chest, Buster heard Bernalyn Dumas step into the living room and close the door. She stepped almost inaudibly across the carpeted living room, then her shoes tapped loudly on the tiled kitchen floor. She left the kitchen again, crossed the living room to the hall, and entered her bedroom still carrying her purse. Immediately Buster was out of the closet and on her with the knife, ordering her to say nothing and forcing her backward onto the bed. Quickly, while she was still shocked, he secured her hands with the stockings and scarf tied to the bedframe, stuffed a stocking into her mouth, and wrapped a pair of panty hose around the lower half of her face. After knotting the hose he pulled the white dickey over her face as a blindfold. Still moving as quickly as he could, he unsnapped the front of her white dress and cut open her underwear with the butcher knife.

At this point, Buster said in his confession, he "molested" Bernalyn Dumas. Under questioning it became clear that he was talking about rape. The detectives did not believe him, knowing that there was no evidence of Mrs. Dumas's having been raped, but he could not be shaken from his story. Asked if he had done anything else to the lower half of her body, he angrily said no. This was the one area in which his confession consistently diverged from the known facts of the killings.

After doing whatever he in fact did to Mrs. Dumas, Buster dumped the contents of her purse onto the bedroom floor. In her wallet he found twenty dollars, which he put into his pocket. Disgusted with this small return for his long and dangerous wait, he set the butcher knife on the dresser, noticing as he did so a pair of scissors lying nearby. Again he searched the apartment, and as before he found no hidden caches of money. At last he gave up and prepared to leave. Mr. and Mrs. Dumas were still alive on their beds.

Buster picked up a handkerchief from the floor and went still again through the apartment. He wiped every surface that he had touched since his arrival hours before, successfully obliterating every fingerprint. He finished in the back bedroom, put on the brown gloves that he had found earlier in Roy Dumas's dresser drawer, and went to Mrs. Dumas's room. She was motionless on the bed, moaning with fright under her gag and blindfold, the muscles of her arms taut against the bindings. He leaned over her, picked up the loose ends of the hose hanging out from under the dickey covering her head, and drew them around her neck. A quickly executed knot held the hose in place and finished the job; Mrs. Dumas struggled briefly and then her body relaxed. Straightening up and turning to leave the room, Buster again saw the scissors on the dresser. He picked them up and stepped slowly to the bed. . . .

Moments later, no longer masked, he entered the back bedroom carrying a gray stocking. He pulled it around Roy Dumas's neck until the flesh stood out in mounds on both sides, and then he knotted it. That done, he went to the living room and opened the front door just enough to see that no one was in the hallway outside. He took off the gloves, dropped them onto the television, and left.

He must have been very calm. His car was on the lot just outside the Dumases' back door, and he could have reached it in seconds by going out through the kitchen. But he realized that if he exited that way someone might see him going from the Dumas apartment to his car. That could raise questions, and eventually it could lead to his arrest. So he went out the front door, and no one saw him step from the Dumas living room into the hallway. From the hallway he went through the building's front door to the sunlit courtyard outside, and if anyone saw him they had no way of guessing which apartment he had been in and no reason to wonder. He went all the way around the Hermitage complex, finally approaching his car by walking toward the Dumases' building. He got behind the wheel, took the hunting knife out of his pocket and slipped it under his seat, and drove away at a normal speed. He was confident that he had done nothing to arouse anyone's suspicion, and of course he was right. His careful departure had made him virtually invisible.

Buster never admitted using the scissors to mutilate Bernalyn Dumas. He spoke at length and with almost flawless memory of how he had murdered her and her husband, and he appeared almost eager to confess that he had raped her. But questions about mutilation made him grow angry and sullen, and so the detectives stopped asking him about that. Too many other things had to be learned while he was so willing to talk.

Long after his confession, in a conversation with Mary at the Shelby County Jail, Buster was just a bit more candid. "I remember tying that woman to her bed," he told Mary, "but from then on it was like some kind of hallucination. It was like I was seeing myself in a movie and not having any control over what was going on. I remember I saw a pair of scissors on a dresser, but I don't know what I did with them. It was all like a bad dream." Mary did not press him for more details. He did not seem at all remorseful about what he had done, and she didn't want to know what he had done with the scissors.

Buster told Mary that his motive was money. He told her he remembered tying stockings around the Dumases' necks, but he said he didn't think he had killed them. "When I left their apartment," he said, "I felt pretty sure somebody would find them before they died."

That was not what he had told the detectives who took his confession. He told them that he had killed the Dumases for the same reason he killed his other victims—because they were the only witnesses to his act of robbery. "I wasn't going to let anybody put me back in prison," he said. "I figured if I killed them they couldn't ever testify against me."

By one of his own explanations, therefore, Buster never intended to kill the Dumases. By another, he killed them simply because they knew he had stolen thirty-two dollars.

On August 16, two days after he killed Roy and Bernalyn Dumas, Buster returned to the blood shop and again sold a pint of plasma for five dollars. He sold another pint two days later, on August 18, and the day after that he was hired as an attendant at the Hudson Oil station on North Bellevue Street. On August 20 he worked at the station from 6 A.M. to 3 P.M. and then drove downtown to sell plasma. On August 22 he reversed that order of business, selling plasma early in the day and working from 3 P.M. to midnight. By this time he was living with Mary in her apartment on Bethel Street—an arrangement explicitly dependent upon his ability to bring money home.

At the gas station Buster became known to the other workers as an agreeable but remarkably quiet young man who did his chores promptly and without complaint. When there were no customers, the station's employees usually gathered in the small glass-walled office to talk and be out of the sun and heat. Buster, however, almost always stayed out-side during daylight hours. "He was a day-dreamer," a middle-aged man who worked with Buster remembered long afterward. "He always wore sunglasses but never wore a hat, and he'd just stand outside for hours on end, just leaning against the pump and staring off into space. He didn't have a lot to say, but he seemed normal enough to me. I'd tell him, 'Boy, you better come in out of the sun,' but he'd just grin and stay where he was. I think he said he wanted to keep his tan."

During his hours alone, leaning against the gas pump and gazing off into the distance, Buster noticed that a 1961 Buick station wagon was for sale outside a transmission repair shop on the other side of North Bellevue. It was neither a hand-some nor a well-preserved vehicle, but he became deter-mined to own it. At 10 A.M. on Monday, August 25, he drove to the Aamco shop and asked the manager, Frank Drew,* how much he wanted for the Buick.

"One hundred dollars," said Drew. "Cash on delivery." Buster did not have a hundred dollars. He was almost broke, in fact. He had not yet been paid at the Hudson station, and the money he had taken from the Dumases was spent. Never-theless, for reasons never explained, Buster wanted the station wagon desperately.

"I really am serious about buying it," he told Drew. "I can pay for it as soon as I get paid. Couldn't you hold it for me till then?"

"No way. I want to get rid of it, and I'm selling it to the first guy who's got a hundred dollars. The only way I can hold it for you is if you give me fifty down. For fifty dollars I'll take the sign off the window."

"I don't know," said Buster. "I'll have to see what I can do. Don't be in a hurry to sell it to somebody else." He left, and on his way back to the center of the city he wondered about where he could get fifty dollars. Picking a house or

* a pseudonym

apartment at random and robbing it no longer seemed like such a good idea after the disappointing results of the Dumas robbery. He needed a place where he would be sure of finding a substantial amount of money, but from which he could escape without trouble. He knew few people in Memphis and had been inside only a few homes in the city, and therefore he did not have to think very long before remembering the old woman from whom he had tried to rent a room more than three weeks before. She would be an easy victim, and she had money. She collected rent from her roomers every Sunday, she had said, and this was Monday morning. It was perfect. Buster couldn't remember the name of her street, but he knew it was around the corner from the hotel he had stayed in after returning to Memphis. He parked near the hotel, started off on foot, and found the house without difficulty. The "Rooms" sign that had caused his first visit to the house was no longer on display, he noticed, but he went up the front walk anyway and knocked on the screen door. It was now 10:30 A.M. Leila Jackson came to the door and greeted him.

"Good morning," Buster said cheerfully. "I stopped by to see if you might still have a room for rent. I was here a while back, last month I think it was, and you showed me one then."

"I remember," said Mrs. Jackson, also cheerful. "I showed you a room in back. It's rented now, though." This was the point at which Mrs. Jackson often turned away men looking for rooms, but perhaps by now she had forgotten her earlier suspicions of Buster, when he'd come to inquire about a room for himself and had been accompanied by a pregnant wife and a small child. Or perhaps she was impressed, this time, with her handsome and polite young visitor. For whatever reason, she did not turn him away. She told him about the room that she was usually reluctant to rent.

"It's up in the front of the house, though," she said, "and

it doesn't have a private entrance or bathroom. If you took it you'd have to share a bathroom with me."

"That might be all right," said Buster. "I don't think that would be such a problem. I'd like to see the room." Mrs. Jackson lifted her hand to the latch, unlocking the door to let him in.

She showed him the bedroom, closing her front door so that he could look in, turning on the overhead light so that he would be sure to see what a large and pleasantly furnished room it was. She said something about the rent, and though Buster wasn't listening he looked at her and smiled. "That sounds fair," he said. "It's a nice room, all right. Can I see the bath?"

Mrs. Jackson led him through the living room and a short hall to the bathroom. He stepped inside, turned around slowly to give the impression that he was considering it carefully, and then returned to the hall. Mrs. Jackson was standing in a doorway, and looking over her shoulder Buster saw a bedroom behind her. Obviously it was her room. She was still talking, but as before Buster wasn't listening. He was deciding whether to make his move. Suddenly decided, he raised both hands and pushed the old woman back in the bedroom. Absurdly but consistently (he had done the same thing in Bernalyn Dumas's room while waiting for her to come home) he pulled back the spread on Mrs. Jackson's bed before throwing her down onto it.

"Mrs. Jackson did fight and scream a little bit, but not too much," Buster said in his confession. "She didn't scratch me or mark me in any way."

He told detectives that he raped Mrs. Jackson. Again he was not believed, but again he insisted. Asked if he had mutilated her with a knife, he put his head down and said nothing. "All right," an officer said, "just tell us about how you killed her."

He tried to strangle Mrs. Jackson with his hands but could

not, he said. To his surprise, he found it impossible to maintain enough pressure on her throat to stop her breathing. Leaving her gasping on the bed, he ran into the adjacent kitchen and grabbed a dishtowel. But when he twisted it around her neck and pulled, it tore. Again he left the bed, and in a drawer he found a nylon stocking. This worked. He wrapped it around her neck, knotted it tightly, and soon her breathing stopped.

He ransacked Mrs. Jackson's bedroom but found no money. He searched the kitchen and found no money there, either. He took a butcher knife and a dull-edged table knife from a drawer and returned with them to the bedroom.

Here again, in the course of his confession, Buster's memory failed him. Evidence found at the scene left little enough to be imagined, however. The butcher knife was inserted into Mrs. Jackson's vagina. Then the bedspread was pulled up to her waist and the knife after being wiped clean of blood, was dropped between her knees. The table knife, apparently not used, was left on the bed beside the body.

Buster did remember seeing a set of keys hanging from the lock on Mrs. Jackson's closet door. He opened the door and found purses on a shelf, and when he pulled them down and started emptying them a billfold fell to the floor. When he examined it, Buster found that the billfold contained what appeared to be a very large amount of money. He put it in his pants pocket and began moving through the house wiping off everything on which he might have left a fingerprint.

By the barest of margins, Buster's luck held. He was just finishing his wiping when a knock sounded on the front door. It terrified him. He ran out the back door without stopping to close it behind him, crossed the back yard to a gap in the fence, and then walked quickly to the corner of Madison and Camilla Streets. From there he slowed and walked the short distance to Baptist Memorial Hospital, went inside, and found a men's room on the first floor. He took the money from Mrs. Jackson's billfold, stuffed it into his pocket, and buried the billfold in a trash can under a pile of crumpled paper towels.

The billfold was never found. It had contained eighty-five dollars. Shortly after noon, less than an hour after fleeing Mrs. Jackson's house in panic, Buster returned to the transmission shop and gave Frank Drew a fifty dollar deposit on the Buick station wagon. Later that afternoon he reported for work on schedule.

On Thursday, August 28, three days after the Jackson murder, Buster went to the blood shop downtown and sold a pint of plasma before starting work at 3 P.M. He was finding it impossible to raise the final fifty dollars to pay off the Buick, and Mary wanted to go to her home in Mississippi. He had promised to take her there for the Labor Day weekend.

Early Friday morning he started off with Mary and Pip for Mississippi. On the way out of Memphis he stopped at the Hudson station and told the manager, Earl Sartis, that he had to take Mary to the doctor and might not be able to start work until 4 P.M. instead of 3 as scheduled. Sartis assented to that, and Buster drove on. When he reached the Bulimore house in Sarah he let Mary and Pip out of the car and then departed alone almost immediately, saying that he wanted to get back to the city and start work as early as possible. Before returning to Memphis, however, he stopped at Blue Goose in an effort to see Clifford. Retha told him that Clifford was at work.

On the highway back to Memphis, Buster thought again about his need for money. Inevitably, he thought that he would have to steal it, but this time he could not think of a possible victim. When he got within the city limits he decided to go to the OK Cafe on Madison to drink beer and try to make plans. The cafe had become his favorite hangout, the place where he spent most of his plasma income.

As it had sixteen days before, when Buster set out on the

first of his robbery-murders, the cafe today proved a good place for thinking. After two or three bottles of Budweiser, Buster began to consider the fact that this was a payday for thousands of people. Many would go home carrying large amounts of cash, he thought, and many of them would be women. Something, perhaps his frequent visits to the blood bank, made him think of all the women who worked downtown. A few minutes after 4 P.M. he finished his last beer and went out to his car. He drove downtown, circled the business district for several minutes, and finally pulled onto the Promenade parking lot at the edge of the Mississippi. The lot was crowded with cars but was far enough away from the office buildings at the top of the bluff to seem a promising place for a robbery. He parked several rows from the street, reached under his seat for Roy Dumas's hunting knife, and slipped it into his belt. Then he waited.

As the minutes passed increasing numbers of men and women came across Riverside Drive, got into cars, and drove away. Buster watched them all carefully, the women especially, but he made no move. Some of the women were not alone, some did not pass close enough to his car to seem accessible, and others he rejected for less clear reasons simply because they did not appear to him to be the kinds of women he was interested in robbing that day.

"After I had been sitting there for about fifteen or twenty minutes," he later confessed, "I saw this dark-headed girl with a yellowish looking dress coming from the steps leading up from the park and get into her car. My car was parked a little behind her, and at an angle. After she got in the car I walked up, like I was going to go by her car, and then when I got even with the door I jerked it open and put the knife on her and told her to scoot over and lay down on the floor. She did."

Glenda Sue rolled herself into a ball under the dashboard on the passenger side of her car, looking up at Buster through frightened eyes as he put the key in the ignition and turned it.

"Down," he said, gunning the engine and holding the point of the knife an inch from her forehead. "Get all the way down and stay there." She lowered her head, brushing the end of the blade with her red hair, and Buster put the car in gear.

Buster had to wait in a line of cars to get off the lot. When he reached the gate he discovered that he needed fifty cents for the automatic turnstile, and he had no change. For a moment he was trapped; other cars were waiting behind him, preventing him from backing up. He put the knife on the seat, looked into the girl's purse, and found two quarters which he dropped into the slot just as someone behind him began to honk. The gate rose and Buster pulled away, turning right onto Riverside and heading south. He had no idea of where he was going, but he wanted to find a secluded place, and the fact that the girl on the floor had neither moved nor made a sound when he was caught at the tollgate now made it appear that there was no need for hurry. He continued south past the downtown area, until Riverside merged into Interstate Highway 55 and became for a while a kind of canyon with high concrete walls on both sides. The rush hour traffic was extremely heavy here, and if the girl had offered any resistance Buster would have been in extreme difficulty; there was no possibility of stopping without becoming a center of angry attention and no place to turn off. He drove with his left hand and held the knife with his right, and the girl did nothing.

After a few minutes the highway rose up out of the canyon, the concrete walls fell away, and the Mustang was on high ground. On the right Buster saw a forested area—exactly what he was looking for. He took the first exit at Mallory Avenue, saw a sign pointing to Riverside Park, and followed its arrow. A minute later he was driving the park's winding and tree-shrouded roads, safely out of traffic for the first time since he had abducted the girl. There were picnickers and ballplayers and children scattered throughout the park, however, and Buster knew that he could not stop beside any of the paved roads without risking trouble. He had never been in the park before.

"I was driving around in these woods on the asphalt roads, and then I saw a little dirt road and drove off into it," he told detectives. *"I remember seeing a rag hanging on a bush, and I think it was blue but I'm not sure. This road made a little bend back to the left and dead-ended. After we parked there, I sexually molested her on the front seat of the car. I know it's bucket seats, but that's where I molested her. I made her take off her panty hose and panties before I sexually molested her. I did not keep the knife on her the whole time I was molesting her. She made me put it outside the car. I did reach a climax inside of her."*

After recovering the knife he helped her put her panties on but did so awkwardly, so that the hem of her slip was caught in the elastic waistband of her panties. He tied her hands behind her back with the panty hose and, gesturing with the knife, directed her to walk deeper into the woods along a footpath leading off from the end of the dirt road. With Buster close behind her, she followed the path downhill and around a curve until they were in a grassy clearing out of sight of the car. There he pushed her down onto her back and straddled her with his knees. He said in his confession that he intended to rape her again.

Buster explained the killing of Glenda Sue Harden as the result of sudden fear. He thought he heard a noise in the bushes nearby, he said, and reflexively raised the knife. The girl stiffened and turned under him when she saw the blade lifted above her head. Her movement increased his fright and he brought the knife down hard, plunging it into the center of her chest. Twice more in as many seconds he pulled the knife up and drove it into her again.

The three wounds were within an inch or two of each other, and any one of them would have been sufficient to kill her. But Buster continued to stab. The fact that he did so made the police doubt his story of killing the girl out of fear; a frightened man, they reasoned, would have run away more quickly. He buried the blade in her neck, then raised himself off her and rolled her halfway over. He stabbed her four times in the side and twice in the head. Finally he turned her onto her face and stabbed her repeatedly in the back. He wiped the knife on the grass, took it with him back to the car, and drove out of the park. Minutes later he was downtown again, leaving the car on the riverfront cobblestones after using his shirt to wipe its interior clean of fingerprints. He walked four blocks south to his own car and drove off the Promenade lot without being noticed. By seven o'clock he was at work.

This had been a hundred-dollar robbery, his most profitable murder. He waited through the three-day weekend, and on Tuesday morning he paid the last fifty dollars on the Buick station wagon and drove it home. That vehicle, for which he had killed two women, never ran again. It sat on the street outside Mary's apartment until after Buster's arrest, and finally the police towed it away.

Earl Sartis, the manager of the gas station where Buster worked, discovered one night early in September that thirty dollars had been taken from the cash register. He was unable to determine which of his employees might have taken the money because several men had worked at the station that evening, but he attempted to isolate the culprit by assigning each suspect to work alone on a different night. If more money disappeared on any of those nights, there would be little doubt about who had taken it.

Thursday, September 4 was Buster's turn. Only he and Sartis worked that night, and after he left at closing time Sartis checked his sales against cash on hand and found that another twenty dollars was missing. When Buster reported for work the next day, Sartis fired him. Buster denied that he had stolen anything but was not believed.

He did not tell Mary about being fired. With the help of his neighbor Ray he got a job at a paint factory, but quit without explanation after only a few hours. But from then on he got up early every morning and left home pretending to be going to work at the factory. Hoping to find another job before the pretense became insupportable, he tried without success to find work at a service station and applied for work as a nursing assistant at the Memphis Medicenter and the B'nai B'rith Hospital for the Aged. He continued to pay for the gasoline and beer that were almost his only daily needs by selling plasma at the blood shop.

Absurdly, with a blithe lack of the simplest common sense, he returned to the Hudson Oil station on September 10 and asked Earl Sartis to lend him money. Sartis refused, of course, and Buster went away disappointed. After four murders he remained as destitute as he had been at the start; the killings had yielded him one broken-down station wagon and about a hundred and fifteen dollars that had quickly been spent on everyday household needs. His career as a bandit was scarcely profitable enough to pay the rent and buy occasional groceries, and it was still possible that Mary would send him away if she learned he had lost his job.

The next morning, on Thursday, he went downtown to sell plasma. He was seated in a chair just inside the blood shop's storefront window when a nurse who had taken his blood several times and was by now almost a friend pointed to the street.

"Isn't that your car?" she asked. "It's getting a ticket." She was right. Buster had not put a coin in the parking meter, and now a meter maid was putting a ticket on his windshield.

"It sure is," he said. "There goes three good dollars down the drain." But as he leaned back in his chair he shrugged and smiled without apparent concern. When he went out to his car minutes later he took the ticket off the windshield and put it in his shirt pocket. He got into the car and drove east to the OK Cafe.

Buster was an established regular at the cafe by now, as well known there as at the blood bank. He received a friendly greeting from waitresses Linda Butler and Gwen Robertson when he arrived at 9:30 Thursday morning, and when he sat down alone at a table two women at the bar turned and tried to draw him into their conversation. Predictably, like everyone in Memphis, they were talking about the murders. Specifically, they were discussing the chilling possibility that at that moment the murderer was walking the streets looking for someone to kill.

"You haven't got a nylon stocking in *your* pocket, have you, boy?" one of the women asked Buster. Her face and voice were both hard, and it was difficult to tell if she was joking. Buster smiled at her and shook his head no, then asked for a beer. During the next two hours he drank half a dozen bottles of Budweiser. One of the waitresses later remembered that he paid for each bottle with a different one-dollar bill, never using his change. He said little but watched the people at the bar and listened to their conversation about the killer.

"I'll tell you one thing," the hard-faced woman said at one point, "he better not come around to Apartment Ten at 1167 Madison Street." She dug into her purse, pulling out a long nail file and pointing it at an imaginary adversary. "He comes to Apartment 10, he'll get his eyes punched out with this." She put the file back into her purse, smiled broadly, and took a long drink from her glass. Buster, safe behind his sunglasses, smiled too.

The woman left the cafe shortly after 11:30, and a few minutes after that Buster left too. He got into his car, put the Dumas hunting knife into his belt, and drove around the block. He parked on a lot behind the 1100 block of Madison and started walking. No one knows with certainty what he did during the next fifteen or twenty minutes.

Some Memphis detectives believe that Buster went to 1177 Madison and tried to find the woman with the nail file. They believe that he had taken her boastful threats to the unknown killer as a personal challenge, and had decided to teach her a lesson. Though such a possibility is supported by the fact that he parked almost directly behind the woman's apartment building, it is nevertheless only hypothesis. Buster never confessed to any such intent.

Retha Putt, Buster's sister-in-law, believes that he went to her apartment two blocks north on Bellevue after leaving the cafe. She believes that Buster intended to kill her, and Clifford Putt agrees with her. Certain details about Buster's mental history and his lifelong relationship with Clifford make this possibility seem at least plausible, but it too cannot be proved. By the time anyone thought of asking Buster about such things, he was no longer talking.

It is possible that Buster wanted to kill both the woman with the nail file and Retha, and that when he was unable to do either he set out to kill the first woman who crossed his path. Certainly he was careless, and certainly he seemed intent upon killing someone that day. At some psychic level, possibly, he wanted to be caught. But none of this can be proved.

Nothing becomes certain until one o'clock in the afternoon, with Buster at the LaBlanche Apartments of Bellevue half a block from Madison. He tried and failed to get into Grace Oldham's apartment there, and as he stepped out of the north wing of the building he saw Mary Christine Pickens coming up the walk.

"I saw this lady wearing a dark suit go into the apartments," said Buster later. "I followed her, and as she was going up the steps I was about five or six steps behind her. She unlocked her door, and when she stepped into the door I pushed her on in and then went in behind her, and she

started screaming and I started stabbing her. Then I heard
someone in the apartment across the hall, and I ran."

Factually, as a convincing account of the murders of Roy
and Bernalyn Dumas and Leila Jackson and Glenda Sue
Harden and Mary Christine Pickens, Buster's confession was
unassailable. It could not have been a fabrication, because it
explained too many things too well. It resolved all questions
about how the first four victims had been slain by a killer
who left no trace of himself and thereby achieved a rapid series of "perfect crimes."

Almost inevitably, considering the complexity of the
twenty-nine-day search for the killer, some questions never
were answered. The fingerprint found on the cake knife in
the Dumas kitchen, for example, was not Buster's and was
never identified though the police tried to match it with the
fingerprints of all possible suspects, including every member
of the Putt family who was in or near Memphis on the day
the Dumases were killed. The police never learned the identity of the woman who had telephoned headquarters and reported that Clifford Putt was the killer. These were fascinating questions, but very minor ones.

Something remains, however. Unless one accepts at face
value the proposition that Buster killed five persons within
twenty-nine days simply to protect himself from a possible
robbery conviction, his confession provides no answer to the
last, most difficult, and most important question of all.

It does not tell why. The answer, if it can be found anywhere, lies in the past.

12

The Making of a Killer

DOCTORS WHO EXAMINED George Howard Putt after his arrest reported that he wished to appear insane but was not. His I.Q. was set at 93—not a high level, but within the normal range and possibly quite good for a man whose formal education had been a shambles and who was not eager to give prosecutors reason to believe that he was competent to stand trial. He was found to be healthy and physically normal, and to possess certain qualities indicating a strong native intelligence. He had a good memory, for example, combined with a fertile imagination.

In short, direct observation of Putt in the months after he was caught made him seem all the more incomprehensible. He seemed, in part because many facts about his early life were not disclosed, to be a sane man who had suddenly become a murderer of strangers. If this was a contradictory portrait, the Memphis newspapers evaded the contradiction by simply covering Putt's trials and reporting only limited, easily obtained information. They brought the story to a superficial conclusion and dropped it without really attempting to understand or explain the man whose activities had for a time obsessed them.

The police did not behave much differently. To some extent this is understandable: the police department's job was to catch the killer, and, once he had been caught and had confessed, to provide the state with as much evidence as possible in order to assure conviction. Nevertheless, it is surprising how little curiosity most of the investigators who had worked on the case displayed about its final mysteries after Putt's confession was in hand. A lieutenant who had helped lead the search for the murderer, who had helped take Putt's confession, and who later hung a picture of the killer on the wall behind his desk, offered in 1973 a typical analysis of the central figure in the biggest case of his career:

"Putt was just a mean son of a bitch. No point in talking about whether he was crazy—he wasn't. He was just mean as hell. I've seen a lot of mean sons of bitches in this job, and Putt was the meanest one of all."

If the lieutenant's opinion is correct—and its correctness is debatable on more than one point—it is nevertheless not helpful. It fails to explain, or even to suggest, why Putt was so "mean."

That question is the final one. Its answer lies in the circumstances that shaped the life and mind of George Howard Putt and made him, in the twenty-third year of his life, a savage killer. An examination of those circumstances makes it plain that Putt did not suddenly become a savage in the summer of 1969 but rather had given repeated warning before he struck. He was, even more than the girl he married, a human being formed and deformed by forces over which he had no control. In his case such forces were so overwhelming that his life was directed very early into paths that could lead to nothing better than a tragic dead end. He seems, when the story of his life has been traced, almost as pitiable as the innocent people he killed.

George Howard Putt was born in the New Orleans charity hospital on March 15, 1946. His birth certificate indicates that he was first named Howard George Putt, but he was given the nickname Buster in infancy and by the time he grew old enough for formal identification his first and middle names had somehow become transposed. He was the third child and third son of Clifford Alva Putt and Ruth Marie Tarver Putt. His elder brothers were John Russell Putt, born in Mississippi in 1943, and Clifford Alva Putt, Jr. (known as Junior in childhood), born in North Carolina in 1944. Later there were five other children, only three of whom are known to have survived. Betty Ruth was born in 1948, Lance (who was severely retarded) in 1954, and Lester in 1955. The other two probably died in infancy but, according to some members of the family, may have been sold by their parents.

Buster's father, born in Mississippi in 1919, was a drifter and petty criminal. One of several children in a respectable family of limited means, he worked in the Civilian Conservation Corps during the mid-1930s and then joined the Army, from which he was discharged in 1941 after four years of service. Soon thereafter he married Ruth Tarver, a seventeen-year-old Louisiana girl whose mother had died when she was small and who had been raised by her father. By all accounts the marriage was a calamity from the beginning. Putt worked intermittently as a truck driver and mechanic but was an alcoholic, a thief, and a seriously disturbed man whose maladjustment often manifested itself in sadism. His wife was an uneducated and almost completely passive girl who accepted abuse without complaint and by stages was made an accomplice in her husband's crimes. As their family quickly grew their life became a bewildering series of sudden moves usually prompted by the need to stay ahead of pursuing police. Putt's specialty was passing bad checks, though the fact that he was arrested more than thirty times suggests that he must have been less than adept. The nature and success of his crimes, at any rate, now matters less than their effect upon his children.

On June 4, 1946, Putt was arrested on a charge of cruelty

to a juvenile. He had, according to surviving reports of the incident, severely beaten his son with a leather strap. The record does not indicate which son was beaten, but members of the Putt family agree that Buster—then not yet three months old—was the victim. His grandfather testified to that effect at Buster's first murder trial 23 years later. Putt was sentenced to a year in jail for the beating, but the sentence was suspended on condition that he leave New Orleans within twenty-four hours.

During most of the 1940s and early 1950s, the Putts fled from place to place, living sometimes in their car and sometimes in cheap hotels, often not having enough to eat. When he was ten months old Buster's parents left him at the home of a woman named Mrs. Cecil Cheek in Tupelo, Mississippi, and did not return for a full year. As Mrs. Cheek grew increasingly fond of the child she decided to keep and raise him, but one day when she was away at work Buster's mother arrived unexpectedly and took him away, not telling the babysitter where she was going. Mrs. Cheek felt bereft but never saw Buster again. Some years later, when she learned that he had been abandoned and was in his first serious trouble, she tried without success to be given custody of him.

His year in the Cheek home was the most tranquil period, and probably the happiest, in Buster's life. The only other good times for him and his brothers were the occasions when they were left with their grandparents, Mr. and Mrs. George Alva Putt. Grandfather Putt operated a cafe in North Carolina when the boys were small, and though he and his wife were in their sixties and less than well-to-do they tried to provide a secure home for Johnny, Junior and Buster—and then for Betty Ruth after she arrived. But more often than they liked the boys found themselves traveling with their parents.

"It wasn't much of a life," Clifford Jr. recalled years later. "There was no home life to speak of at all, and we weren't treated right by our father or our mother either. Our father was outside the law, you know. I understand it better now than I did then. I knew what he was doing then, but I didn't understand that it was wrong—cashing checks here and there and not having money in the bank. We got lots of beatings. My father would have killed us all one time when he was drunk if it wasn't for my mother stopping him. He like to have strangled us to death with a belt. He beat us with his fist, even.

"Buster just reacted like anybody would. We were scared to death of our father and we wouldn't dare to say anything about it. We'd just hold it in, but it had to come out somehow. When we were growing up we didn't have a say-so at all. If anything got did, we'd get the blame for it. If we said we didn't do it, we'd get slapped in the face."

On one occasion, which Clifford remembered with particular clarity, the boys were left alone in a hotel room all day without food. Buster was two or three years old at the time, and he became hysterical. He, and finally Clifford and Johnny too, ran around the room screaming. They cried for hours, until someone heard them and alerted the hotel manager. This must have happened in North Carolina, because the manager was able to call Grandmother Putt, who came and got the boys and took them home with her. Except for the happy ending, the incident was not an unusual one. In Clifford's words, "We were left like that all the time."

When Buster was eight years old, his parents were convicted on a forgery charge and sent to prison. The children all moved in with their grandparents, who by now had sold their cafe and moved to Richmond, Virginia, to be near a relative who was sick and needed assistance. This was a better situation for the boys but far from a perfect one, since Grandfather Putt was himself no longer in robust health and his wife was working part-time at an ice cream parlor. Both of them were growing visibly old, and they found it difficult to manage four growing children unaccustomed to the routine disciplines of ordinary home life. The boys were insubordinate and often into mischief, and when their grandparents struggled to bring them under control they became defiant. One recurrent problem was similar to a difficulty that the boys had earlier experienced in living with their parents: no one, it seemed, would listen to them. As he recalled these years, Clifford spoke affectionately of his grandparents and their sacrifices. He expressed understanding of their difficulties. But he stopped a little short of describing them as ideal guardians.

"We sassed our grandmother like boys do, especially if they don't have a father around," he said. "The reason we did it was they wouldn't listen to us. My grandmother, she whipped us, but usually we deserved it. But if she thought we did something and we wanted to explain, she wouldn't listen. That gets under you after a while." In this period Clifford came to feel very close to Buster, to regard him as his ally and one good friend. Buster gave the appearance of reciprocating these feelings, though he was already developing a shell of reserve. Their brother Johnny was a solitary youth, remote from both of them.

In November, 1957, Clifford and Buster shot out the windows of a neighbor's house with a stolen air rifle and were arrested. Their grandmother was extremely upset by the incident and arranged to have the boys—five of them now, their parents having delivered the infants Lance and Lester to Richmond during renewed wanderings following their release from prison—admitted to a school for parentless children in a small town far from Richmond. Betty Ruth was kept at home, but Johnny, Junior, Buster, Lance and Lester were sent away. They ranged in age from fourteen to two.

As Clifford described the school some sixteen years after his arrival there, it was in the mid-1950s like something conceived in the dark side of Charles Dickens' imagination. A big and gloomy place, frightening to youngsters, it housed several hundred boys and girls and subjected them to a stern, sometimes terrifying disciplinary system. Religious services called "devotions" were held nightly and involved public confessions of rule violations (which were called "sins"), and sinners were beaten both for what they confessed and for what they failed to confess. Going into town without permission was a sin; playing in nearby caves without permission was a sin; so were dancing and seeing a movie.

At devotions, the children were assembled in a large hall where they were instructed to sit on the floor and lower their heads between their knees for a period of prayer. Next came confession, followed by switchings for whatever had been confessed. Finally the sinners who had not confessed—the ones who had been seen coming out of a movie but did not know they had been seen, for example—got their beatings. "The indoor beating was done by a housemother," Clifford recalled. "I remember she was called Miss Granite, granite rock, and she was rock all right." The Putt boys quickly learned to hate the place, and the three eldest all decided to escape. According to Clifford, they were frequently in trouble for doing things without permission because they could not get permission to do anything. "That's why we had to sneak," he said.

Not very long after their arrival, Buster and his big brothers walked to a nearby highway where they tried to hitchhike a ride toward their grandparents' home, which they guessed was about 400 miles away. No cars would stop for them, and as they were standing beside the road with their thumbs out a young man named J. B. Stites* drove past in a flatbed truck used to haul things at the school. They knew Stites and were frightened when he saw them. He was an older adolescent who had been raised at the school and had become a kind of overseer there. The boys were relieved when he drove past them without stopping, but minutes later he returned in a pickup truck and parked it on the shoulder of the highway. Johnny, Junior and Buster fled down an embankment into a creek and Stites ran after them.

"He caught Buster first, ducked him under the water, and

* a pseudonym

dragged him on out," said Clifford. "He caught me on the other side of the creek. But Johnny kept running and J. B. Stites had to chase him on into the woods before he caught him. We got beaten for that. It was a standing rule. You knew that if you ran away you'd get beaten. J. B. Stites beat us that night with a big old switch. It was a stick, really."

Soon Johnny ran away alone, successfully this time, getting all the way to his grandmother's house and never returning. Miss Granite told Clifford and Buster, very sternly, that their brother had been expelled. When they were alone the two boys laughed and agreed that expulsion was a funny punishment for breaking out of prison. They were not amused to be still at the school themselves, however. But they stayed, and in time they learned that their parents had separated. Mrs. Putt went to New Orleans and eventually remarried. She had once promised Buster that they would be reunited after her release from prison, and her failure to keep that promise was a painful, possibly damaging blow to the boy.

"Buster and me never stopped despising that school," said Clifford. "They worked us like we was some kind of animals. We were sent out to work in the fields every day to hoe or pick corn, and you had to do so much or you'd get beaten. This J. B. Stites, his job went to his head. If you was working in the cornfield and he didn't like the way you were doing it, he'd take a cornstalk and whip you with it. And I didn't mind the work as much as the way they'd steal off you. They'd break into your locker and take your things, the things your people sent you. My clothes would get stolen and I'd know who did it, but when I told Miss Granite nothing would happen.

"Buster and me, we stuck together and got tough. Every time we'd fight, we'd fight together, and finally nobody would mess with us. The only time we'd fight then was if somebody stole something off us or messed around with one of our little brothers."

But although they had found a way to protect themselves,

and although J. B. Stites eventually departed (either for college or the Army, Clifford remembered), the boys continued to hate the school. Clifford devised a plan by which, with some help, he might escape. He recruited Buster, naturally, as his helper.

Clifford's major problem was that he wanted to take his belongings with him. He had a big, battered suitcase, but getting off the school grounds and through town while carrying luggage was practically impossible. Someone was sure to see and stop him. There was a way, however, one that no one had ever tried, as far as Clifford knew. The creek across which J. B. Stites had chased the boys at the end of their first escape attempt ran past the school and around the town to the highway. If Clifford could reach the creekbed, he could follow it to the highway and get away unseen with his suitcase.

As soon as he felt confident that the plan could work, Clifford took his brother aside. "Buster," he said, "I'm not going to take this any more. I'm leaving, and I need you to help me." There was no argument from Buster as Clifford explained his plan. The next morning, when all the boys were marched as usual to breakfast, Clifford stayed upstairs in the dormitory and hurriedly packed his suitcase. Then, with Buster standing watch on the stairs, he slipped out of the building and clambered down the creek's steep bank until he was out of sight. He made it safely past the town, and when he reached the highway and put out his thumb a car stopped and the driver gave him a ride as far as a town called Princeton. He was on the outskirts of Princeton trying to get another ride when a state police car stopped and the officer behind the wheel told him to get in. When the officer learned that his rider was a runaway, Clifford was taken to the Princeton jail and held there for three days. Then a man from the school arrived and took him back to school.

Clifford expected to be beaten when he reached the school, but he wasn't. Nobody in authority said anything about his escape, in fact, except to ask in a friendly way how he had managed to get away in broad daylight carrying that big suitcase of his. Buster had not told on him, and apparently no adult had yet discovered the creek's usefulness as an escape route. Clifford didn't tell, either; he thought he might try it again. For three weeks he waited to be punished and nothing happened. Then Buster ran away, and that was the end of the school for both of them.

Buster's sudden flight was far less a serious escape attempt than a childish escapade. One night he and three young inmates of the girls' dormitory left the school grounds together. Instead of running for the highway, however, they merely crossed the road in front of the school and climbed to the high ground of a nearby graveyard. They hid there for a while, and then they began playing and throwing empty tin cans down onto the road. Neighbors heard their laughter and the clang of the cans hitting the pavement, and the police were called. Buster and the girls were chased back to the school, and when they arrived all four were screaming in pain. In their hurry to get through the dark cemetery and back to the school they had somehow disturbed a beehive and were covered with stings.

Again there was no beating. Buster was even told that he would not be beaten for what he had done, so he did not have to wait and worry as Clifford had. He was surprised and pleased. Then, after a few days, the punishment was announced. Buster was expelled from the school, and Clifford was expelled with him. They were both put on a bus and rode to their grandmother's house in a state of high jubilation. They regretted nothing except the fact that Lance and Lester, still quite small and now without protectors, had not been expelled also.

For several months after their expulsion, the boys lived with their grandparents in Richmond. They were much bigger now than they'd been when they first went away, of course, and they were far more independent. Grandmother

Putt, older and more frail, found them impossible to control. Life at home became increasingly unpleasant for all of them. Ruth Tarver Putt was still in New Orleans, Clifford Sr. was still moving from town to town and trying to keep out of the hands of the police, and Johnny had gone off on a career that would within a few years lead him to a term in federal prison for transporting a stolen car across state lines.

Clifford Jr. had a friend in school, an orphan boy named Bobby Jones, and he told Bobby about the problems at home. "You ought to come live where I do, at the Richmond Home for Boys," Bobby said. "It's a real nice place. They treat you nice, and they even have a swimming pool." Clifford told his grandmother what he had learned, and she went to the Henrico County Welfare Department to make inquiries. When she got home she told the boys that they could move to the home. They arrived there in September, 1959.

"That school was the best place I was ever in," Clifford said. "I liked it and Buster did too. We lived at first in a cottage with some other boys and a housemother named Miss Gillespie who'd do anything for you. If you ripped your clothes, you know, she'd sew them up. She was a nice lady, and I think she liked Buster better than anybody.

"Two or three boys lived together in each room, and every boy had his own closet to keep his things in and nobody ever stole from you. They even gave you an allowance. I remember my allowance was a dollar and seventy-five cents when I was fifteen years old. That was a lot of money for a boy who never had anything except what his grandma could give him and you could see a movie for fifteen cents. The home even had donations money from somewhere for sending boys to college."

A report on Buster written by his sixth grade teacher described him as very athletic and noted that "he liked art, and he liked to write gruesome stories. He was probably the cleanest and neatest boy in the sixth grade class. Everything had to be just right about his appearance." Buster took two baths every day, the teacher said.

This same report contains one of the first suggestions that Buster did not return Clifford's affection. Buster "had a very poor relationship with his brother at Boys Home, but this brother proved to be very loyal," the report stated. "George worried about his brother who was in a home in North Carolina and stated that this was his only family." At this point, apparently, Buster was reserving his affection for one or the other of his younger brothers and already felt alienated from the "loyal" Clifford. This alienation, however, was carefully veiled.

After a while Clifford was moved to a cottage for older boys, but though Buster stayed behind with Miss Gillespie the brothers continued to spend a great deal of time together. They were tough and athletic—the toughest boys at the school, according to Clifford—and together they joined the boxing team. Then they joined the swimming and football teams. With four other youngsters who were good at sports they formed an intimate, exclusive clique. Though not a particularly good student, Buster was regarded as a leader and was popular with boys and girls his age.

One night, during a football game between the Richmond Home for Boys and a local school, Buster was kicked in the forehead and lost consciousness. Clifford and two other players carried him off the field and laid him on the grass near the sideline, and though he did not awaken for many minutes Clifford could not remember that he received any medical attention. In any case, he was alert by the time the game ended and seemed to have fully recovered. But it was not long after this that his behavior began to change strangely.

"He'd get spells, you know, blackouts," Clifford remembered. "Many a time Miss Gillespie would send a boy down from her cabin at a dead run to get me because Buster was having a fit. He'd pick up a chair with one hand and throw it across the room. One time he tore a towel rack off the wall. I'd get him into bed and he'd go right to sleep and wake up the next morning and not remember anything. Sometimes he'd sleepwalk with his eyes open. One time I caught him on the road at night, walking along in a trance. I stopped him and asked him where he was going and he said he was going to see Cecilia. Cecilia was the girl he was going with. I took him back to the cottage and put him in bed and he closed his eyes and went straight to sleep."

Buster's seventh grade report noted the change. It described him as still an excellent athlete, but as a poor student now, and it stated that he was afflicted with kidney infections, severe headaches, dizzy spells, and blackouts that lasted as long as forty minutes. According to the report, Buster loved horror movies and stories about Caryl Chessman, the convicted California murderer who was waging a long and ultimately unsuccessful court battle to evade his death sentence.

Because of these symptoms Buster was given psychiatric tests in 1960, and the resulting report stated that he was "seriously disturbed in contrast to the placid facade which he presented in the interview. His thinking is at times bizarre and so frequently do his perceptions vary from the normal that reality testing must be quite poor." He displayed, a psychiatrist said, "morbid preoccupation with blood and gore."

All this came to a climax late on a summer day long after Buster's football injury. Clifford was listening to the radio when a boy burst into his room and said that Miss Gillespie needed him immediately. Seventeen years old now and almost fully grown, Clifford went on the run, and when he reached Miss Gillespie she told him that Buster had disappeared and had to be found as quickly as possible. Clifford knew where to look: a graveyard not far away where Buster sometimes went to be alone. He found Buster sitting on the ground with his back against a tree. He was wearing a pair of light green pants cut off near the knee, and one of the legs was stained with something dark.

"Hey, Buster," said Clifford. "What you doin'?"

"Hi, Junior."

Clifford, who was trying to shed his nickname, pointed in annoyance at the stain. "How'd you get that?" he asked.

"What?" Buster looked down at his pants. "Oh. I don't know where that came from."

"Listen, Buster, Miss Gillespie is looking all over for you. You better come back to the cottage."

"No, Junior," Buster replied. "I ain't going back now." Clifford asked him again, but Buster just shook his head.

When Clifford reported that Buster had refused to return with him, Miss Gillespie told him that Buster had been accused of attacking two girls and was being hunted by the police. Clifford ran back to the graveyard, but when he reached it Buster had disappeared. He told Miss Gillespie, then went to his cottage and waited for a while, trying to decide what to do. Then he went up to the home's administration building and tried to call his grandmother. Miss Gillespie was in the building talking with two policemen.

Clifford dialed and got a busy signal. Then he remembered, from something he'd been told, that his grandparents were visiting relatives out of town. If nobody was home but the phone was busy, Buster must have gone there. He must be trying to call somebody. Clifford told the policeman what had happened and they drove him out to the house.

Nobody answered when Clifford rang his grandmother's doorbell. The front and back doors were locked. He looked in a window and saw something, a shadow, move. He tried a side door, found it unlocked, and interpreted this as a sign that Buster wanted to be found. Because they did not have a search warrant, the policemen asked Clifford to enter the house first. They found Buster under a bed, staring out at them with dazed eyes, and when Clifford asked him to come out he shook his head. "Come on out," one of the officers said. "We only want to talk to you." Buster muttered that he didn't want to talk in front of his brother, so Clifford left the house and walked back to the Richmond Home. That night Miss Gillespie told him that his brother had been arrested.

Early one morning about three weeks later, dressed only in his underpants, Buster returned in a taxicab to the Richmond Home for Boys. A dumbfounded Miss Gillespie paid his fare as Buster ran into her cottage and hid in a linen closet. When some of the boys who lived at the cottage looked into the closet at him, he asked one of them to get him clothes and another to run and tell Clifford that he had escaped.

By this time, Clifford had begun to fear that he had made a mistake in telling the police about the busy signal. As the days had passed and bits of news were relayed by Miss Gillespie, it had become clear that Buster was in serious trouble and might not be allowed to return to the home. So when he learned that Buster had run away from wherever he had been held, Clifford decided that he had better keep running. When he reached Miss Gillespie's cottage he gave Buster some money that he had been given to see a dentist and told him to leave town before the police found him again. A man who worked at the home saw Clifford hand the money over and told him he couldn't do that. Clifford ignored him and told Buster to hurry. The man warned Clifford that he could be expelled. "You can go to hell," Clifford snapped, "my brother needs this money more than I do. If you don't like it, I'll leave with him." The man said that if Clifford left he would be expelled and reported to police as a runaway. That didn't make any sense to Clifford. How could he be a runaway if they expelled him? He decided that he had better go with Buster. They took off together, running.

Later, when they were in hiding, Buster told Clifford that he had not attacked anyone. Some girls had been throwing rocks at the windows of a nearby school, he said, and he had

chased them off. That was all. Clifford got the impression
that Buster wanted to say more about the incident, but he
never did. That was the last Clifford ever heard of the matter, from Buster or from anyone. When the police caught
them, the attack was not mentioned.

After leaving the boys' home Clifford and Buster lived
briefly as fugitives, moving almost constantly, sleeping in
hiding places, buying food with the dentist money and
scrounging when it was all spent. They stole corn from a
field and boiled it in an old bent pot, picked half-ripe apples
when no one was looking, and once or twice sneaked back to
the home and were given food by their friends. The friends
were eager to help.

"Every boy who was in that place the same time as us
knew there was something wrong with Buster, that he had a
mental block or something," Clifford said. "They seen it in
him with their own eyes. But they all liked him. He was a
good boy, and he'd do anything for you."

Buster delighted Clifford and their friends with the story
of how he had escaped in his underpants. He said he had
jumped out a second-story window at a detention home
while waiting for a medical examination, had hidden in a
tree all night while people searched for him, and had
climbed down and caught a taxi shortly after dawn.

One night during their moving and hiding, Clifford and
Buster found themselves caught outdoors in a chilling rain.
Starved and exhausted, they tried to get into a dark church
building and discovered that a basement door was unlocked.
They slept that night on the floor of the church's furnace
room, and the next morning they crept upstairs and found
soft drinks, crackers and beans in a pantry. Astonished at
their sudden good luck, they ate everything and explored the
rest of the building. Then they went outside. No one was
around, the early sun was shining brilliantly, and it all
seemed too good to be true. Clifford said maybe they could

stay there a few days without being detected. Buster agreed and announced that he was going to climb up to the roof and sunbathe. Clifford shrugged, unable to think of a better idea. The church walls were of brick, and some of the bricks protruded for decorative effect; Buster used these as a ladder, leaving muddy tracks on the wall as he climbed. Clifford watched him until he was over the top and out of sight on the flat roof but didn't follow. He walked aimlessly around the building for a few minutes, then stripped off his shirt and lay down in a pile of leaves. He fell asleep.

Clifford was awakened by a policeman sitting on his chest. "Good morning," the officer said. "Where's your buddy?" Clifford turned his head and saw another policeman nearby. "C'mon," the man sitting on him said, jerking himself up and then coming down painfully on Clifford's chest. "We know there's two of you. Where'd your buddy go?" Clifford said nothing. He assumed that Buster was still on the roof and didn't want to give him away. The policeman stood up, pulling Clifford up with him and marching him to a police car where he was put in the back seat. Two officers got in with him and immediately began to ask questions. "I don't know what you're talking about," said Clifford. Through the windshield he could see the church. He saw an officer come out of the basement door with a pistol in his hand.

"Hey look," a young officer in the front seat exclaimed. "There's mud on that wall." He looked back at Clifford and smiled. "You don't suppose that's fresh mud, do you?" He looked over the top of his seat at Clifford's shoes. They were muddy, like Buster's. "I think I'll just check that out," said the young officer. He got out of the car and started toward the church, but before he had gone more than a few steps Clifford shouted at him.

"That's my brother," he yelled. "The boy you're looking for, that's my brother. If you find him you better not shoot him." He tried to make it sound like a threat. The policeman stared at him briefly before going on to the church,

where he talked with the man who had come out of the basement. Both of them hitched up their pants, climbed carefully
up the wall to the roof, and disappeared. Seconds later Clifford heard a shot. A few minutes after that the two officers
reappeared at the edge of the roof and climbed slowly back
down to the ground.

"The little fucker got away," the young officer said when
he returned to the car. "No use trying to chase him. He was
laying up there flat on his back when we got onto the roof,
but then he sat straight up and saw us. He jumped right off
the goddamn roof and got away before we could do
anything."

Clifford was relieved and angry. "You shot at him, didn't
you?" he demanded. "I heard you shoot at him." Neither
officer answered him. He was taken to jail and charged with
breaking and entering and theft. Later the same day Buster
learned of Clifford's arrest and turned himself in. He too was
put in a cell and charged with breaking and entering and
theft, but after a short time he was taken away to another institution. Clifford was released when the pastor of the church
where he and Buster had slept refused to press charges.

Clifford learned of Buster's next escape in January. He
was sitting in his grandmother's kitchen one afternoon when,
happening to glance out a window, he saw policemen running from the back yard to the front of the house. More
afraid than curious, he opened the door and asked the men
what they wanted.

"Who are you?" an officer asked sharply. He had stopped
running and put his hand on the revolver holstered at his
side.

"I'm Clifford Putt."

"You sure you're *Clifford* Putt?" Crouching slightly and
keeping his hands at his side, the officer started slowly toward
the house. Clifford wanted to run but decided it would be
suicide.

On the way to police headquarters, Clifford was told that

his brother had again slipped out of custody and was accused of using a knife to rob and rape a woman. Clifford was jailed and held as a suspect for a while, until a woman was brought to look at him. When the woman said he was not the youth who had assaulted her, he was permitted to go home. He did not see Buster again for more than five years.

Clifford's recollection of these events was necessarily limited to his own experiences. Police and psychiatric reports provide supplementary information and make the record considerably more complete. According to such reports, Buster first became a fugitive after he accosted two ten-year-old girls in a school yard, took one of them into a weed patch, stripped her, lay atop her without raping her, and forced her to put his penis in her mouth. He fled when the girl's father came looking for her, and after being found under his grandparents' bed by Clifford and the police he was charged with forcible sodomy. Doctors who questioned and examined him after his arrest diagnosed him as "a character disorder with a possibility of central nervous system damage." Commitment to a mental hospital was recommended. "George's feelings toward his parents are antagonistic," a doctor wrote. "He does not want to see them, he feels they have let him down, and that they do not care about him."

Buster jumped out the window in his shorts after learning that the doctors wanted to put him in a mental hospital. Days later, after Clifford was caught at the church and he turned himself in, he was sent to the Southwestern State Hospital for further examination. There he was diagnosed as a "sociopathic personality disorder, antisocial reaction," a condition attributed primarily to "almost unbelievable physical and emotional deprivation during his lifetime." Declared fit to stand trial on the sodomy charge, he was transferred to the Henrico County juvenile detention home in Richmond. He escaped from there on December 22, 1961, and almost immediately became involved in a series of increasingly serious crimes.

On January 5, 1962, a thirty-year-old woman told police that she had been abducted at knifepoint from Richmond's Village Shopping Center, robbed of thirty-five dollars, and raped. She described the rapist as a smallish, fair-haired teenage boy whose face was pocked with acne. The description fit Buster perfectly and new warrants were issued for his arrest. Before the police could begin searching for him, however, he left Virginia and headed for the Southwest. First he went to New Orleans and tried to find his mother; an uncle, when Buster telephoned, said Ruth Putt did not want to see him. From there Buster continued west into Texas. He had the idea that his father was in Mexico, and he hoped to locate him there.

Though Buster's pathetic efforts to make contact with his parents contradicted his earlier expressions of hostility for them, those efforts also echoed a poignant report written at the Richmond Guidance Clinic in January 1961, a year before he left Virginia. A psychiatrist who examined Buster at that time described him as "an appealing-looking, brightish boy who, like so many children who have had a pillar-to-post existence, seems to be yearning for his own parents. . . . George does not appear to be a deeply disturbed child, but a youngster who is yearning for what it is impossible for him to have, that is, his own family. Rather than a particularly rebellious and defiant boy, he seems to be a rather frightened child." If he hated his parents for abandoning him, he nevertheless clung for a long time to the hope that they might yet admit him to their lives.

On his way to Mexico, Buster burglarized a home from which he took a pistol. On January 13 he abducted a woman in Laredo, Texas, used the pistol to force her to drive him out of town, and escaped on foot when the woman intentionally crashed her automobile. Two nights later he climbed into the window of a Laredo apartment and, again using the pistol, abducted another woman by threatening to kill her sleeping children if she refused to cooperate. He was attempting to drive the woman out of town in her car when he saw a police van, panicked, and crashed. Again he escaped on foot, but now the police were searching for him and he was arrested the next day while leaving a movie theater.

Buster was held in Laredo's Webb County Jail for thirteen months, spending his sixteenth birthday there. Again he was examined by a psychiatrist, and he was diagnosed as being sociopathic, antisocial, and afflicted with severe separation anxiety. A report from this period indicates that he expressed longing for his mother mixed with resentment over her past submissiveness to his "brutal father." He said he did not smoke or drink because he did not want to be like his father in any way. This same report noted that Buster displayed hatred for his brother Clifford based on the belief that in early childhood Clifford had been closer to their mother. Clifford, meanwhile, still in Virginia, was mournfully assuming that Buster needed and missed him.

On February 28, 1963, Buster was transferred from jail to the Terrace School in Laredo. He spent his seventeenth birthday there, escaped in October, and was caught and sent to a more secure institution called the Hilltop School, where he became eighteen. On June 25, 1964, he was placed in an "adjustment center" after authorities learned that he had hatched a plan by which he and three other inmates were to kidnap the school's female librarian and escape in her car. He was examined, described as having "earmarks of a psychopath in his makeup," and tranferred to a top-security juvenile detention facility in Gatesville, Texas. There too he was examined, and a 1965 report described him as a psychopath, as antisocial, and as a youth with "no loyalties to any person or any group" and little chance of adjusting satisfactorily to life on the outside. Later diagnoses were no better, but when his twenty-first birthday came he was routinely discharged. He quickly proved that he was indeed incapable of adjusting to freedom.

He went first to Tupelo, where his grandparents were again living after an unsuccessful move to Arizona in search of milder weather, and he found a job as a hospital orderly. After only a few days he was accused of stealing a hundred dollars from a nurse's purse and fired. Because he made restitution for the missing money, he was not arrested. Next he went to New Orleans, and a few days after his arrival there he was accused of stealing a checkbook from a room in the Roosevelt Hotel. On May 5, in Orange, Texas, he was accused of stealing forty-six dollars from a cafe cash register. The money was found in his sock when he was arrested, but the cafe owner did not press charges. He moved on to Juarez, Mexico, spent a week there, and finally went north to Houston, Texas. He remained in Houston for many weeks, working one day as a hospital orderly and at other times supporting himself by unknown means. If he committed additional crimes in this period, he was not caught and left no record of them. In the fall of 1967 he returned to Mississippi and met Mary Ruth Bulimore when Clifford brought her to the Putt family reunion.

During the years that they were separated, Clifford was kept informed of Buster's recurring difficulties by his grandmother, who received occasional reports from Texas authorities. The information was usually vague and there never was much of it, but it always reminded Clifford of the strange behavior that had started his brother's trouble in the first place. Mixed with Grandma Putt's fragments of second-hand news, Clifford's memories made him increasingly apprehensive.

"Even when I was seventeen and Buster was down there in Texas, I thought he was capable of killing somebody," Clifford said in 1973. "I used to think about that, and I wondered how it would affect me if he did. I didn't want to admit it, but I knew he needed help and I thought he would never stay in one place long enough to get it."

These fears evaporated when he saw Buster in Tupelo late in 1967. "He seemed in good spirits the day I got to Tupelo," Clifford remembered. "He was really happy. We sat up all night and talked. We didn't go to bed the whole night. We talked about old times, all the things we'd done together, and Buster didn't seem any different than I remembered except he was in a better way than he'd been when he got into trouble in Richmond. I tried not to ask him questions about his trouble. I didn't want to bring up bad memories or nothing."

Thus when Mary and Buster announced that they were getting married, Clifford did not tell her about Buster's past. Buster seemed fully recovered, and there was nothing to suggest that he might ever again cause trouble for anyone. Rather, Clifford later insisted, he feared that Mary would be bad for Buster. He took Buster aside and tried to dissuade him from getting married—told him that Mary was selfish, fickle, cold-hearted and greedy. Buster, not interested, said he didn't want to hear such things, so Clifford decided to keep silent. Buster seemed to know what he was doing, and when Grandmother Putt learned about the wedding she said delightedly that a bride was exactly what Buster needed.

As things turned out, it appeared in the months after the wedding that Clifford's worries had been unjustified. The marriage seemed to work, and so far as Clifford could tell Buster seemed quite happy. By the standards of the Putt family at least, life became tranquil and remained that way for ten months.

The old troubles began to return on October 12, 1968, the day that Clifford and Retha Redd were married in Blue Goose. At this time Buster and Mary were living in Houston, Mississippi, and working at the hospital there. Buster came to the wedding alone, and afterwards he said he had to go to Memphis to pick up a baby bed at Mary's Uncle Edward's house. He left in his car and did not return all night. The next morning Clifford received a telephone call. It was from Buster, and he was weeping.

"Junior," Buster said. "I'm in the jail in Memphis. They impounded my car and I need some money to get out." He was speaking very softly and choking painfully on his words.

"For what? What did they get you for?"

"Oh," Buster began, but before he could continue he broke down again, making a series of gasping sobs into the phone. "Oh, Junior, I attacked this nigger woman at a red light. Don't ask. I can't get out of here 'til I pay them fifty-two dollars."

Clifford was broke, but Retha had some money which she gave him to take to Memphis. Buster, when he was released, said no more about the incident. "He didn't explain, and I didn't press him," Clifford said later. "I figured if he wanted to tell me, he would." Later, under far more serious circumstances, both brothers would behave in exactly the same way, one saying nothing and the other not asking the obvious questions.

Police records of this incident are scanty. An arrest report indicates only that at 10:40 P.M. on October 12 George Howard Putt was taken into custody by two officers who had observed him beating a Negro woman with his fists at the intersection of Third Street and Belz Avenue. "Complainant stated that she pulled her car up to the left rear side of defendant's car and he jumped out and told her to move over," the report stated. "He then pushed her over to one side and got in and began beating her." Perhaps because the victim was black, there appears to have been no effort to determine why Buster had suddenly attacked a stranger, and the case apparently was given no attention between his arrest and his release. The fact that this outburst occurred on the night of Clifford's wedding is tantalizingly interesting, in view of the complexity of the relationship between the brothers. Obviously the two events may have had some connection.

Not long after their wedding, Clifford and Retha went to Houston. They moved in with Buster and Mary, and Clifford got a job at the hospital. If he sensed Mary's unhappiness about his arrival, he did not admit it later. He insisted that everything seemed fine, that "Buster kept quiet about

Mary, but they seemed to get along okay whenever I saw them together." They were both now living with the child who was Clifford's son biologically and Buster's by law, and this appears to have produced tensions that the brothers did not acknowledge to one another. Clifford said later that he had been troubled by the fact that Pip seemed to be afraid of Buster. Buster, during questioning by police after his arrest on murder charges, said he had always felt uneasy about seeing Clifford and Pip together.

Buster had an old Bell & Howell movie projector at his house in Houston—Clifford said he didn't know where it had come from—and suggested that the two of them take it to Memphis and pawn it. They had no use for a projector, so Clifford readily agreed. He was accustomed to pawning things; once he had pawned his wrist watch for a single dollar. They drove to Memphis and parked near a pawn shop, and Clifford waited in the car while Buster went inside. He waited a long time, growing more and more impatient and wondering what Buster was doing. Finally he got out of the car and went to the shop intending to make Buster hurry, and when he got inside he found Buster being questioned by a pair of detectives. One of the detectives explained that a quantity of office equipment had been stolen recently and the projector might be part of the loot. The Putt brothers proclaimed their innocence but were arrested and booked on suspicion of burglary.

"They kept us in jail for two days and then let us go," Clifford recalled. "They just sent us home without apologizing or anything." Upon returning to Houston he and Buster learned that they had been fired from their jobs.

"When he found out we'd been fired, Buster was mad and hurt," Clifford said. "I was too. I think anybody would be, when they hold you in jail and try to get you to admit something that you didn't do and then you lose your job over it." Police records indicate that Buster and Clifford had been released after officers were unable to trace the projector or prove that it had been stolen.

Clifford and Buster went to Jackson after losing their jobs, taking their wives and Pip with them and applying for work at another hospital. The hospital was short-handed and hired both of them immediately as orderlies, routinely asking for references while putting them to work. Somehow, they did not hesitate to list the Houston hospital as part of their work experience. When administrators at the Jackson hospital called Houston and learned about the burglary charges, Clifford and Buster were fired again.

"The way they treated you," Clifford said of this, "the only way you could get work was to lie and cheat." Perhaps Buster felt the same way.

The brothers got jobs at service stations in Jackson, but from this point things rapidly became worse. Mary and Buster fought, separated, and after a complicated series of adjustments that were not clear in Clifford's memory they reconciled and moved into a rundown house in Crenshaw. This was early in 1969, and for a while there were no more difficulties. Or so it seemed to Clifford. Annie Bulimore, Mary's mother, knew differently.

On three occasions in the weeks following his reconciliation with Mary and the move to Crenshaw, Buster attacked Mrs. Bulimore when they were alone together with the apparent intention of raping her. Mrs. Bulimore was sixty years old then, a hard life had given her an even older appearance, and she was astounded to find herself the object of violent advances by a twenty-two-year-old boy. The first attack occurred late one night as she was getting out of the bathtub at her home in Sarah; Buster, who had been sleeping with Mary on a folding bed in the kitchen, suddenly entered the bathroom and threw his arms around her in a tight hug. Days later, when she and Buster went together to inspect a house for rent, he grabbed her again, tried to pull her into a bedroom, and told her he loved her. It happened the third time at her house in Sarah while Mary was away shopping. Each time, Annie Bulimore said, Buster appeared to be out of his senses; when he entered the bathroom on the first occasion, she recalled, he had "kind of a skim over his eyes," and later that night she found him alone in the living room, huddled on the sofa with his head between his knees, rocking slowly back and forth. He stopped each attack when she ordered him to, and she told no one about what had happened until long afterward; Mary had too many problems already, the old woman explained, and didn't need more. Also, Mrs. Bulimore felt a strong affection for Buster, and though his behavior baffled her she was far more concerned for him than afraid of him. "He was one of the nicest young men I ever saw and one of the craziest I ever saw," she said after Buster had been convicted of murder. "If he hadn't been the kind of person he was, he could have made anything of himself."

On April 27, 1969, shortly after Buster's last assault on his mother-in-law, a man was stabbed to death under mysterious circumstances at his home in Jackson. The man was a socially prominent bachelor with a reputation for striking up brief acquaintanceships with young men passing through town; he had been stabbed fifteen times; his house was a short distance from a service station where Buster had been working when Mary left him. The murder was never solved and there is no direct evidence linking Buster to the case, but investigators in both Jackson and Memphis have expressed strong suspicions that he was the killer. This is speculation, however, and is likely to remain so forever.

That murder was discovered on Sunday; the next day Buster ran off with Eileen King. When he was caught early in May, Clifford and Retha departed for Virginia, where they stayed at the home of Grandmother and Grandfather Putt. After Buster's escape from the Hinds County prison farm he too went to Virginia. Almost immediately upon his arrival there he began to behave in ways that alarmed the entire family.

"Buster seemed sort of funny, you know, when he came back up to Richmond," Clifford said afterward. "Things just didn't seem right between him and me. There were arguments here and there that I'd rather not talk about. Buster argued with my sister Betty Ruth—things I'd rather keep in the family. His moods would change. He'd be real happy sometimes and sometimes he'd sit real quiet and just not talk at all. He'd go out in the sun in the middle of the day and lay on top of the car for what seemed like hours."

Young Lester Putt, also staying with his grandparents at this time, had an experience that he recounted months later when questioned by Memphis detectives. One night Buster borrowed Clifford's car and went out. The next day, cleaning the car, Lester found blood-soaked and sand-spattered men's clothing (a shirt and a pair of trousers, he recalled) on the floor under the back seat. Later that day, he heard that the body of a murdered woman had been found at a beach near Richmond. Memphis officers wrote to Richmond requesting information about any such murder but received none.

Clifford and Retha had been working at Johnston-Willis Hospital in Richmond when Buster arrived. They helped him to get a job there, and he started work on July 8. On July 22, when Clifford announced that he and Retha had decided to go to Chicago and look for better-paying jobs, Buster said he wanted to go with them. The three of them left for Chicago the next day, but when they stopped for gas at Ashland, Virginia, Buster said he had decided to telephone Mary to see how she was. He went into a phone booth, stayed there for several minutes, and then walked slowly back to the car.

"Listen, Junior," he said after a long hesitation. "I just talked to Mary, and she said she's bleeding and thinks she's going to have a miscarriage. I think I've got to go down there. I'm going to stay here and see if I can catch a bus to Memphis."

Clifford believed him. "Well, hell," he answered, "there's no need for you to take the bus. Retha and me can run you down to Memphis. Can't we, Retha?" He looked into the back seat and Retha nodded anxiously. Buster got into the car and they started for Tennessee. Not knowing that Buster was lying about the call, Clifford had made a decision that would almost cost Retha her life.

Clifford and Retha were living in Blue Goose when the Dumases were murdered, but they often drove into Memphis to see Buster and Mary. A few nights after those first murders, the four of them went out to play miniature golf. Buster, driving, took a circuitous route to the golf course, putting his arm out the window at one point and gesturing toward a handsome brick building on a high lawn above the street.

"See that apartment there?" he asked. "Right on the first floor at this end, that's where those Dumas people got killed the other day. Right there in that building."

"Huh," said Clifford, only mildly interested. He glanced at the building as the car swept past it, then turned his eyes to the front and began talking about other things. Buster's remark had been a harmless observation, and there was nothing particularly odd about his knowing where an already-famous murder had occurred. But later that month, after Leila Jackson was killed, something similar and more troubling happened.

"You know that old lady who got killed here?" Buster asked when he and Clifford met again. "That Mrs. Jackson? I knew her—didn't I tell you about her before? I tried to rent a room from her. She gave me a real hard time, got real smart and raised the rent on me so I couldn't afford it. She was a real witch, that woman."

Now Clifford was concerned. Buster seemed unnaturally agitated. Anger and bitterness were in his voice, and something in the way he spoke made Clifford think that he had more on his mind than he was saying. As usual Clifford asked no questions, but he drove across the state line into Mississippi that night thinking about Buster's past.

From then on, Buster and the Memphis murders were frozen together in Clifford's mind. He thought about the murders often, and he was unable to think about them without thinking of Buster at the same time. He became alert for signs of trouble and thus was prepared to react quickly when, late on a Friday afternoon several days after Mrs. Jackson's death, he arrived home from work and learned from Retha that Buster had been trying to find him.

"How long ago?" he asked. He'd had a hot and tiring day and had looked forward to a bath before supper, but Retha's news erased his fatigue and replaced it with anxiety. "When was he here?" he asked again.

"I'm not sure," said Retha. "The middle of the afternoon some time. He said he had to get to work but wanted you to come see him."

Forgetting about bath and supper, Clifford told Retha that they were leaving for Memphis. Minutes later he was doing seventy miles an hour on the highway, wishing that he dared to go faster and certain that Buster had something important to tell him. He reached the city limits about 7:30 P.M. and pulled into the Hudson station where Buster worked. Buster, the reflection of neon lights gleaming in the lenses of his sunglasses, watched his brother brake to a stop and walked over to the car.

"Well, hi," said Buster. He leaned down into the car window, folding his arms and smiling. "I didn't expect to see you tonight."

"Retha said you wanted to see me."

"Yeah," Buster said in a half-surprised way, as if he had forgotten his stop in Blue Goose. "That's right. I wanted to show you something. Come on over here for a minute."

The something was a battered old Buick station wagon parked across the road. "I got it for a hundred dollars," Buster said proudly. Clifford didn't know what to say. The car looked worthless to him. He stood at the edge of the road staring at it, not even trying to appear enthusiastic. He wondered where Buster had got a hundred dollars, and why he had driven all the way to Blue Goose to tell him about a piece of junk.

Buster walked around the car and slapped his palm on a

fender. "Hey," he said. "Did you hear? We had another one of those killings."

"No, I didn't hear that." Clifford was surprised. He had listened to the radio all the way into town and had heard nothing about a murder. "I must have missed it," he said. "I been at work all day." He looked across the top of the station wagon and thought he saw something expectant in the set of his brother's mouth. He became certain that Buster was struggling with himself, and somehow it began to seem very important that the conversation not be permitted to die. Clifford asked Buster who had been killed. At that moment a car pulled into the station, ringing the pneumatic bells, and Buster ran back to work.

"I believed then that he wanted to tell me something," Clifford said long afterward. "But he didn't know how to break it to me."

Mary and Pip were in Sarah that weekend, and when Buster invited Clifford and Retha to stay with him they accepted. They went to the zoo when Buster was at work on Saturday and watched television with him after he got home. There was no more talk about a new murder, and no news of one on television. They awoke early Sunday morning, and after breakfast Buster said he wanted to go out for a newspaper. Clifford had no interest in papers—and he'd never known Buster to read them—but he said he'd go along for the ride. They drove until Buster spotted a newspaper box and parked the car. He bought a paper, gave part of it to Clifford, and got behind the steering wheel to read the front page. Clifford looked over and saw that the top story was about a killing.

"She was only twenty-one years old," Buster said after a moment. He turned to an inside page and resumed reading.

"The girl who got killed?" Clifford asked.

"Yeah. The paper says she was only twenty-one years old."

"That's terrible," Clifford replied. "That's the youngest one yet. But they'll catch him."

"Who?"

"The guy that's doing all this. They'll catch him."

Buster closed the paper and turned to look at Clifford. His jaw was clenched and his mouth was set in a hard line. "Junior," he said in a low voice taut with anger, "those cops ain't as smart as you think." He dropped the paper into Clifford's lap and started the car.

On the way back to the apartment, Clifford looked quickly through the story about the murder. It said that Glenda Sue Harden had disappeared on Friday afternoon, and that her body had been found on Saturday. Buster had told him about a new killing early Friday night. Clifford folded the paper neatly and placed it on the seat next to Buster. When they reached the apartment he said a quick goodbye and started back to Blue Goose with Retha. By the time he got there he decided that a man couldn't report his own brother to the police unless he was absolutely sure. Especially not if the brother was wanted for escaping from prison. Clifford told himself that he was not absolutely sure.

Buster drove to Sarah the next day to get Mary and Pip, and when he arrived at the Bulimores' house he sat down in the living room to talk with Annie.

"Did you hear?" he asked. "We had another one of those awful murders."

"Yes, I heard about it," said Annie. "But you know, Buster, one of these days they're going to catch that bastard."

Buster jumped to his feet, an expression of total confusion swept over his face, and he dropped back into his chair. He remained there for several minutes, apparently still confused, then hurried Mary and the baby out to the car and away.

Clifford had decided that he should be close to Buster. He left the furniture factory, moved to Memphis with Retha, and went to work at a service station. Buster seemed delighted by his brother's decision to move into the city, though he didn't know the reason for it, and he invited

Clifford and Retha to come by for a visit Tuesday night. "You come over to our place," Clifford answered. "We want you to see our new apartment."

Buster and Mary arrived with the baby a few hours after supper. Pip was put to bed, and then the four of them went into the living room to watch television. Retha turned out the lights so they could see the screen more clearly, and Buster, as usual, kept his dark glasses on. Clifford took a chair near Buster's and discovered that, from where he sat, he could turn his face in the direction of the screen but see Buster out of the corner of his eye. Then he made another discovery. The light from the television penetrated Buster's sunglasses in a way that permitted Clifford to see his eyes. It was like getting a secret glimpse into a forbidden place.

Buster faced the television, but his eyes were looking to the right at something else. It wasn't Mary, Clifford could tell, because she was beside Buster on the sofa where he couldn't have seen her without turning his head. It was something between Mary and the television.

It was Retha. Buster was watching Retha and pretending not to. Clifford felt himself grow tense.

"This ain't a bad place, you know?" Buster said casually.

Clifford looked down quickly, to avoid Buster's eyes in case he took them from Retha. "It ain't too bad," he answered. "It'll do." When he looked up again he saw that his brother was still staring at Retha. She, oblivious, was absorbed in the television show. Buster kept his eyes on her and said, "Yes sir, this is a real nice place."

They went on this way for a long time, the women watching television and Buster watching Retha and Clifford watching Buster. Occasionally Mary and Retha would laugh at something, and then Buster would laugh and Clifford would laugh too and pretend that he knew what was funny. The chain of eyes was broken periodically by fragments of trivial conversation. Mary talked about how tired and sick she'd been feeling. Buster asked Clifford how he liked his new job, and Clifford answered that he didn't know yet but he guessed it would be okay. Buster asked what hours he was working, and Clifford said that starting tomorrow he'd be working from noon to midnight. As soon as he said it, he was sorry. He wished that he'd lied. "That's a long day," said Buster.

Clifford felt relieved when Buster and Mary got the baby from the bedroom and went home. He locked the door carefully behind them, and he and Retha went to bed. Before falling asleep, Clifford told Retha that when he was at work she was not to open the door for anyone. "Not even Buster," he said. "If Buster comes to the door, don't you let him in."

The next morning Clifford went to a hardware store and bought a big new lock. He put it on the apartment's front door, and before leaving for work he reminded Retha that she was not to let anyone in. When he got home hours later Retha was waiting up for him. Nobody had knocked all day.

The day after that, Clifford repeated his warning to Retha and left for work a few minutes before noon. He had been gone about an hour when Retha heard footsteps in the hall. They stopped, apparently not far from the door. Retha waited for a moment, and when the steps did not resume she tiptoed to the keyhole and looked out. Someone was there, but she couldn't see who it was. Then the someone knocked.

Retha straightened up. "Who is it?" she asked, forcing herself to use her most casual singsong voice.

"Open the door," a friendly voice replied. It sounded a lot like Clifford. Or Buster. The brothers had similar voices.

"I'm not opening the door for anybody till you tell me who you are."

"It's me."

"Who?"

"Santy Claus."

"Well . . . I'm not opening the door."

This time the voice didn't answer. Retha stood motionless, looking at the locked door for what seemed a long time. Then she heard steps again, walking away down the hall.

Perhaps half an hour later, she heard sirens.

Clifford was at work when he heard on the radio that another woman had been murdered. The news frightened him. The next bulletin said the woman had lived on Bellevue, and his fright began to turn to panic. He was wondering whether he should go home when it was announced that a suspect had been arrested and that the dead woman was fifty-nine years old. Hearing that, Clifford relaxed; nobody would mistake Retha for a fifty-nine-year-old woman, and Buster could not be the suspect because he was at work. Later there were more details about the woman and the arrest, and Clifford stayed in the station office in a group of other men around the radio. Finally, when the radio said the suspect was a young man identified as George Howard Putt, Clifford didn't wonder about what to do. He ran for his car.

When he reached his apartment, the police were already there. Ignoring them, he took the stairs three at a time and found Retha sitting on the sofa in the living room. The front door was wide open, and Retha was crying. She had heard about the killing, she said, and about Buster being arrested. She said the police wanted to search their apartment. Then she told Clifford about the visit from "Santy Claus" earlier in the afternoon.

"I think it must have been Buster," she sobbed. Clifford was sure she was right.

In the years after that, Clifford clung to the conviction that Buster had wanted to communicate with him about the murders, that he had been trying to ask for help. "I believe if we'd had a little more time, and if I'd been around more, he'd have told me," Clifford said. "To this day I don't know what I'd have done if he'd told me. I know I'd have wanted to know why he done it. I still hurt over it. I think about it all the time. Sometimes I go to bed and think about it for hours before I can go to sleep. I always think of Buster as my good brother, my closest brother. Buster and me weren't just brothers, we were buddies. We were never separated until Buster got into trouble."

Clifford was ignorant of many things. He did not know

that for years Buster had concealed from him the feelings of anger and resentment that he repeatedly disclosed to doctors and counselors. He did not know that while at the Hinds County prison farm Buster had written these words to Mary: "Baby, you let me know if Junior ever lays a hand on my baby or you. If he does I won't wait for him to hit me. Don't let him see this letter—I may need his help to get out some time." Clifford did not know that in the eyes of his "good brother" he was someone to be used.

Buster Putt, who could have been anything "if he hadn't been the kind of person he was," who had been so twisted in childhood that he became incapable of coping with the world, lived as a free adult for a very short time. His freedom began in the spring of 1967 when he was released from detention in Texas, and it ended in the summer of 1969 when he was caught with blood on his hands in Memphis. During his two and a half years at large he caromed from one calamity to another, was repeatedly in and out of the hands of the law, and finally, with something approaching inevitability, brought death to at least five people and terror to a city of almost a million people. Then he was returned to confinement, to wait for his own death. If ever a life was a total waste, his was.

A few days after Buster was caught, with Memphis celebrating its relief in an almost carnival-like way, the city council passed a resolution praising everyone who had taken part in the chase that led to his arrest. The policemen and private citizens named in the resolution were invited to attend the council's next meeting and receive citations. But a state criminal judge loudly protested that such demonstrations of civic gratitude were unjustified until the defendant had been tried, and so the awards ceremony was called off.

Days after that, amid much publicity, the suddenly and unhappily famous Mary Putt gave birth to a son. He was given the name Robert. Later, in another state and without any such attention, Retha and Clifford Putt also had a son. He too was named Robert.

Buster spent more than three and a half years in the Shelby County Jail and was kept in the same cell that earlier had held James Earl Ray, the confessed killer of Martin Luther King. In October 1970, in the same courtroom where Ray had pleaded guilty to the King slaying, Buster was brought before Judge William H. Williams to stand trial for the murder of Mary Christine Pickens. His lawyers pleaded that he was innocent by reason of insanity, but psychiatrists testified for the prosecution that he was legally sane. The trial lasted only a few days and its result was never seriously in doubt. Buster's confession was presented in evidence, and an FBI specialist testified that Buster's fingerprints had been found on Mrs. Pickens' purse and on the doorframe of her apartment. On October 27 a jury of twelve men found him guilty of first-degree murder, and Judge Williams sentenced him to death. Buster, hands in pockets, shrugged and calmly sat down. Execution was set for February 25, 1971.

Buster was not put to death on the scheduled date. His conviction and death sentence were appealed all through 1971 on grounds that he had been insane when he committed the murder and mentally incompetent when he confessed. Early in 1972 the conviction was upheld by the Tennessee Court of Criminal Appeals and a new execution date was set. In June, however, the death penalty was struck down as unconstitutional by the U.S. Supreme Court, and Buster's sentence was commuted to ninety-nine years with automatic eligibility for parole after thirty years.

Late in 1972 someone smuggled a saw blade into the jail and Buster used it to cut a bar out of a cell window. He was discovered before he could escape.

In April 1973, after renewed but again unsuccessful claims of insanity, Buster was put on trial for the murders of Roy and Bernalyn Dumas. He knew before the trial began that the two strongest pieces of evidence against him were his own confession and the fact that Michael Dumas was prepared to testify that the knife used to kill Mary Christine Pickens had belonged to his father, and when Mary Putt visited him in jail he asked her to hire someone to kill young Dumas. Mary, who had divorced Buster by now and was living with her two sons in a St. Louis slum, refused. Dumas testified, and on April 27 Buster was convicted on two additional counts of murder. He was sentenced to serve 199 years in prison on each count—a total of 398 years. His earlier ninety-nine year sentence from the Pickens trial brought the grand total to 497 years. Altogether it was the longest sentence in the history of Shelby County.

Judge Williams, again presiding, ordered that Buster's three sentences would be served consecutively so that he would not be eligible for parole until he had served ninety years. This was done, the judge said, because George Howard Putt was "a dangerous human being to other human beings" and "should never walk the streets again."

Buster, his last hope of ever again being free destroyed, looked down and giggled as the judge finished speaking. After the trial he was taken to the state penitentiary in Nashville, where, presumably, he will live for forty or fifty or sixty years and die of natural causes after paying for his crimes, and the crimes of his parents, and crimes that cannot be blamed on any individual persons but contributed to making him what he was.

Two trials and three sentences removed from free society the man commonly regarded as the most feared murderer in the history of Memphis, Tennessee. They did not remove, however, whatever Buster Putt was a symptom of. On the very night that Putt was found guilty of murdering the Dumases, a twenty-three-year-old high school teacher was murdered in Memphis. She was stabbed to death in her apartment at 1135 South Cooper Street—next door to the apartment in which the Dumases had died. The case has not been solved. The police found no clues, no suspects, no motive.

A Final Note

N O C H A R A C T E R and no incident in this book is an act of the author's imagination. The book is based on almost a year of interviewing, research and careful cross-checking, and each chapter is as accurate as the author was able to make it.

The book had its genesis in 1972 when Mary Bulimore Putt telephoned the author, who had never met her or heard of her or the Memphis murders, and communicated to him her desire to tell her story in return for financial compensation. Somewhat skeptically at first, the author interviewed Mrs. Putt and made preliminary inquiries into the validity of what she said. There followed months of additional and prolonged questioning of Mrs. Putt, followed by travel in search of documentary material and other persons who had been involved in the story. After considerable difficulty the author was able to find Clifford Putt in Chicago and interview him. Mrs. Annie Bulimore was interviewed in St. Louis, and the author made numerous visits to Memphis to examine records, question people with information about the story, and visit the places at which the story occurred. Newspaper files were of value chiefly as reflections of the mood in Memphis during the time when the murders were taking place and the later trials were being held. The most valuable and reliable information—information which confirmed the oral accounts provided by Mary and Clifford Putt and other persons—was found in the files of the Memphis Police Department. Officers of that department's homicide bureau, the author learned when at last he was given access to the files, had done a remarkably thorough job of reconstructing the details of the killings and of the killer's life.

The author is indebted to many persons for their cooperation in the preparation of this book. He is particularly grateful to Captain Robert Cochran of the Memphis Police Department, whose interest in presenting the truth about a remarkable case to the public made him a hospitable and dependable source of information, and to George Lawler, whose patience and intelligence as an editor helped to lighten months of toil. Most particularly, he is grateful to his wife Pamela and his three children, whose faith and forebearance made the toil possible. To them this book is dedicated.

GERALD MEYER
Kirkwood, Missouri